NON-PROLIFERATION EXPORT CONTROLS

For Yvette
for six moves in eight years
on two continents

Non-Proliferation Export Controls

Origins, Challenges, and Proposals for Strengthening

Edited by

DANIEL JOYNER
University of Warwick, UK

ASHGATE

Published by
Ashgate Publishing Limited
Gower House
Croft Road
Aldershot
Hampshire GU11 3HR
England

Ashgate Publishing Company
Suite 420
101 Cherry Street
Burlington, VT 05401-4405
USA

Ashgate website: http://www.ashgate.com

British Library Cataloguing in Publication Data
Non-Proliferation export controls : origins, challenges,
and proposals for strengthening
1. Arms control 2. Export controls 3. Arms transfers -
Government policy
I. Joyner, Daniel
382.4'56234

Library of Congress Cataloging-in-Publication Data
Non-proliferation export controls : origins, challenges, and proposals for strengthening / edited by Daniel Joyner.
p. cm.
Includes index.
ISBN-13: 978-0-7546-4460-6
ISBN-10: 0-7546-4460-X
1. Nuclear nonproliferation. 2. Nuclear weapons (International law) I. Joyner, Daniel.

KZ5675.N66 2006
341.7'34--dc22

2006018466

ISBN-13: 978 0 7546 4460 6
ISBN-10: 0 7546 4460 X

Printed and bound in Great Britain by MPG Books Ltd, Bodmin, Cornwall.

Contents

Foreword

Gary K. Bertsch,
University Professor
Director, Centre for International Trade and Security, University of Georgia

Weapons of mass destruction are proliferating, in large part through normal channels of international commerce. The revelations about A.Q. Khan's proliferation network effectively dispelled any doubts on that score. If illicit trafficking in the technology and substances needed to build nuclear, biological, chemical or radiological arms goes unchecked, it could make life in the twenty-first century a nasty, brutish prospect.

Alongside their many benefits, the modern science, technology and commerce that permeate today's global economy raises new challenges for international export controls and non-proliferation. Individuals across the globe now have access to the technologies, equipment and know-how they need to produce weapons of mass destruction. Such items can be bought and sold through normal channels of international commerce, as the Khan affair showed. If these commodities are not carefully controlled, they may well find their way into the hands of those intent on terrorist acts of catastrophic proportions.

Governments, international organizations and other bodies must do a number of things to stave off such catastrophes. Bolstering export controls is one of these. Goods, technologies and services now flit around the globe at incredible speeds. These include dual-use technologies and materials that not only have legitimate commercial uses but are integral to nuclear, biological, chemical and other advanced weapons, as well as to missiles that can carry these weapons across state borders.

Responsible businesses and governments around the world acknowledge that export controls reduce the likelihood of harmful transfers, but they find the practice of export control extraordinarily difficult in this interconnected world. With so many goods, technologies and services passing so quickly through so many borders, detecting and quashing the few transactions intended for weapons of mass destruction is like searching for the proverbial needle in a haystack. Our present-day policies, practices and institutions, most of which were crafted in and for the Cold War – an age far different from the one we encounter today – do not help matters.

While national export control systems and international arrangements, such as the Nuclear Suppliers Group and the Missile Technology Control Regime, continue to play a critical role in stemming weapons proliferation, they are woefully unequal to today's proliferation challenge. The Khan affair and other experiences shone a spotlight on the shortcomings of these institutions. The good news is that many influential people now recognize these problems, national and international export controls can be and are being improved, and analysts such as those who have contributed to this book are making critical contributions.

My colleagues and I at the Centre for International Trade and Security at the University of Georgia have been working on these issues for nearly two decades. We have witnessed the end of the Cold War and the advent of the War on Terror. We have evaluated the use and utility of export controls, both past and present. We have found that export controls play an important role in controlling the spread of weapons of mass destruction. And we know that export controls remain vital. They definitely have a future – but what will that future be?

This book brings together a group of distinguished analysts of non-proliferation, hailing from several regions and numerous countries around the world. International experience, perspectives and analysis are critically important when examining the future of international export controls, the central topic of this book. The inhabitants of different regions and countries tend to appraise the practice of export control differently, just as they appraise the problem of terrorism differently. The international community's efforts to counteract terrorism and proliferation benefit greatly from international research, dialogue, communication and understanding.

This volume contributes significantly in this regard. The experience and analysis found in these pages raise and address in depth a host of critical issues surrounding international export controls. The authors present insight and analysis regarding national systems, international institutions and the economic, political and security contexts in which export controls operate. Taken together, the chapters that follow provide much of what we need to know to reconfigure export controls to meet the challenges of the twenty-first century.

I commend the editor, Professor Daniel H. Joyner of the University of Warwick, and his contributors for producing a book that speaks truth to power. They have drawn on their scientific training and practical experience, calling attention to issues that policymakers must address if we are to avoid weapons proliferation that we and our children may live to regret. The topic of this book is of critical importance. The analysis within it is of great value. *Non-Proliferation Export Controls: Origins, Challenges and Proposals for Strengthening* makes an important contribution on one of the critical endeavours of our day.

Gary K. Bertsch
Athens, Georgia, USA
February 2006

Introduction

Daniel H. Joyner
Lecturer, University of Warwick
Senior Research Fellow, Centre for International Trade and Security, University of Georgia

As edited volumes tend to do, this one has evolved in its scope and theme due to the individual perspectives of the authors on their subjects. And while for an editor this can cause some initial concern, in the end inevitably the result is a richer collection of contributions, and a better overall work.

The theme of this volume was originally intended to be an analysis of the multilateral export control regimes (MECR), growing out of work in which I was involved, along with a core group of researchers at the University of Georgia Centre for International Trade and Security. As we pursued our research into the MECR, we were very fortunate to receive the support and advice of officials in a number of national governments, as well as colleagues in other academic institutions and non-governmental organizations. This research network of scholars and regime experts became the nucleus of the contributors to this volume.

Thus, I originally chose as a theme for this volume *The Future of Multilateral Non-Proliferation Export Control Regimes*. However, as work progressed on the authors' contributions, and as other authors from various disciplines were invited to participate, I observed that a number of authors were writing very interesting and original pieces expanding on this theme in very useful ways, and broadening the treatment to consider not just the regimes themselves but also a variety of issues in national systems and in international law and policy that have an effect on, and are affected by the MECR.

I was extremely gratified by this expansion of scope, as I thought it gave a more comprehensive and well-rounded view of the regimes themselves, as well as, importantly, the national and international legal and political contexts in which the regimes operate.

The title *Non-Proliferation Export Controls: Origins, Challenges and Proposals for Strengthening* has therefore been chosen to reflect this greater diversity of issues examined. It is meant to encompass institutional analysis of the MECR (Gahlaut, Lipson, Jones), analysis of national export control systems and their relationship with the MECR (McEldowney, Anderson and Svankjaer Thagaard), challenges facing the MECR from global economic dynamics (Smith and Garcia-Alonso), trends in regionalization of international export control norms (Yamamoto), as well as a number of other perspectives, ranging from the highly practical to the highly theoretical, on how the MECR and international export controls generally can be strengthened (Scheinman, Cupitt and Jones, Joyner, Kelle).

I hope that this broader coverage will enhance the contribution of this volume to the wider literature on export controls and non-proliferation studies more generally. I further hope that it will promote greater attention to the role of export controls in the international community's overall non-proliferation programme.

Export controls are an element of national regulatory frameworks which receive little notice, and even less rigorous scrutiny from high levels of official pay grades, until they fail in a spectacular way. This phenomenon was brought to the world's attention in alarming fashion in early 2004, when it was revealed that the father of Pakistan's gas centrifuge programme, Dr Abdul Qadeer Khan, had been masterminding a long-standing, clandestine international smuggling ring in nuclear materials and related dual-use goods. It has since become clear that through this complex system of middlemen and trans-shipment points, both fissile materials and an array of both tangible and intangible technologies fit for use in nuclear weapons programmes, were transferred to countries including Libya, Iran and North Korea.

The inherent limitations of export controls, and export control regulation on both the national and international levels are well known. Since not all states have effective export control systems in their national law, there is a strong collective action problem present in the system, and a danger of economic undercut.

In terms of the multilateral regimes (which could be technically referred to as plurilateral, as accession must be approved by the standing membership) there are many states who are either unwilling to become members of the regimes, or who have not been allowed membership by existing regime members. This non-universality therefore limits the influence of the regimes in harmonizing export control standards in national systems.

A further limitation of the MECR, inherent as well in the treaties to which they are related (most notably the Nuclear Non-proliferation Treaty, the Chemical Weapons Convention and the Biological Weapons Convention), is the fact that all existing restrictions within these regimes upon manufacture, possession and trafficking in weapons-related technologies are addressed to states. Thus, at the international level there is no substantive restriction on private parties, including business entities as well as other non-state actors, engaging in any of these activities.

These problems of the universality of the non-proliferation 'treaties and regimes' system, as well as its state-centric regulatory character, were precisely the problems which the United Nations Security Council sought to address through Resolution 1540, passed on 28 April 2004.

Notwithstanding these limitations, export controls and the multilateral regimes which seek to harmonize and standardize them, have been, and continue to be, a vital component part of the international non-proliferation legal and policy framework, and their value and importance should not be underestimated.

While their precise impact can never be calculated due to the absence of control case, it is strongly persuasive, both from anecdotal evidence and from what empirical evidence has been gathered, that for the past 40 years national export controls have had a significant effect in slowing the proliferation of WMD-related items and technologies to states and non-state actors of concern to export-controlling countries.[1] The MECR, in turn, have played a very significant role in providing normative standards for the coordination and harmonization of national export control regulations, and in fleshing out the details of the spirit of the treaty instruments to which they are related.

However, as a number of the authors in this volume point out, national export control systems and the multilateral regimes which seek to harmonize them, face unprecedented challenges due to changing global political and economic realities. The concern is expressed by a number of contributors that, unless more attention is paid to their proper maintenance and rigorous application, the usefulness of export controls will be diminished as a result of these forces, resulting in a likely increase in both the speed and scope of the problem of WMD-related materials proliferation.

It is hoped that the analysis of these challenges, as well as proposals for strengthening international export controls included in the chapters of this volume, will contribute to both scholarly and policy-oriented discourse on this important subject.

Daniel Joyner
Coventry, United Kingdom
February 2006

[1] For research into the effectiveness of export controls, see the University of Georgia Centre for International Trade and Security website at http://www.uga.edu/cits/home/index.htm.

PART I
Introduction to International Export Controls

Chapter 1

Multilateral Export Control Regimes: Operations, Successes, Failures and the Challenges Ahead

Seema Gahlaut
Senior Research Associate,
Centre for International Trade and Security, University of Georgia

The international non-proliferation community has been grappling with a number of challenges over the past few years. Recent research suggests that terrorist groups are becoming interested in acquiring weapons of mass destruction (WMD), that state actors continue to remain interested in developing latent WMD capability (if not the weapons themselves), and that the black market in materials and technologies that can assist both types of actors in this quest continues to thrive. This situation persists even as we see a growth in the number of international agreements and initiatives to control the proliferation of nuclear, chemical, biological weapons and missiles. Within these, the agreements to regulate trade and transfers of sensitive dual-use technologies have been under maximum strain. Globalization of liberal free market ideology, the diffusion of advanced technologies to an ever larger number of states, and the transnationalization of the high-tech industry have together created an environment where controls on export of sensitive technologies are hard to legislate upon, and even harder to implement and enforce at the national level. Reaching and sustaining export control agreements between nations has become correspondingly more difficult. Despite these trends, the four major multilateral export control regimes: the Nuclear Suppliers Group (NSG), the Missile Technology Control Regime (MTCR), the Australia Group (AG) and the Wassenaar Arrangement (WA) have survived, and are engaged in efforts to re-equip themselves to face the changed environment (see Table 1.1). In order to assess whether, and to what extent, they will succeed in their mission, we must examine their origins, operations, successes and failures.

Origins of Multilateral Export Control Coordination and Cooperation

The first post-Second World War attempt to coordinate export controls resulted in the establishment of the Coordinating Committee on Multilateral Export Controls (COCOM) by the United States and its allies. Yet the objective of export controls in COCOM was not the prevention of WMD proliferation in general: the focus was primarily on denial of technology to the opposing Communist Bloc – the Soviet Union, China and members of the Soviet-led alliance.[1] In time, the focus expanded to include states that were either considered sympathetic to the Communist ideology or were deemed to be potential conduits of western technology to the Communist Bloc.

Within two decades of the formation of COCOM, during the late 1960s, negotiations on the Nuclear Non-proliferation Treaty (NPT) produced near-identical drafts from the United States and the Soviet Union regarding the broad contours of the proposed treaty: the two ideological adversaries recognized their common interest in preventing the proliferation of nuclear weapons technology to other states. The final form of the NPT text, however, had no specifics on how to implement and enforce Article 2 commitments.[2] Suppliers within the NPT formed the Zangger Committee to create guidelines on regulating nuclear exports within the mandate of NPT.[3]

The nuclear test by India in 1974 necessitated the creation of an alternate arrangement that would regulate nuclear trade *more strictly* than the NPT-bound Zangger Committee. Thus was born the first of the multilateral export control regimes in 1975: the London Suppliers Club – later renamed the Nuclear Suppliers Group (NSG).[4] Subsequently, two other parallel regimes came to be established: the Australia Group (AG) to regulate trade in chemical and biological technologies in 1985[5] and the Missile Technology Control Regime (MTCR) in 1987.[6] The fourth regime, the Wassenaar Arrangement (WA) was established in 1995 (Smith and Udis 2001, 81–92). It was a refurbished and updated successor to the COCOM which, by 1993, had already lost its *raison d'être* as the primary targets of this regime – the Soviet Union and the Warsaw Pact – disintegrated.

Table 1.1 The Four Multilateral Export Control Regimes[7]

The Nuclear Suppliers Group (NSG) is an informal agreement established in 1975. Currently, 45 states are members (with the European Union as an observer). NSG members agree to common guidelines governing exports of nuclear materials, technologies and related equipment. NSG seeks to ensure that civilian nuclear trade does not contribute to nuclear weapons acquisition. The Group's actions are viewed as complementary measures in support of the 1971 Nuclear Non-Proliferation Treaty and the 1954 International Atomic Energy Agency (IAEA). The IAEA first published the NSG guidelines on nuclear export in 1978. There are two sets of NSG Guidelines: the first one governs the export of items that are especially designed or prepared for nuclear use, while the second one includes items that can make a major contribution to an unsafeguarded nuclear fuel cycle or nuclear explosive activity, but which have non-nuclear uses as well. The Group has no charter or constitution. It operates by consensus. Members voluntarily adhere to the guidelines, and share information on nuclear proliferation concerns. Recently, NSG members have begun to consider proposals for responding to the threat posed by nuclear terrorism. Website: <www.nsg-online.org>.

Table 1.1 continued

The Australia Group (AG) is an informal agreement established in 1984. Currently, 39 states are members (with the European Union and Singapore as observers). AG members agree to common guidelines governing chemicals, pharmaceuticals and pathogens, and related technologies and equipment. AG seeks to ensure that exporting or transshipping countries do not inadvertently assist chemical and biological weapon (CBW) proliferation. Members meet annually in Paris. The Group's actions are viewed as complementary measures in support of the 1925 Geneva Protocol, the 1972 Biological and Toxins Weapons Convention and the 1993 Chemical Weapons Convention. The Group has no charter or constitution. It operates by consensus. Members voluntarily adhere to the guidelines, and share information on CBW proliferation concerns. Recently, AG has become the first regime where members have agreed to adopt catch-all controls as a means for ensuring greater government–industry partnership in controlling sensitive exports to suspect end-users. Website: <www.australiagroup.net/>.
The Missile Technology Control Regime (MTCR) is an informal agreement established in 1987. Currently, 34 states are members. MTCR members seek to prevent the proliferation of unmanned delivery systems that may be used for delivering weapons of mass destruction. It controls exports of missiles (and related technology) whose performance in terms of payload and range exceeds stated parameters. There are two categories of items controlled. Category I includes complete systems and subsystems capable of carrying a payload of 500 kg over a range of at least 300 km, and specially designed production facilities for such systems. Category II includes missile-related components such as propellants, avionics equipment and other items used for the production of Category I systems. The Group has no charter or constitution. It operates by consensus. Members voluntarily adhere to the guidelines, and share information on missile proliferation concerns. Members meet annually in Paris. Website: <www.mtcr.info/>.
The Wassenaar Arrangement (WA) is an informal agreement established in 1995. Currently, 39 states are members. WA members seek to prevent destabilizing accumulations of conventional weapons and sensitive dual-use goods and technologies. Accordingly, WA was designed to promote transparency, exchange of views and information, and greater responsibility among supplier states. The Group has no charter or constitution. It operates by consensus. Members voluntarily adhere to the guidelines, and share information on conventional weapons and dual-use proliferation concerns. The institution has no list of target countries or restricted entities, although it does (since December 2001) target 'terrorist groups and organizations, as well as individual terrorists'. There are, however, agreed lists of items: a munitions list that consists of the same basic categories of major weapons-systems as the UN Register on Conventional Weapons; and a dual-use technology list that is broken into two tiers. Tier 1, the basic list, is made up of sensitive items and technologies; and tier 2 consists of very sensitive items that are subject to more stringent monitoring. Final interpretation and implementation of these lists is left to the national discretion of participating states. There is a small secretariat located in Vienna, and there are several expert and technical working group meetings held each year in addition to the plenary in December. The Wassenaar Arrangement replaced the Cold War export control mechanism (COCOM) that sought to deny military-related articles to the Soviet Union and its allies. Website: <www.wassenaar.org/>. Information is current as of September 2005.

There were a few common factors that formed the bases for the creation of these four regimes. Each regime arose as a response to the perceived gap in the existing formal non-proliferation treaty that regulated state behaviour with regard to a particular type of technology. Each regime sought to overcome the implementation and enforcement weaknesses in the existing arms control and non-proliferation agreements. Each defined its own practices and procedures based on the assumption of a rosy future in which the capabilities and the motivations of the target states would be contained primarily through supply-side controls and strengthening non-proliferation norms on the one hand, while on the other, the technological oligopoly of its members would continue unchallenged into the distant future. Finally, participants/members of each of these regimes shared a unity of purpose which came from a mix of shared security and commercial concerns.

Table 1.2 Basic Principles of Multilateral Export Control Regimes[8]

Principle/ Regime	NSG	AG	MTCR	WA
Prevent proliferation of WMDs	Nuclear weapons	Chemical and biological weapons	Ballistic and cruise missiles	Advanced conventional weapons and WMD-relevant dual-use technologies
Support the relevant international treaty	NPT, CTBT, IAEA	CWC and BWC		UN Arms Register, EU Code of Conduct on Conventional Weapons
Monitor and regulate exports of WMD-relevant technology	Fissile material, nuclear weapons technology, related dual-use materials and technology, nuclear power plant equipment	Chemicals, plant, animal and human pathogens, and industrial and laboratory equipment used for manufacturing these	Missiles, satellite launch vehicles, missile components, composite materials	
Not interfere in legitimate civilian trade	Export licences granted for qualified end-users, and under certain conditions	Export licences granted for qualified end-users, and under certain conditions	Export licences granted for qualified end-users, and under certain conditions	Export licences granted for qualified end-users, and under certain conditions

Operations of the Multilateral Export Control Regimes (MECR)

Each of the four regimes aims to stop proliferation of (a particular type of) WMD-technology, while ensuring that civilian trade in these technologies is not unduly hampered (see Table 1.2). Each regime claims to support international non-proliferation norms and treaties, and exhorts non-members to adopt guidelines similar to its own. Each has a detailed and fairly specific control list of items, mostly graded into lists or tiers denoting their level of sensitivity. Export of more sensitive items requires stricter scrutiny of the recipient's antecedents by the exporting member. All items on a control list require members to exercise caution when exporting outside the group, and to institute conditions that a recipient (importing) state and/or entity must agree to before the export can be licenced. These could vary from the requirement of end-use/end-user certification in the pre-licence phase to the requirement of post-shipment verification by the exporting state after the export has taken place. Yet, in all cases, the agreements only set the guidelines for export licensing for their members – the actual licensing decision is made by the individual member state and is not a collective decision.

Table 1.3 Common Rules of Operation

Rule/Regime	NSG	AG	MTCR	WA
Informal	X	X	X	X
Closed membership	X	X	X	X
Consensus	X	X	X	X
National discretion	X	X	X	X
Annual plenaries	X	X	X	X
Detailed control lists of items	X	X	X	X
Broad guidelines for export conduct	X	X	X	X
Technical working groups	X	X	X	X
Episodic review of control list	X	X	X	X
Episodic review of guidelines	X	X	X	X
Rotating chairmanship	X	X	X	X
Permanent secretariat	–	–	–	X
Permanent point of contact	X	X	X	–
Secure database of shared information	X	X	X	X

Each of the regimes has certain common rules under which it operates (see Table 1.3).[9] Each is an informal political arrangement among its members. There is no document that a state has to sign in order to become a member. Membership in each of the regimes is restricted: all members have to agree to allow a new member to join. All decisions within the regime require unanimity and consensus. For instance, revisions of the control list (whether adding or deleting or further detailing an item) cannot take place unless all members agree. Each member is free to exercise 'national discretion' when making a particular export licensing decision. Thus, while regime guidelines are the same for every member, implementation and enforcement details of the same are left to the national level agencies. For example, although all members of the MTCR might agree to its guidelines that members should not export item X to a country that might use it in a WMD programme and almost all members agree that country Y fulfils this risk criterion, an individual member could use its national discretion to licence export of item X to country Y because it deems the risk of diversion to a WMD programme to be minimal. In such a situation, dissenting members might criticize the offending member in bilateral or group meetings, but the group as a whole has no formal mechanism to either veto the export, or establish that a violation has occurred, or even be able to punish the violating member.

Much of the actual nuts and bolts work of a particular regime, such as revisions of guidelines or control list, takes place within Technical Working Groups (TWGs) that meet several times through the year. Review and revisions of guidelines and control lists are episodic and not mandated to be regular and periodic. If one or more members believe that some revision or modification is necessary, a TWG is established to discuss and debate all aspects of the proposed change. The TWGs are theoretically open to all members, but in practice, tend to have just a few members, especially those that have a direct interest and expertise relating to the issue–item being discussed. The agenda of a TWG is mostly set by the member state that has proposed a particular change. Much of the debate and negotiation on the issue–item happens within the TWGs, and only consensus decisions are tabled at the plenaries where the rest of the members have the option to agree or disagree with the proposed change. Even one dissenting vote means that the matter goes back to the TWG for further debate – which now includes the dissenting member. Depending on the depth of the dissent, contentious revisions sometimes take years to be resolved and accepted into the group's guidelines – although individual members sometimes adopt the change unilaterally, even before formal acceptance by the entire group.

Members share aggregate information about their dual-use exports and export denials, as well as intelligence about proliferation programmes of target states. Theoretically all members are supposed to share such intelligence with all other members. In reality, however, members with more intelligence resources share more information, and do so selectively – more sensitive information is shared among only those members that work together closely in other related fora.

Table 1.4 Membership (as of September 2005)

NSG	AG	MTCR	WA
Argentina	Argentina	Argentina	Argentina
Australia	Australia	Australia	Australia
Austria	Austria	Austria	Austria
Belarus	–	–	–
Belgium	Belgium	Belgium	Belgium
Brazil	–	Brazil	–

Table 1.4 continued

NSG	AG	MTCR	WA
Bulgaria	Bulgaria	Bulgaria	Bulgaria
Canada	Canada	Canada	Canada
Cyprus	Cyprus	–	–
China	–	–	–
Croatia	–	–	Croatia
Czech Republic	Czech Republic	Czech Republic	Czech Republic
Denmark	Denmark	Denmark	Denmark
Estonia	Estonia	–	Estonia
Finland	Finland	Finland	Finland
France	France	France	France
Germany	Germany	Germany	Germany
Greece	Greece	Greece	Greece
Hungary	Hungary	Hungary	Hungary
–	Iceland	Iceland	–
Ireland	Ireland	Ireland	Ireland
Italy	Italy	Italy	Italy
Japan	Japan	Japan	Japan
Kazakhstan	–	–	–
Korea, South	Korea, South	Korea, South	Korea, South
Latvia	Latvia	–	Latvia
Lithuania	Lithuania	–	Lithuania
Luxembourg	Luxembourg	Luxembourg	Luxembourg
Malta	Malta	–	Malta
Netherlands	Netherlands	Netherlands	Netherlands
New Zealand	New Zealand	New Zealand	New Zealand
Norway	Norway	Norway	Norway
Poland	Poland	Poland	Poland
Portugal	Portugal	Portugal	Portugal
Romania	Romania	–	Romania
Russia	–	Russia	Russia
Slovakia	Slovakia	–	Slovakia
Slovenia	Slovenia	–	Slovenia
South Africa	–	South Africa	–
Spain	Spain	Spain	Spain
Sweden	Sweden	Sweden	Sweden
Switzerland	Switzerland	Switzerland	Switzerland
Turkey	Turkey	Turkey	Turkey
Ukraine	Ukraine	Ukraine	Ukraine
UK	UK	UK	UK
USA	USA	USA	USA
45	**39**	**34**	**39**

Membership (see Table 1.4) in the regimes is by invitation, and all members must approve of the decision to induct a particular new member. Each regime, broadly, has a set of basic qualifications that a prospective member must have before it can be considered for membership. All regimes require that members must be signatories of major international non-proliferation treaties or their equivalent bilateral or multilateral agreements. They must all be treaty signatories in good standing. They must commit that they will not proliferate WMD technologies and must have or will establish strong national export control systems to implement and enforce this commitment. Despite the restricted membership rules and the essentially self-selecting nature of the regimes, membership in each has grown substantially in the past two decades. This expansion, however, has come with its own set of problems.

The export control regimes originated with groups of like-minded supplier states, notably the United States and its allies in western Europe and Japan, who agreed on the nature of the threat and appropriate responses. Since the end of the Cold War, the number of states participating in the regimes has grown, but at the cost of diluting the original membership criteria. From being exclusive groups of western industrial states, membership has expanded to include former Soviet states (including Russia), developed Asian states, and a number of Eastern European states. This expansion was driven primarily by the euphoric belief within the non-proliferation community that the end of the Cold War had inaugurated an era in which former Warsaw Pact states would make common cause with the West to squelch WMD proliferation (Beck and Gahlaut 2003). Another factor was the consolidation of the European Union (EU) into a common economic market with few barriers to the movement of goods and services. The extension of the export control regimes to include the EU thus became almost automatic.[10] Interestingly, although the regimes began as groups of like-minded supplier states, that is, states that had the capabilities to produce, export and control exports of WMD-relevant dual-use items, a large number of later entrants are neither suppliers nor have strong export controls, or are particularly like-minded! Indeed, some of the new entrants have been invited solely because they have political and economic agreements with major supplier states which make them potential transit and trans-shipment points for exports from the major supplier states.

Successes

Some of the practices that one or more of the regimes established have had salutary impact on the international non-proliferation arena. By providing a forum for technology suppliers to share information and concerns about proliferation, and by establishing some rules (see Table 1.5) to coordinate their exports better, the regimes have helped develop habits of cooperation among states that might otherwise have engaged in mutually destructive competition to sell dangerous technologies. The practice of regular information sharing, inter and intra-state consultations and the pro-active identification of proliferation-sensitive technologies, equipment and processes all helped establish the minimum common expectations about others' behaviour.

Table 1.5 New Rules for a New World

New Rule	NSG	AG	MTCR	WA
No undercut rule	Yes	Yes	Yes	No
Prior notification of export licence granted	Yes	Yes	Yes	No (only post-facto notification)
Periodic notification of export licence denials	Yes	Yes	Yes	Yes (aggregate; for past 3 years)
Share data on approvals	No (except for dual-use items)	No (except via CWC)	No	Yes (but only aggregate)
Catch-all controls	Yes 2004	Yes	Yes 2003	Yes 2003 (but only re UNSC embargos)
Controls on intangible technology transfers	Yes	Yes	Yes 2004	Yes 2001
Black list (terrorist groups)	–	Yes	–	–

To the extent that the regimes are essentially suppliers' cartels, they have successfully managed the issue of selective denials and controlling the supply of proliferation-sensitive technology that have uses in civilian sectors. The international non-proliferation treaties accept the right to civilian uses of dual-use technologies and prescribe minimum conditions that signatories have to meet in order to access technology for civilian uses. However, treaty-mandated provisions for detecting violations of these prescriptions, for establishing wrongdoing, and for resultant denial of access to technology are mostly complicated and have loopholes that cheating signatories can exploit for years. Export control regimes closed this loophole by asserting their identities as separate from treaties: thus they assert their right to go beyond treaty-mandated criteria and processes. They can deny a treaty signatory state access to technology even when it apparently meets the basic minimum conditions.

These regimes, despite being outside the framework of established non-proliferation treaties, have helped establish some recognizable non-proliferation norms and best practices. The idea that responsible states not only have laws that uphold commitment to non-proliferation but also clear and specific control lists has gained currency as the regimes have developed more comprehensive control lists. They have had an impact on members as well as non-members' behaviour: states have unilaterally adopted/adapted regime control lists and guidelines and some have declared themselves to be adherents (although they are not members).[11] As such, regimes have gained growing legitimacy vis-à-vis the formal treaty system. Their actions have been acknowledged as effective in slowing proliferation programmes: monitoring and denials by major suppliers of technology have raised the costs of proliferation for many states.

Again, their non-treaty-based nature has allowed the regimes to be flexible and adaptable. They have, in some cases, become informal channels of give and take on non-proliferation issues with prospective members.[12] They have been successful in recruiting disparate states to their cause: former enemies and targets have been co-opted as fellow members or adherents. As a new technology environment was identified or as new proliferation patterns were seen, the regimes were able to respond relatively quickly: they have the flexibility to adapt control lists to new developments.

Challenges

Despite their apparent success in slowing proliferation, socializing new members into their norms, and converting more non-members to consider becoming members, the regimes also suffer from certain inadequacies that might hamper their effectiveness in the future. For some scholars, unless they respond to the challenges posed by globalization, alternative suppliers and terrorism, the regimes will ultimately be overtaken by events.[13] First, the high technology industry is now truly globalized, where much of technological innovation takes place in the private sector and is driven by teams of scientists and engineers who work across national boundaries. Most of the innovative companies are multinational, not only in terms of physical location, but also of workforce, management, ownership and target markets. Members of the export control regimes, therefore, need to define their rules and regulations more clearly and coherently, keeping in mind the need to balance non-proliferation requirements with the realities of high-tech commerce. Yet we have a constellation of four separate regimes that essentially do the same things to control different technologies relevant to weapons of mass destruction, while maintaining minor differences in procedures. This situation not only makes it harder for industry to comply, but also threatens to leave loopholes for future A.Q. Khans to exploit.

Second, the private sector in developed economies has replaced the state as the locus of technological innovation and market expansion, and dual-use technologies claim a growing share of exports in most dynamic economies. The civilian markets for these technologies are now global in scope and immensely lucrative. They also show how economic liberalism can be an engine of prosperity in the world. Controlling civilian dual-use trade on the basis of fuzzy or unilateral foreign policy considerations puts domestic industry at a disadvantage. Globalization has created more markets in states outside the comfort zone of the regimes. Members increasingly use national discretion to interpret regime guidelines in ways that favour their domestic industries and manufacturers.

Third, as defence budgets shrink everywhere in the developed world (except in the United States), manufacturers of high technology are forced to compete for foreign markets. The economic and security interests of the regimes' members overlap less and less. Serious implications for the regimes' cohesion and unity of purpose could result from divergent interests. The rift within the Wassenaar

Arrangement between exporters of conventional weapons and exporters of dual-use technologies, for instance, has stymied reform in the past. States such as China, India and Israel have emerged not only as possible alternative suppliers of such goods, but also as attractive markets for technology-embedded capital investment and as useful partners for collaborative development of certain technologies. The regimes will find it increasingly difficult to allow these countries to collaborate in one technology sector while forbidding collaboration in another, because many dual-use technologies are fungible across sectors.

Finally, international concern about state-to-state proliferation has grown in the recent years and few states would like to attract international opprobrium. Therefore, it is increasingly likely that in the future proliferation may take place either with covert official blessing or via unauthorized collusion among significant domestic actors within states. North Korea, Pakistan, Malaysia, South Africa and the United Arab Emirates have already become – willingly or unwillingly – the alternative sources of high-tech goods and/or conduits for proliferation networks (Albright and Hinderstein 2005). Either way, these states will pose a unique challenge to the regimes as secondary suppliers from the developing world. Their technologies may not be advanced but might be just enough for non-state actors seeking either weapons of mass disruption or for economic and political blackmail.

Failures

Despite the changes in their external environment and internal composition, regimes seem content to maintain their original rules and practices. From a modernization perspective, this stasis would increasingly undermine the adaptability of the regimes over time.[14] While there has been a severe dilution of the original membership criteria (like-mindedness and supplier capability) within the regimes, yet each of the regimes maintains rules unsuitable for a growing and diverse membership (unanimity, discretion, response to violations, and arbitrary and/or vague criteria for membership).[15]

Continuation of the consensus voting rule is a perfect example. This rule reflected the character of the regimes at their inception, when they were all groups of like-minded suppliers of WMD-relevant technologies. Now, however, membership in the regimes has expanded to include states that are either not suppliers or are not like-minded or do not have the domestic consensus to abide by all regime guidelines. Consensus voting might prove counterproductive under such circumstances. The intransigence of a single member can stymie updates to the control lists or guidelines, causing the regimes to lag behind developments in technology, bringing them to the same level of inefficiency plagued by international treaties.

Controls on exports of dual-use items and technologies can only be effective, and will only earn the willing support of domestic industry, when all *relevant* actors adhere to them. Yet the regimes allow their members unlimited national discretion: members are free to interpret regime guidelines according to their national interests, with little care for how fellow members' economic and security interests might be undercut by self-serving interpretations (Beck and Gahlaut 2003).

Despite the growing clamour for transparency and accountability within treaties and agreements in various spheres, export control regimes have not been able to significantly change their members' behaviours. The regimes still do not require their members to fully disclose which exports they have approved and which they have denied, causing opacity that sometimes allows one member to supply a controlled item that was denied by another. For example, a recent US General Accounting Office (GAO) report noted that many governments that participate in the Nuclear Suppliers Group have yet to share any information on export denials. Nor have they shared even the informal suggestions they have issued to businesses advising them not to pursue contracts with suspect end-users (see US GAO 2002). The GAO report also drew attention to problems of *timely* information sharing. The report noted that the United States did not report any of 27 Australia Group-related export licence denials between 1996 and 2001 and also pointed out that nearly half of the Wassenaar member states failed to submit information on export denials within established reporting timeframes. The report observed, furthermore, that regime members often failed to incorporate the decisions reached within the regimes into their national export control regulations quickly and uniformly. There have been cases in which some countries, including the United States, have taken as long as a year to make the agreed-upon changes to their national laws (ibid., 23).

Finally, although there is no dearth of discussion about corporate accountability today, the export control regimes have no mechanism for prosecuting violations by members. In effect they rely on individual members to rebuke and bring pressure on violators through bilateral diplomacy. Violations have typically elicited little more than protests and demarchés from some members. Diplomatic action generally has little impact, since offenders choose to interpret unilateral protests as subjective, politically motivated, or contrary to the principle of national discretion (Gahlaut and Jones 2004). This does not bode well for the future regime cohesion and effectiveness.

In their efforts to regulate or deny dual-use technology to non-members, all four export control regimes face criticism from non-members for being opaque, part of an exclusionary club based upon discrimination against the Third World, subjective, and going beyond the mandates of existing non-proliferation treaties.[16] These criticisms are unlikely to subside in the near future, especially now as the control lists of the regimes expand to accommodate terrorist-relevant (that is, relatively unsophisticated) technologies (Van Diepen 2002).

However, there have been a few positive developments in this context during the past few years. First, the informal export control regimes have communicated their goals and methods with significant non-members. Such outreach has lessened suspicions of developing nations somewhat.[17] Second, several regime studies have attempted to counter criticisms by gathering data on the actual quantum of licence denials for sensitive items, thereby placing the onus on the critics to provide counterfactual evidence to support their claims that the regimes limit economic development. Third, several major critics, such as Argentina, Brazil, China, South Africa, have been admitted as members in the informal regimes. Fourth, there is growing realization within the informal regimes that they should have mutually supportive operational relationship with international organizations that are engaged in monitoring, verification, and other enforcement activities relevant to trade and transfers of sensitive items. Some scholars now see the World Customs Organization, the IAEA, the Organization for the Prohibition of Chemical Weapons (OPCW) as complementary organizations with whom the regimes ought to have greater interaction via periodic sharing of expertise and information (Agersnap 2004; see also Feakes 2001). Clearly, multilateral export control regimes are not adequately working with other non-proliferation organizations. The Director General of the IAEA, Mohammed ElBaradei recently noted, '… there is no linkage between the export control system and the verification system. Export control information is not systematically shared with the IAEA, nor even fully among the members of the Nuclear Suppliers Group' (ElBaradei 2004).

Finally, the added advantage of closer cooperation with established non-proliferation organizations would be that the regimes will gain greater legitimacy – something they have tried to claim unilaterally in the past by a one-way relationship: the submission of 'notification of intent' to treaty-based organizations like the IAEA and the OPCW by individual members. These legitimacy claims will become more acceptable to the sceptics if the informal regimes find ways to have a genuinely mutual relationship with the formal elements of the non-proliferation regime.

Beyond the above challenges and failures, the regimes have had some unintended consequences: on the one hand, these consequences suggest that the regimes were successful in their mission, but on the other hand, the very success may have spawned new conditions that alter the future operative environment of the regimes. For instance, in most cases of opportunistic proliferators, the regimes helped raised the costs of acquiring WMD capabilities. One could argue that de-proliferation by states such as Argentina, Brazil, Ukraine, South Africa, Kazakhstan, Belarus and Libya was at least partially induced by the tightening rules of the regimes. At the same time, the more determined targets of the regimes, such as China, India, Israel, Iran, Pakistan and North Korea, hardened their resolve to increase their self-reliance. In the process of resisting the regimes they have developed capabilities that might no longer be as susceptible to technology-denials in the future. In turn, these programmes have also developed the capacity to be alternate suppliers and to form supply-chains that defeat the regimes' rules. China, Pakistan and North Korea have already proven their capability and intent for horizontal proliferation,[18] while Iran remains on the brink (Ghattas 2005). China has been co-opted by the regimes to some extent: it is now in the NSG and efforts continue to bring it into the MTCR in the near future.[19] However, thus far, India and Israel continue to exercise restraint unilaterally, based on internal political decisions.[20]

Choices before the Multilateral Export Control Regimes

The world of technology is changing exponentially. The biggest challenge that the export control regimes face is keeping abreast of technological developments and institutional innovations in the field of business. National boundaries no longer circumscribe how technology-innovation and export is managed in the private sector. At a time when businesses are streamlining their operations to innovate, produce and export faster, the members of the control regimes must streamline their own regulatory efforts if they hope to keep up. This could conceivably be done in several ways. One would be to update internal procedures and establish cross-regime linkages and information sharing. A more radical means would be to establish one unified export control regime (instead of the current four), which is empowered to establish objective procedures to determine when a violation has taken place and how a collective reprimand should be administered.

The regimes are essentially at the crossroads of several procedural paths. They have to choose between increasing formality of commitment versus continuing to allow national discretion. As their membership becomes more diverse, the rules of unanimity and informality will perpetuate existing problems of delays in adapting to emerging situations. If the regimes are to be truly effective, members will need to establish and enforce common standards for export licensing, ensuring that national commercial considerations do not triumph over collective decision, that free-riding by some members is curtailed, and that industry has a level playing field across increasingly integrated markets. Accordingly, the scope of national discretion within the regimes will have to be narrowed somewhat and more specifically defined.

So long as the regimes were primarily focused on preventing state-to-state transfers, they created control lists based on technology trajectories that some of their own members went through. The common assumptions behind such lists were that states interested in developing credible WMD capability will look for advanced technology that will allow them to develop precise and battle-useable weapons. The recent intelligence about growing interest of terrorist groups in acquiring WMDs has changed the equations: terrorist groups are typically not interested in precise and advanced weapons. Their objectives are crude and direct: hit the enemy – to destroy and to cause mayhem – and, if required, to die in the operation. Precision, stealth, proven kill-capacity and battle-hardiness are irrelevant for such operations. This would imply that old, obsolete technologies and easily available materials might be enough to fashion crude WMDs. The consequent challenge for the regimes would be to begin controlling relatively low-level items and technologies as well. In essence, widening the control lists at a time when industry is demanding more streamlined lists of more strictly controlled items. The related challenge for regime members is to focus on import-monitoring as well. Thus far, regime members do not scrutinize exports to fellow members, because they are considered trustworthy. However, experts are suggesting that terrorist groups might find it easier to assemble a weapon in the target country itself rather than build it in another country and attempt to launch it from there or to import an assembled weapon into the target country. Regime members will have to institute procedures to scrutinize orders for dangerous items – even when they emanate from a fellow member state – verify their end-use/end-user and inform the national authorities of the importing state of the transfer.

Regimes now face a challenge in terms of choosing a specific path towards shoring up their effectiveness. They can institute stronger guidelines and internal procedures that deepen the commitment of existing members. For instance, they can develop a unified, coherent strategy for dealing with potential secondary suppliers and strongly encourage member states to share information freely with respect to acquisition strategies used by state and non-state actors linked to these states. Alternatively, they can focus on widening the membership by co-opting some of the secondary suppliers. In this case, it would make sense not to make the internal rules harsher and risk scaring away relevant new members who might not be ready to commit to such rules.

A more crucial trade-off that the regimes face relates to their attempts to gain legitimacy. Thus far, the regimes have responded to charges of illegitimacy – which usually cite their secrecy of operations and self-selection – by increasing transparency about their motives, functioning and guidelines. This has been done primarily in two ways: establishing websites and releasing consensus decisions at the end of plenaries on the one hand, and by engaging in outreach on the other. A related strategy of establishing legitimacy has been to harden their linkages with non-proliferation treaties. For instance, all four regimes assert that their objective is to uphold the norms and objectives of one or more treaties; NSG members routinely submit letters to IAEA affirming their adherence to some change in NSG guidelines; WA members refer to the UN Register and EU Code of Conduct in their operations; all four regimes set membership in the NPT or equivalent non-proliferation agreement as a crucial criterion for membership and for receipt of sensitive exports.

However, in the attempt to burnish their links with not just the norms but also the principles (legal commitments) of the formal treaties, the regimes might be boxing themselves in, perhaps becoming less flexible. The original intent behind the formation of the regimes was to have more flexibility – the ability to forge non-traditional/innovative solutions to proliferation problems – which formal treaties did not have. Ever closer and direct linkages with the treaties – while gaining the regimes more acceptance among their critics – would circumscribe their independence of action. A good example of these trade-offs is the issue of civilian nuclear cooperation with India. The July 2005 bilateral agreement between the United States and India (United States 2005) goes against the NPT norm[21] as well as makes an exception vis-à-vis the NSG full-scope safeguards requirement.[22] The NSG membership has yet to approve of this US initiative, although a few individual members have welcomed the deal (Chandrasekar 2005; White 2005; Willard 2005). A major institutional argument in support of the deal is that NSG is the only forum which was designed to be adaptable to new circumstances and to fill the loopholes that treaty-bound NPT cannot. In short, the more closely tied NSG is to NPT, the harder it will be for the NSG to maintain its flexibility to innovate.[23]

The final challenge the regimes face is that of the growing gap between their mandates and expectations from them. Political and public assessments of output and outcomes tend to be critical of the regimes – especially as new cases of proliferation come to light. However, much of this criticism stems from a lack of popular understanding about what regimes were designed to do and what 'power' they have, and consequently, unreasonable expectations from the regimes. For instance, disclosures of proliferation from the A.Q. Khan network led to sharp criticism of NSG based on the common assumption that NSG rules failed to control the actions of non-members (such as Pakistan, Iran, Iraq, China and so on).[24] When most NSG members did not sanction Russian nuclear cooperation with India and Iran, NSG was seen as a failure – without any realization that the voluntary nature of NSG commitments and the national discretion allowed to members precludes a unified response or even a mandatory response by all NSG members. Critics of WA focus on high levels of conventional arms exports by some members, even though WA is merely a transparency regime and not strictly a non-proliferation regime. The bottom line is that most members of the public and even the policymakers expect the regimes to stop proliferation – whereas the regimes have been set up to merely delay proliferation. Regimes are expected to perform like treaties – especially when fellow members are deemed to be in the wrong – yet individual members are loath to cede their own decisional independence. They often cite the informal nature of the regimes in support of their own actions that go beyond common understandings and guidelines! Regimes can minimize this duality of expectations only through public outreach within the member states.

Conclusion

The four multilateral export control regimes have performed reasonably well in curtailing the enthusiasm and ability of proliferators in the past decades. However, their operational environment is changing slowly in some cases (character and nature of the hard cases they have to focus on) and rapidly in others (technological innovation and globalization). Consequently, experts have presented a range of proposals to help the regimes renew and refurbish themselves. These range from the incremental changes within the regimes to meso-level changes in supporting institutions to the radical proposal of merger.

Incremental change proposals usually relate to the nuts and bolts issues within each regime – where better coordination and better specification of guidelines can improve implementation (Heine et al. 2004). Meso-level proposals take two tracks: first, a focus on improving national export control implementation among members and second, initiative to improve regional export control implementation such as United Nations Security Council Resolution 1540 and targeted outreach to regime non-members. Other proposals at this level include ideas for creating new micro-regimes (Cevasco 2001) and loose codes of conduct[25] on specific sub-categories of dual-use items or technologies. The proposal of merger is based on the argument of efficiency and consolidation: maintaining four separate information sharing systems and piecemeal sharing of information on WMD procurement efforts negates international efforts in the past decade to streamline the non-proliferation regime as a whole as well as efforts to integrate the activities of the export control regimes (Gahlaut et al. 2004).

It is not clear which path of reform the export control regimes are going to choose in the near future. However, some emerging issues in export control would continue to require multilateral coordination – whether inside the regimes or outside them. Among these are the dilemmas posed by the emerging suppliers, by terrorist groups, and by the transnational black market in WMD technologies. Each of these dilemmas further underlines the need to sensitize multinational industry regarding the modus operandi of suspect procurers. These also necessitate the training and equipping of customs, immigration and border security agencies to filter suspect transactions from vast volumes of legitimate ones, and to coordinate with their counterpart agencies across national boundaries in pursuit of proliferators. Recent meetings of regimes have attempted to establish such cross-regime linkages, but the question remains: will such piecemeal adaptations be able to overcome the new proliferation challenges facing the regimes?

References

Agersnap, L. (2004), 'Non-Proliferation and the Coordination of International Efforts', Occasional Paper, Centre for International Trade and Security, University of Georgia, Athens, GA, July 2004.

Albright, D. and Hinderstein, C. (2005), 'Unraveling the A.Q. Khan and Future Proliferation Networks', *The Washington Quarterly*, Spring 2005.

BBC, 'Chinese Firms Punished Over Iran', 18 January 2005, <news.bbc.co.uk/go/pr/fr/-/2/hi/americas/4183717.stm>.

Beck, M. and Gahlaut, S. (2003), 'Creating a New Multilateral Export Control Regime', *Arms Control Today*, April 2003.

Blackford, J. (2004), 'Asher Karni Case Shows Weakness in Nuclear Export Controls', *ISIS Brief*, 8 September 2004, <www.isis-online.org/publications/southafrica/asherkarni.html>.

Broad, W.J. and Sanger, D.E. (2004), 'Warhead Blueprints Link Libya Project to Pakistan Figure', *New York Times*, 4 February 2004.

Burr, W. (ed.) (2004), 'China, Pakistan, and the Bomb: The Declassified File on U.S. Policy, 1977–1997', *National Security Archive Electronic Briefing Book*, No. 114, 5 March 2004.

Cevasco, F. (2001), 'Survey and Assessment: Alternative Multilateral Export Control Structures', Working Paper No. 3, Study Group on Enhancing Multilateral Export Controls for US National Security, Henry L. Stimson Centre, April 2001.

Chandrasekar, V.S. (2005), 'Russia Endorses Civilian Nuclear Energy Pact', *Rediff.com*, 16 September 2005, <www.rediff.com/news/2005/sep/16pmun8.htm>.

DeSutter, P.A. (2003), 'China's Record of Proliferation Activities', Testimony by Assistant Secretary for Verification and Compliance Before the US–China Commission, 24 July 2003, Washington, DC.

ElBaradei, M. (2004), 'Nuclear Non-Proliferation: Global Security in a Rapidly Changing World', Presentation at the Carnegie Endowment for Peace, Non-Proliferation Conference, 21 June 2004, Washington, DC.

Feakes, D. (2001) 'Export Controls, Chemical Trade, and the Chemical Weapons Convention', Paper No. 62, SPRU Science and Technology Policy Research, University of Sussex, February 2001.

Frank, G. (2004), 'Speech to IAEA 48th General Conference by Director General of the Israeli Atomic Energy Commission', September 2004, <www.iaec.gov.il/pages_e/dover_04-09b.asp>.

Gahlaut, S. (2005), 'US–India Nuclear Deal Will Strengthen Non-Proliferation', *PacNet Newsletter*, 37, 31 August 2005, <www.csis.org/pacfor/pac0537.pdf>.

—— (2002), *Strengthening Multilateral Export Controls: A Non-Proliferation Priority*, Report from the Centre for International Trade and Security, Athens, GA, September 2002.

Gahlaut, S., Beck, M., Jones, S. and Joyner, D. (2004), *Roadmap to Reform: Creating a New Multilateral Export Control Regime*, Report from the Centre For International Trade and Security, University of Georgia, Athens, GA, November 2004.

Gahlaut, S. and Jones, S. (2004), 'Multilateral Export Control Regimes Must be Modernized', *Export Practitioner*, 2004.

Gahlaut, S. and Srivastava, A. (2005), *Non-Proliferation Export Controls in India: Update 2005*, Center for International Trade and Security, University of Georgia, Athens, GA, July 2005.

Gahlaut, S. and Zaborsky, V. (2004), 'Do Multilateral Regimes Have the Members They Really Need?', *Comparative Strategy*, Vol. 23, Fall 2004.

Ghattas, S.F. (2005), 'Iran May Give Nuclear Aid to Other Muslim Nations', *The Boston Globe*/Associated Press, 16 September 2005.

Heine, P., DuFresne, J., Weiss, L., Breland, N., Perry, T. and Walker, C. (2004), 'Building Effective Systems for Nuclear Export Control: Controlling Transit Trade through the Baltics, Caucasus, and Central Asia', Paper Presented at the Institute for Nuclear Material Management 45th Annual Meeting, 18 July 2004.

Hersh, S.M. (2003), 'The Cold Test: What the Administration Knew About Pakistan and the North Korean Nuclear Programme', *The New Yorker*, 27 January 2003.

Jones, S.A. (2003), 'EU Enlargement: Implications for EU and Multilateral Export Controls', *The Nonproliferation Review*, Summer 2003.

Kampani, G. (2002), 'Second Tier Proliferation: The Case of Pakistan and North Korea', *The Nonproliferation Review*, Fall/Winter 2002.

Mastanduno, M. (1992), *Economic Containment: COCOM and the Politics of East-West Trade*, Cornell University Press, Ithaca, NY.

Mistry, D. (2003), 'Beyond the MTCR: Building a Comprehensive Regime to Contain Ballistic Missile Proliferation', *International Security*, 2003.

Perry Robinson, J. (1992), 'The Australia Group: A Description and Assessment', in H.G. Brauch, H.J. van der Graaf, J. Grin and W. Smit (eds), *Controlling Military Research and Development and Exports of Dual Use Technologies as a Problem of Disarmament and Arms Control Policy in the 1990s*, VU University Press, Amsterdam and St Martin's Press, New York.

Schmidt, F. (1994), 'The Zangger Committee: Its History and Future Role', *The Nonproliferation Review*, Fall 1994.

Smith, R. and Udis, B. (2001), 'New Challenges to Arms Export Control: Whither Wassenaar?', *The Nonproliferation Review*, Summer 2001.

Srivastava, A. (2005), 'China's Export Controls: Assessing the Domestic and International Dimensions', *Arms Control Today*, November 2005.

Thorne, C.E. (1997), 'Multilateral Nuclear Export Controls: Past, Present and Future', Keynote Speech, Session 2, *International Seminar on the Role of Export Controls in Nuclear Non-Proliferation*; 7–8 October 1997, Vienna International Centre, Vienna <www.nuclearsuppliersgroup.org/PDF/SeminarControl1.pdf>.

US General Accounting Office (2002), 'Strategy Needed to Strengthen Multilateral Export Control Regimes', GAO-03-43, General Accounting Office, Washington, DC.

United States (2005) 'Joint Statement Between President George W. Bush and Prime Minister Manmohan Singh', <www.whitehouse.gov/news/releases/2005/07/20050718-6.html>.

Van Diepen, Vann (2002), 'Strengthening Multilateral Non-Proliferation Regimes', Testimony of the Director, Office of Chemical, Biological, and Missile Non-Proliferation, Before the Senate Governmental Affairs Committee Subcommittee on International Security, Proliferation and Federal Services, 29 July 2002, Washington, DC.

White, M. (2005), 'Blair Backs Improved Nuclear Cooperation with India', *The Guardian*, 9 September 2005.

Willard, A. (2005), 'France Promises India Nuclear Energy Help', Reuters, 13 September 2005.

Notes

1. For a comprehensive look at COCOM's origins and evolution, see Mastanduno (1992).
2. NPT Article I states: 'Each nuclear-weapon State Party to the Treaty undertakes not to transfer to any recipient whatsoever nuclear weapons or other nuclear explosive devices or control over such weapons or explosive devices directly, or indirectly; and not in any way to assist, encourage, or induce any non-nuclear weapon State to manufacture or otherwise acquire nuclear weapons or other nuclear explosive devices, or control over such weapons or explosive devices'. Article IIIb states: 'Each State Party to the Treaty undertakes not to provide: (a) source or special fissionable material, or (b) equipment or material especially designed or prepared for the processing, use or production of special fissionable material, to any non-nuclear-weapon State for peaceful purposes, unless the

source or special fissionable material shall be subject to the safeguards required by this article'.

3. For more, see Schmidt (1994).
4. For a more detailed look at the successive establishment of Zangger Committee and NSG, see Thorne (1997).
5. For one of the earliest detailed descriptions and analyses of AG, see Perry Robinson (1992).
6. For a comprehensive examination of MTCR, see Mistry (2003).
7. Adapted from Gahlaut et al. (2004).
8. This table summarizes the information available at the official websites of the four regimes. For NSG, see <www.nsg-online.org>; for AG, see <www.australiagroup.net>; for MTCR, see <www.mtcr.info>; and for WA, see <www.wassenaar.org>.
9. This draws from author's collaborative research at the University of Georgia, see Gahlaut (2002).
10. For more on the implications of EU expansion on export control regimes, see Jones (2003, 81–9).
11. India, Israel, Singapore and China are some of the countries that have 'harmonized' their control lists with those of the NSG and MTCR. China had declared itself an adherent to the MTCR in the mid-1990s – although it had a somewhat different understanding of some of the MTCR guidelines, which have led to numerous protests and sanctions on China by major MTCR members until now. See BBC (2005).
12. The primary means of this communication have been outreach activities undertaken by some regime members on behalf of the group. NSG uses a troika – a group of three – consisting of past, present and future chairs, who have engaged states with the potential of proliferation (such as India and Israel) and those that have pledged to stem proliferation (China and Pakistan). MTCR and AG use a similar strategy aimed at relevant non-members. The regimes also hold seminars or other interactive events to exchange views regarding proliferation threats and non-proliferation 'best practices' with non-members.
13. This section borrows heavily from Gahlaut and Jones (2004).
14. This section draws upon Gahlaut et al. (2004).
15. For a detailed look at the implications on diverse membership, see Gahlaut and Zaborsky (2004, 73–91).
16. AG, for instance, has been attacked in the Biological Weapons Convention (BWC) and the Chemical Weapons Convention (CWC) by some members of the non-aligned movement seeking to abolish export controls on CBW-related goods (see van Diepen, 2002). However Argentina, Brazil, China, India, Iran, Pakistan and South Africa were some of the major members of the non-aligned movement that routinely criticized the NSG for denying technology to developing states, based on commercial rather than non-proliferation concerns. Argentina, Brazil, China and South Africa, of course, went on to become members of NSG and India seems intent to follow suit!
17. The fact that significant non-members like India and Israel have begun voluntarily to incorporate NSG and MTCR control lists into their national export control lists is a good indicator of this trend.
18. When Libya decided to give up its WMD programmes in 2003, it turned over all the relevant materials and documents to the United States and the IAEA. One of the interesting finds in this material was a blueprint of a Chinese warhead that Dr A.Q. Khan had supplied to Libya, from among the technologies Pakistan had acquired from

China in the 1980s. See Broad and Sanger (2004). For details on China's proliferation to Pakistan, see DeSutter (2003) and Burr (2004). For the missiles-for-enrichment technology swap between Pakistan and North Korea, see Hersh (2003) and Kampani (2002, 107–16).

19. For more on this, see Srivastava (2005).
20. For India's policy and behaviour regarding horizontal non-proliferation, see Gahlaut and Srivastava (2005). A new Israeli export control order entered into force on July 2004: 'It fully incorporates the NSG Trigger List and the List of Nuclear-Related Dual Use Equipment, Materials, Software and Related Technology. The Israeli legislation goes beyond NSG lists and includes a "catch-all" clause' (Frank 2004).
21. The NPT itself does not forbid civilian nuclear cooperation with a non-member – it only stipulates that the transfers be under safeguards.
22. Since 1992, NSG has required that a recipient state accept IAEA safeguards on all its civilian nuclear activities.
23. For more on this argument, see Gahlaut (2005).
24. One report was specific in limiting the blame to South Africa's lapses (see Blackford 2004). However, most reporting on the case did not make this distinction.
25. For example, the Hague Code of Conduct was established to shore up the missile non-proliferation commitments of MTCR-non-members.

Chapter 2

The Economics of Arms Export Controls

Ron Smith
Professor of Applied Economics, Birkbeck College, London

Maria Garcia-Alonso
Lecturer, University of Kent

Introduction

The economic analysis of 'bads', such as illicit drugs, alcohol in prohibition in the United States and Islamic countries, and the proliferation of weapons of mass destruction, shares many features with the more standard economic analysis of goods. In both, it is important to identify the forces that drive demand and supply and thus determine price and quantity. However, whereas with goods, the focus is on ensuring that supply equals demand at reasonable prices, with bads, the focus is on acting on demand or supply to ensure that price is high (for example through taxes on alcohol and tobacco) and quantity is low. As a result, things that are regarded as problems in goods markets (for example, monopoly or cartels, excessively high prices or inadequate supply) tend to be regarded as solutions in bads' markets. Brzoska (2003) discusses taxation of the arms trade, Becker, Murphy and Grossman (2004) the more general economic theory of illegal goods.

The bads we are concerned with are military. They can be roughly divided into weapons of mass destruction (WMD), typically nuclear, biological and chemical (NBC); major weapons systems; small arms and light weapons; dual-purpose goods, which have both military and commercial applications (NBC and others); and services including intangible technology transfer. As with drugs, not everybody agrees that they should be regarded as bad; and those who agree that they are bad do not agree whether the best way to deal with the problem is by demand-side or supply-side actions. Whereas with illicit drugs, the demand prompting concern is largely from rich countries while the supply is largely from poor countries; with the military products, the demand prompting concern is largely from poor countries and the supply largely from rich countries. For weapons and related technologies, the demand may be from states or non-state actors. The non-state actors are mainly legitimate, for example, nuclear, biological and chemical industries, but may be illegitimate, such as terrorist groups. As with illegal drugs, there are large international externalities in arms transfers; what is done by one country has effects on other countries, so there are benefits from coordination.

There has been a substantial economic analysis of arms exports but most of it has been mathematical or econometric within quite specific, often game theory, models. Some of the implications of game theory analysis for arms export control are discussed in a non-technical way in Smith and Udis (2001). The economic analysis has used elements of new trade theory and regulation theory with the added elements of security perceptions and procurement theory to analyse how export control policies interact with other more traditional policy instruments and objectives. The technical nature of the literature has probably inhibited communication with other disciplines. In this chapter, we try to set out the issues within an economic framework and briefly summarize some of the conclusions of our work in a non-technical way.

The framework that we use first discusses the context, the particular nature of the arms trade, and then asks:

- how do we distinguish legitimate demand (for civilian use or to meet internationally recognized security needs) from illegitimate demand?
- what are the possibly conflicting interests of supplier countries and their firms that may lead them to want to control arms exports?
- to what extent do supplier countries have common interests, what are their incentives to coordinate their controls and not cheat on their international obligations?
- given that controls are in place, what are the possible unintended consequences of those controls?

The Arms Trade

The arms trade is subject to more extensive controls than trade in most other goods. Almost all countries regulate arms exports to some extent, if only to ensure that the arms they produce are not used against them. These unilateral national control systems are the foundation for multilateral controls, which vary from relatively informal clubs of suppliers, to very formal systems embodied in treaties and involving extensive monitoring systems like that associated with the nuclear Non-Proliferation Treaty (NPT).

We can divide export controls into *quantitative* and *qualitative* controls (see Panofsky [1990] for a similar classification). Quantitative export controls include total or partial restriction of weapons exported to a single country or a group of countries. Qualitative export controls include controls on the transfer of state-of-the-art technologies that allow exporter countries to maintain a technological edge over potential adversaries, and controls on the transfer of very sensitive technologies, for example of weapons of mass destruction. For instance, when exporting advanced systems, the US often 'black-boxes' the software, not providing the source code, so the buyer cannot find out how the system works or change it. The United Kingdom Ministry of Defence could not use the Chinook HC3 helicopters because it was unable to verify the software (NAO 2004).

A central issue is how these controls interact with the patterns of supply and demand. Even in markets for goods it can be quite difficult to determine the relative importance of demand and supply factors on the evolution of prices and quantities, for example, whether the high oil prices of 2004 were primarily due to demand or supply. For bads, it can be even more difficult, because of the secrecy associated with the decisions. Consider the proliferation of nuclear weapons. Initially the evolution of ownership as indicated by tests of nuclear weapons was almost linear: US 1945, USSR 1949, UK 1952, France 1960, China 1964. This speed of diffusion was limited only by supply constraints: these countries acquired them as rapidly as they could. Extrapolation might have suggested a new country every five years. Mid-1960s predictions based on supply-side capabilities (who would be able to make bombs) suggested a much faster spread of nuclear weapons. This was captured in Tom Lehrer's mid-1960s song *Whose Next?* which ended: 'We'll try to stay serene and calm; When Alabama gets the bomb'.

In fact, since 1965, only two countries have announced they were conducting tests of nuclear weapons: India and Pakistan. There is some question as to whether two other nuclear weapons states, Israel and South Africa, did carry out tests. South Africa denuclearized as did the former Soviet Republics of Belarus, Ukraine and Kazakhstan. The status of North Korea and Iran is currently uncertain. Clearly what stopped proliferation in cases such as that of Sweden and Japan were not supply-side constraints as both could easily build nuclear weapons, but demand-side factors as they did not see large benefits from doing so. The number of countries capable of building nuclear weapons fairly quickly is estimated to range from 25 upwards, including all those countries with civil nuclear reactors. But most of those countries have no desire to acquire nuclear weapons. In 1965, such a lack of proliferation would have seemed a low probability prediction. But, even with hindsight, it is difficult to determine how much of the non-proliferation was the result of the supply-side constraints associated with the NPT and the Nuclear Suppliers Group and how much was demand-side judgements about the limited benefits of possessing nuclear weapons.

Supply-side controls tend to increase the cost of the product to the potential acquiring country targeted by the export control. This can be done through direct price increases, prohibition of exports or economic sanctions to restrict the potential of the demanding country to develop the weapons themselves. As all controls can be evaded at a price, effective controls are those where the price is too high to be worth evading. Supply-side controls influence equilibrium demand by raising prices. By demand-side factors, we mean factors that change the demand for weapons at a given price. These may include a peace agreement or a change in perceived threats that will change demand for weapons even if prices are constant.

The most common economic model for demand is an arms race between two antagonists. In this case, the restriction of arms supply to one antagonist has the indirect benefit of reducing the derived demand for arms by the other antagonist. The economic literature is less effective in modelling other reasons for export controls, such as embargos imposed in response to internal repression or human rights violations.

Although we speak about price, this is a simplification. Arms export contracts are complicated packages that include not just the weapons systems themselves, but munitions, spares and training. They are often paid for by counter-trade (or barter, for example, the UK al Yamamah arms export package to Saudi Arabia is paid for in oil) and have associated offsets (for example, the seller promising to set up production in the buyer country), plus soft loans to finance the sale. Brauer and Dunne (2004) provide details on counter-trade and offsets. Evidence on the financial details of arms contracts is difficult to obtain. The contract is usually the start of a long-term relationship since weapons will need munitions, spares, upgrades and so on in the future. A crucial part of the relationship will be whether the supplier is willing to continue supply in time of conflict.

Legitimate and Illegitimate Demand

The demand for arms of various types is influenced by security perceptions of internal or external threats and by price and income, which determine what a state can afford. States then choose whether it is more cost effective to develop and produce the weapons domestically; to develop and produce them in collaboration with other countries; to produce under licence systems developed elsewhere; or to import the desired arms. If they decide to import, they have to choose between competing systems available on the world market. Bribery and corruption are endemic in the arms market and a policy issue for supplier countries is to what extent they can or will take anti-corruption measures. In December 2004, the UK government announced a loosening up of anti-corruption controls within the Export Credit Guarantee Department in response to the pressure from defence companies. However, while the decision-makers who make these choices may be self-interested and, quite possibly, corrupt, their choices are constrained by the security and economic situation. Prices matter and the main factor constraining the proliferation of major weapons systems is that few countries can afford them. Smith and Tasiran (2005) provide econometric estimates of the demand for arms imports as a function of military expenditure (a proxy for the threat), a (very inaccurate) measure of price and the income of a country. On these estimates, demand is sensitive to price. For constant threat, a 1 per cent increase in price causes a roughly 1 per cent fall in the demand for arms imports.

During the Cold War, the western allies had a clear security interest in stopping transfers of arms to the Soviet bloc. The Coordinating Committee for Multilateral Export Controls (COCOM) was set up in 1949 to restrict the flow of technology and weapons to the Eastern bloc. It was wound up in 1994, being replaced in 1996 by the Wassenaar Arrangement on export controls for conventional arms and dual-use goods and technology that includes Russia. Within the western alliance during the Cold War, military preparations had elements of a public good, the forces of one country having had spillover benefits for other countries. There was therefore also a security interest in encouraging sales of arms to allies to increase their capability and enhance interoperability. In practice, the application of these security principles through COCOM and burden-sharing debates was fraught with tensions, though COCOM tended to work better when the Soviet threat seemed greater. During the Cold War period, sales to non-aligned countries were often seen through a Cold War perspective. After the Cold War, the security interest became less clear and there were fewer general principles.

Given the right of states to self-defence, embodied in the United Nations (UN) Charter, they have a legitimate right to import arms and few would criticize, for instance, the US supply of arms to the UK during the Second World War under the lend-lease programme. However, the international community has tried to establish criteria whereby the import of arms is not legitimate. A typical set of criteria is provided in the 1991 guidelines agreed by the five permanent members of the UN Security Council, discussed by Pierre (1997). These indicate that restrictions on exports are required where the transfer would be likely to: prolong or aggravate an existing armed conflict; increase tension in a region or contribute to regional instability; introduce destabilizing military capabilities in a region; contravene embargos or other relevant internationally agreed restraints to which they are parties; be used other than for the legitimate defence and security needs of the recipient state; support or encourage international terrorism; be used to interfere with the internal affairs of sovereign states; or seriously undermine the recipient states' economy. Other factors may include situations where the transfer has an adverse effect on national security of the exporter or other countries; facilitates internal repression or breaches of human rights; or encourages the proliferation of weapons of mass destruction. These criteria are quite vague and will involve subjective judgement, about which there may be disputes.

To illustrate the issues in determining legitimacy, consider the case of China. China agreed to the Security Council guidelines listed above in 1991, but withdrew cooperation in 1992 in the response to the decision by President George W. Bush to allow the sale of F-16s to Taiwan. Since Taiwan is regarded by China as part of China, China regarded this as interference with the internal affairs of a sovereign state, in contravention of the guidelines. China was itself subject to a European Union embargo introduced after the Tiananmen Square massacre of 1989. At time of writing, in early 2005, the EU was discussing removing the embargo, while at the same time strengthening the arms export Code of Conduct discussed below. Removal of the embargo faced strong opposition from the US, which was concerned both with the growth of Chinese military power and its threat to Taiwan. The large European arms manufacturers were ambivalent. China is a large and potentially profitable market and they have a chance to displace Russia and Israel, China's traditional suppliers. But they feared that sales to China would close off access to US markets and technology, and that by transferring technology to China they would be creating a new competitor in the international arms market.

It can also be quite difficult to judge when the development of nuclear, biological or chemical industries by particular states reflects legitimate commercial judgements or are covers for illegitimate acquisition of weapons of mass destruction. Potential recipients of the arms may recognize the interest of the supplier groups in restricting the flow of destabilizing weapons, but they are also likely to accuse the suppliers of forming 'cartels' to restrict the flow of goods or technology in order to raise prices and maintain military dominance and joint monopoly.

Interests of Supplier Governments and Firms

The primary instrument supplier governments have to meet their objectives in this area is their national export control systems. At a minimum, countries do not want to be threatened by their own weapons that they have supplied to enemies. During the First Gulf War after the Iraqi invasion of Kuwait, French Mirages had to be withdrawn from the conflict because they were indistinguishable on radar screens from those France had sold to Iraq. National export control systems typically have a number of elements: lists of products that require a licence; lists of countries to which exports can or cannot be made; lists of criteria used to judge particular cases; customs procedures to stop unlicenced exports; and some system to guarantee the 'end use' of the product to stop it being re-exported. The UK produces a quarterly strategic export controls report on licences granted and refused, available at <www.dti.gov.uk/export.control>. However, governments in arms producer countries also promote arms sales through organizations such as the Defence Export Services Organization in the UK, and through export credits and guarantees, such as those offered by the Export Credit Guarantee Department in the UK.

Governments have a variety of objectives. These include not only national security and international stability, but also maximizing exports by domestic firms, which may generate profits, employment and tax revenue. It is often argued that arms exports help maintain a domestic defence industrial base and reduce costs to the domestic defence ministry by spreading overheads, such as research and development (R&D), and taking advantage of increasing returns to scale and learning curves. The various objectives of the government may or may not conflict in particular cases, and where objectives do conflict, it often appears as conflicts between the government departments responsible for export control. In the UK, the Department of Trade and Industry is the lead department, but the Ministry of Defence, the Treasury, the Foreign Office and the Department for International Development will all have positions. In a number of cases, there will be pressure on the armed forces to buy equipment that they do not want in order to enhance its export potential. This was a particular problem in France, where the military repeatedly complained that they were forced to buy equipment designed with export markets in mind (Kolodziej 1987). This has also happened on occasion in the UK. Where an export contract is very large, such as the UK sales to Saudi Arabia under the al Yamamah contract, it may shape foreign policy.

There has been a substantial debate about the extent to which arms export sales have been subsidized by supplier governments. For many systems, there is overcapacity in the arms industry and legitimate sales are very competitive. In 2003, the French government instructed arms suppliers not to offer products at prices below production cost in order to win contracts. The 1993 order for 436 Leclerc tanks from the UAE sold for US$3.4 billion, resulting in a loss of US$1.2billion (SIPRI 2004, 457). In 2003, Portugal chose German rather than French submarines after the French producer increased prices by 15 per cent, presumably in accordance with government instructions. Ingram and Isbister (2004) argue that arms exports are bad for Britain, both because of the subsidies and the distortion of procurement choices.

In the past, it was common for national arms firms to be almost an extension of the state, and they were often publicly owned. There has been a trend for the arms firms to become increasingly independent from their national governments, a move that was initially taken to increase the efficiency of weapons production. Such a situation increases the importance of asymmetric information between firm and government. Within game theory models, information differences between the two parties to a transaction, asymmetric information, can lead to a range of market failures, cases where markets cannot be relied upon to allocate resources efficiently. Of course, even when the firm is owned by the state, the firm may capture the part of government, nominally controlling it, and firm interests come to determine policy. This seems to have been the case with a number of French procurement choices. The balance of information and interests becomes more of an issue as competition grows in the international arms market, arms firms become more internationalized, and collaborative projects between countries become more common.

Most high technology industries which require large investments in research and development are concentrated and globalized, with a few multinational firms dominating the global industry, for example, Airbus and Boeing for large civil airliners, and Intel and AMD for micro-processors. This is not the case in the arms industry because of the desire by national governments to protect their defence industrial base. The Stockholm International Peace Research Institute (SIPRI) list of the 100 largest arms producing firms shows that in 1990, the five largest firms accounted for 22 per cent of the market. This is a very small percentage compared to other industries. The end of the Cold War was followed by a merger wave, with the appearance of multinational arms firms which operate in a number of countries, such as Thales, BAE Systems, EADS and Lockheed Martin. In 2003, the five largest firms accounted for 44 per cent of the market. Although concentration has doubled, it is still not high in comparison to similar civilian markets. Increased competition can go along with increased concentration and fewer firms. As competition increases, profit margins fall and the weaker firms are driven out.

National governments now face a further information asymmetry, not only with respect to its own firms, but also with respect to the firms and governments of other exporter countries. This globalization of production can raise difficulties, for example, when 'Head Up Displays' for F-16s were supplied by the UK to the US and the F-16s were then sold to Israel, when it is unlikely that direct sales from the UK to Israel would have been allowed. The Foreign Secretary explained on 8 July 2002, in response to a parliamentary question prompted by this case, that '[t]he restructuring of the defence industry presents new challenges for the Government's approach to export licensing. Many export licence applications are for goods which are to be incorporated in defence equipment in a second country, which thereafter may be exported to a third country' (Written Answers to Questions 2002).

There has also been a tendency towards the development of dual-use technologies that could spin-off from or spin-in to weapon technology. Dual-use technologies make it more difficult to identify a military product as such. Many crucial components within weapons systems or equipment used to produce weapons systems also have legitimate civilian uses. Under the COCOM regime, the Toshiba sale of machine tools to the Soviet Union, which could be used to produce very quiet submarine propellers, was an example of the ambiguity (Mastanduno 1992).

The lack of transparency between governments and national champions over the quality exported generates incentives on the side of profit-maximizing firms to export forbidden technologies or to export to forbidden countries. This would force governments to introduce a penalty system strong enough to discourage firms from infringing export controls. However, the existence of limited liability on the side of possible infringers of export control regulations imposes constraints on the implementation of such punishments. Governments may be unwilling to drive firms into bankruptcy, and therefore the expected value of cheating to the firm is increased, because the penalty if they are caught is smaller. Asymmetric information may not always have negative effects on the implementation of export controls. If the source of asymmetric information is the procurer government being unsure about the cost-effectiveness of the domestic firm, the quantity of exports may decrease. The reason for this is that it will be more difficult for the government to give incentives for firms to behave efficiently. This will result in costs being higher and, therefore, optimal prices going up and equilibrium exports going down (see Garcia-Alonso and Levine 2004). Another example of a positive effect of asymmetric information on export controls (broadly defined) would be a case in which the importer government is unsure about the quality of the imported military product or whether future replacement needs will be covered (see Garcia-Alonso, Levine and Morgan 2004). This will reduce demand. There is often pressure on the exporting government to buy the weapons, even if it does not need them, to signal quality to potential importers.

There are also substantial compliance costs on private firms from arms export controls, though they are difficult to estimate. In the UK, the Export Control Organization (ECO) has to return half of all applications to the exporter, either for more information or because the application has been completed wrongly. The ECO document, 'Export Licence Applications: Common Pitfalls' dated 9 November 2004 illustrates this complexity (ECO 2004).

There is a substantial dispute about the extent to which supply-side or demand-side forces drive consumption: whether arms exports are driven by the machinations of the merchants of death or the legitimate security needs of the recipients. Both forces operate within a context set by the supplier state, but if one supplier state does not make the sale, there is the danger that others will. Therefore coordination is important.

Coordination by Supplier Governments

The main coordination mechanism on trade is the World Trade Organization (WTO). The WTO is probably the most extensive rule-based system in international relations. However, unlike most other trade, the trade in arms is exempt from WTO rules as it was from the previous General Agreement on Tariffs and Trade (GATT) rules. Therefore practices, which would be illegal for other manufactured goods, for example export subsidies, are not illegal for arms. This exemption is recorded in the General Agreement on Tariffs and Trade (GATT):

> ... nothing in this Agreement shall be construed ... to prevent any contracting party from taking any action which it considers necessary for the protection of its essential security interests:
> (i) relating to fissionable materials or the materials from which they are derived;
> (ii) relating to the traffic in arms, ammunition and implements of war and to such traffic in other goods and materials as is carried on directly or indirectly for the purpose of supplying a military establishment;
> (iii) taken in time of war or other emergency in international relations ... (GATT, Article XXI).

At a formal level, the situation within the European Union is similar. Article 296 (formerly Article 223) of the Treaty of Rome states:

> 1. The provisions of this Treaty shall not preclude the application of the following rules:
>   (a) No Member State shall be obliged to supply information the disclosure of which it considers contrary to the essential interests of its security;
>   (b) Any Member State may take such measures as it considers necessary for the protection of the essential interests of its security which are connected with the production of or trade in arms, munitions and war material; such measures shall not adversely affect the conditions of competition in the common market regarding products which are not intended for specifically military purposes.
> 2. The Council may, acting unanimously on a proposal from the commission, make changes to the list which it drew up on 15 April 1958, of the products to which the provisions of paragraph 1(b) apply.

This makes the arms industry and arms trade exempt from community rules, for example on government procurement and competition. However, given the single market, it is essential that the EU does coordinate its trade. Thus, the EU has spoken with a single voice in international negotiations on trade policy, when it has not been able to establish a single voice in other areas. The same applies to arms export controls. Coordination is essential, otherwise arms could be transferred from a country with strict rules to a country with less strict rules under the single market and exported from there. This was an issue for the export of Tornado aircraft to Saudi Arabia. Although the aircraft was partly built in Germany, it was exported under the less strict UK rules (Anthony 1991). The EU Code of Conduct on Arms Exports was adopted in June 1998 and has been extended since. Enlargement has raised particular issues in respect of the need to bring the acceding countries within the Code. Some of the new members did not have strong arms export control systems. The Code is a political commitment but is not legally binding. Various proposals to strengthen the Code were under discussion in early 2005.

Other forms of coordination by supplier governments in arms export controls take a large variety of forms, which overlap with other non-proliferation and more general arms control measures. These forms range from formal treaties through to political commitments to informal understandings between groups of countries, as well as measures to increase transparency, such as the UN register of arms transfers. Their effectiveness will differ depending on the payoffs to the participants of complying or cheating; the monitoring capability of the participants (how easy it is to detect cheating); and the consequences of being detected as cheating. Informal arrangements driven by common interests where compliance or non-compliance is transparent may be more effective than more formal arrangements which are legally binding but are difficult to enforce. Examples of informal regimes are the Nuclear Suppliers Group, Australia Group, Missile Technology Control Regime, Wassenaar Arrangement and the EU Code of Conduct. No undercutting rules play a major role in such agreements – if one country does not grant an export licence, it notifies the other countries, each of whom should at least consult with the country that denied the export licence before proceeding with the export. The UK government is committed to securing a legally binding global arms trade treaty. This is something that a number of non-governmental organizations, for example Saferworld, have championed, but the negotiations are likely to be complex.

As the disadvantages of non-cooperation become apparent, the benefits for weapon exporters of entering into cooperative agreements to restrict quantity and quality of weapons exported grow. However, implementation of coordination in setting export controls is not an easy task because countries have incentives to deviate unilaterally from such agreements unless the right punitive mechanisms are put into place. As a consequence, international agreements and institutions have an important role to play in restricting trade, just as they do in the case of the WTO with its aim of expanding trade. As Maggi (1999) notes, multilateral institutions have an important role to play in: assisting coordination; verifying violations of the agreement and informing third parties in order to facilitate enforcement; and promoting multilateral rule-making procedures in the place of a web of bilateral negotiations.

The interaction between weapons exporters aiming to control weapons exports is often characterized by what game theorists call prisoners' dilemma games. These games describe situations in which parties could increase their payoffs if only they could devise mechanisms that ensure cooperation. Groups of states have a collective interest in restricting supply to all their potential antagonists. State A benefits if State B does not supply to State A's antagonist, just as State B benefits if State A does not supply State B's antagonist. However, if antagonists differ, or if the threat from the antagonist to the different states varies; there is a classic prisoners' dilemma problem. State A does best, if State B does not supply State A's antagonists, while State A gets the profits from supplying State B's antagonists.

This is a classic collective action problem. As Sandler observes:

> The trading country achieves a net benefit from trade-associated employment, profits, scale economies, learning by doing economies, while creating security externalities to any country placed in harm's way by its weapons trade. A trading country *only considers its share of the security risks and ignores the risks imposed on others when deciding its trade in weapons*; consequently too much arms trade results. The dominant strategy to trade, stemming from the trader specific joint products, is not a desirable outcome from the community of nations' viewpoint (Sandler 2003, 215).

The same situation arises when producer countries decide on the amount or quality or weapons exported, even if they share the same antagonists. As these countries only see the negative impact that the exports have on their own security, they each export more than they would jointly have decided to export if they could have implemented cooperation. The fact that military goods are exempted from WTO rules means that countries competing in the exports market then have unilateral incentives to give export or R&D subsidies so as to increase their market share. This results in both security and less welfare for both exporter countries and recipients. Garcia-Alonso and Levine (2002, 2004) and Garcia-Alonso (1999, 2000) provide examples of models that capture these interactions.

An exporter may even create a technological arms race with itself, having to develop new generations of weapons that are superior to the ones it previously exported. The inability of producer countries to coordinate in the setting of export controls can sometimes lead to almost counter-intuitive situations, a security-minded country may want to develop sensitive technologies which it does not want to see exported, not because it needs them but just to keep a qualitative edge relative to other maybe less technologically advanced exporters. These exporters may then find it not worth their while to try to develop such technologies and they would be likely to be 'beaten' in the exports market should they decide to develop them anyway (see Garcia-Alonso 2000).

There are a number of factors affecting the incentives of individual countries to defect from multilateral export control agreements, such as: information asymmetries (within and between countries); the structure of the arms exports market (profits to be made out of weapons exports); asymmetry of security concerns among exporters; the number of countries having access to the restricted military product; the type of weapon to be controlled or the credibility of punishment strategies on defecting firms or countries. These issues are discussed in Garcia-Alonso and Hartley (2000). In simple game theory models, defection can easily be detected, and punishment is credible. This is often not the case in arms export controls. Other countries might expect the defecting country to argue: I did not sell dangerous weapons to X; even if I did, the sale was justified; and even if you do not accept those justifications, trying to punish me is going to hurt you more than it does me. Thus cooperation can unravel.

Controlling some weapons may be made easier by the fact that the negative impact of exporting them on any of the exporters' security is likely to be high and therefore individual incentives to deviate are lower. This probably applies to nuclear weapons, because of their destructive potential, and to small surface-to-air missiles, so called man-portable air-defence systems (MANPADS), because of the vulnerability of civil aviation. However, even in these cases, there may be individual firms or countries who think that they will not be targeted, as did the US in supplying Stinger missiles to Afghan insurgents during the Soviet occupation.

Agreements that help control the quantity or quality of weapons exported are not always export control agreements as such. Cooperative agreements among exporters, such as cartels and international mergers, would tend to increase export prices and therefore decrease exports in the same way as export taxes. If there is a monopoly or tight oligopoly, it is profitable to restrict the quantity for commercial not arms control reasons, Levine and Smith (1997) provide an analysis of cartels. Mergers and cartelization also reduce the number of potential deviators and decrease asymmetric information issues, thereby reinforcing export control agreements. Such agreements and other collaborative agreements among weapons producers, such as research joint ventures, might result in higher R&D investments and, therefore, higher levels of potential quality to be exported unless combined with a direct qualitative export control, that is, cooperation between firms alone could result in more quality being exported unless regulated by cooperating governments. This issue is modelled in Dunne et al. (2004a).

Another example of an agreement that could in principle help export controls is for arms trade to be included within WTO rules prohibiting export subsidies. The fact that the arms industry has been exempted from WTO rules tends to produce more arms exports than otherwise as individual producer countries have incentives to give export subsidies. In addition, these subsidies may increase the incentives that individual producer countries would have to defect from standard export control agreements as a given deviation may then result in higher increases in profits. This is modelled by Garcia-Alonso and Levine (2004).

While there are clear incentives for formal coordination among exporters, and coordination takes the form of both conventions and treaties, such as the NPT, which are formal and open to all, and of supplier groups, sometimes called regimes, such as the Nuclear Supplier Group (NSG) which are informal with restricted membership, what is surprising is that there are so many different organizations. There are no different organizations to regulate trade in agriculture and cars, so why are there four different organizations to regulate trade in ballistic missiles, conventional arms, chemical and biological weapons and nuclear supplies? This is particularly surprising given that the membership of the regimes overlaps to a considerable extent. SIPRI (2004, 738) lists the membership of the four main regimes and the Zangger

Committee. There are 42 countries who belong to at least one of the five, with the numbers in each group ranging from 33 in the Australia Group and the MTCR to 40 in the NSG. There are 27 countries who belong to all five regimes and this number will probably increase as China and the new EU states enter more regimes.

Responses to Export Controls

The overall effect on the welfare of an importing country subject to export controls is complicated. Although qualitative or quantitative export controls may reduce conflict if applied to all parties involved, the increase in the cost of acquiring these military products (sometimes prohibitory) will reduce consumption not just of weapons but also of other goods, especially if the price elasticity for weapon imports is low. The positive impact on security can potentially offset the negative impact on consumption and therefore result in a positive welfare effect (see, for example, Levine and Smith 1997; and Dunne et al. 2004a).

However, even if the welfare of importer countries was increased via export controls, they may still have an incentive to unilaterally search for alternative ways to build military capability that would give them an edge with respect to their adversaries. The problem of course would be that their adversaries would do exactly the same, resulting once again in conflict escalation. It is this situation which explains why export controls can sometimes have unintended consequences. States subject to embargo or control, or who fear that they may be subject to embargo in the future, may develop their own arms industry to produce the weapons that they cannot import. South Africa is an example and the French embargo on Israel has also increased the Israeli desire for domestic self-sufficiency. Levine and Smith (2000), Levine, Mouzakis and Smith (2003) and Mouzakis (2002) discuss the interaction between export controls and proliferation. States subject to export controls may develop weapons of mass destruction as a substitute for or supplement to conventional weapons, and again Israel and South Africa are examples.

As with other industries, high prices and restricted supply encourage new entrants. States that are tightly integrated into the international community may find the reputational costs of supplying illegitimate weapons too high to be worth risking. In cases where the international community has little leverage over a state, it may become a major source of illegitimate supply; for example, North Korea has become the main exporter of ballistic missiles. Controls can be evaded and may provide incentives for the development of illicit supply channels, such as the nuclear network run by the Pakistani scientist Abdul Qadeer Khan. Embargos invariably prompt the development embargo-busting networks. The development of such networks may have longer-term implications for the viability of criminal or terrorist organizations.

If one supplier is very strict in its applications of controls, as the US was during COCOM period, other suppliers try to design out the components subject to control. Most of the other weapons-exporting countries have tried to avoid using US components during this period for this reason (Mastanduno 1992). It is still an issue. In January 2004, a consortium led by EADS won a UK contract for in-air refuelling aircraft which would be leased by the RAF when needed and used commercially as a cargo or charter aircraft at other times. A protracted dispute followed about the terms of the contract, in which one issue was the US State Department's decision to treat the aircraft as military even when being used commercially. Because the aircraft would have a significant number of US parts, this would allow the US government to restrict the places the aircraft could fly and who could fly it. In response to this, the *Financial Times* reported that the Ministry of Defence project team leader, Kevin Johns, wrote to EADS stating, '[i]t is vital that you significantly reduce your dependence of your solution on export licences for US military list equipment … This needs to include identifying the required European licences for inclusion … and identify the risks to obtaining the relevant licences' (Spiegel 2003).

A recent development in the security perceptions of weapon exporters that may actually affect the impact that export controls have on the exporter security is asymmetric conflict. The traditional export control agreements implicitly assume that all countries' technological defence needs would develop following a pattern similar to that of the exporter countries. Recent events have shown though that this pattern can be broken. Despite having massive technological and military superiority, the US withdrew from Lebanon in 1983 after a suicide bombing killing 241 troops, and from Somalia in 1993 after a battle in Mogadishu in which television covered the brutal treatment of two American corpses and one injured prisoner. The bombing of *USS Cole* in Yemen in 2000 and the attack on the World Trade Centre on 11 September 2001 demonstrate US vulnerability to certain sorts of asymmetric attack. Traditional export control systems were not designed with such attacks in mind.

Ensuring that the technology states retain in their own weapons is greater than that in the systems they export may then no longer be enough to shield states from future enemies who cannot afford high cost traditional weaponry and may therefore decide to use non-traditional methods of aggression. This does not mean that export controls have become redundant. Many conflicts in the world use traditional weaponry, which cost developing countries valuable resources, and it is these conflicts that may later need external intervention. The weapons that kill the most – small arms and light weapons – are some of the most difficult to control. It is important to see also that it is not export controls that have provoked asymmetric conflict but the increase in the cost of traditional weapon systems resulting from many decades of weapon escalation. Dunne et al. (2004b) discuss the difficulties involved in managing asymmetric conflict.

Conclusion

Arms export controls have a long history. Anthony (1991, 8) notes that in the eighth century, Charlemagne declared the death penalty for Frankish merchants selling swords to the Vikings. It is now taken for granted that governments have a legal obligation to control the movement of arms to ensure that they do not fall into unauthorized hands. However, the economic interests of some actors to sell arms conflict with the security interests of other actors against whom those arms may be used. Individual governments have the responsibility of trying to reconcile that conflict at a national level but, to be effective, the controls have to be international. Thus, supplier governments have a common interest in establishing some mechanism, a regime, to coordinate their export control procedures. For such coordination to be effective, governments have to establish a consensus about how decisions will be made. These decisions will cover what items are to be controlled; what constitutes legitimate and illegitimate demand; which countries can be members of the regime and what standards their national regulation must meet. Coordination will be enhanced by mechanisms to share information about potentially illegitimate uses and to monitor compliance by members. To the extent that these mechanisms are effective, they will establish credibility and legitimacy. This provides incentives for members to comply with the agreements since failure to comply carries a high cost in lost reputation. Such incentives will tend to encourage suppliers who are members of such regimes to put more weight on long-term joint security interests relative to short-term individual economic interests. However, to the extent that such export controls are effective, states subject to control have incentives to establish their own arms industry, substitute weapons of mass-destruction for conventional weapons, and adopt asymmetric warfare. Effective controls also increase the incentive for illegitimate sources of supply to develop.

References

Anthony, I. (ed.) (1991), *Arms Export Regulations*, Oxford University Press for SIPRI, Oxford.

Becker, G.S., Murphy, K.M. and Grossman, M. (2004), *The Economic Theory of Illegal Goods*, Working Paper 10976, National Bureau of Economic Research (NBER).

Brauer, J. and Dunne, J.P. (eds) (2002), *Arming the South*, Palgrave, Basingstoke.

—— (eds) (2004), *Arms Trade and Economic Development: Theory, Policy and Cases in Arms Trade Offsets*, Routledge, London and New York.

Brzoska, M. (2004), 'Taxation of the Global Arms Trade? An Overview of the Issues', *Kyklos*, Vol. 57, No. 2.

Chalmers, M., Davies, N., Hartley, K. and Wilkinson, C. (2002), 'The Economic Costs and Benefits of UK Defence Exports', *Fiscal Studies*, Vol. 23, No. 3.

Dunne, J.P., Garcia-Alonso, M., Levine, P. and Smith, R. (2004a), 'Military Procurement, Industry Structure and Regional Conflict', Discussion Paper, University of Kent.

—— (2004b), 'Managing Asymmetric Conflict', Discussion Paper, University of Kent.

Export Control Organization (ECO) (2004), 'Export Licence Applications: Common Pitfalls', 9 November 2004.

Garcia-Alonso, Maria (1999), 'Price Competition in a Model of the Arms Trade', *Defence and Peace Economics*, Vol. 10, No. 3.

—— (2000), 'The Role of Technology Security in a Model of Trade with Horizontal Differentiation', *International Journal of Industrial Organisation*, Vol. 18, Issue 8.

Garcia-Alonso, M. and Hartley, K. (2000), 'Export Controls, Market Structure and International Coordination', *Defence and Peace Economics*, Vol. 11, Smith (2003).

Garcia-Alonso, M. and Levine, P. (2002), 'Domestic Procurement, Subsidies and the Arms Trade', in Brauer and Dunne (eds) (2002), *Arming the South*, Palgrave, Basingstoke.

—— (2004), 'Arms Export Control Regimes, Export Subsidies and the WTO Exemption', *Scottish Journal of Political Economy*, forthcoming.

Garcia-Alonso, M., Levine, P. and Morgan, A. (2004), 'Export Credit Guarantees, Moral Hazard and Export Quality', *Bulletin of Economic Research*, Vol. 56, No. 4.

Ingram, P. and Isbister, R. (2004), *Escaping the Subsidy Trap, Why Arms Exports Are Bad for Britain*, BASIC, Saferworld and Oxford Research Group, London.

Kolodziej, E.A. (1987), *Making and Marketing Arms: The French Experience and its Implications for the International System*, Princeton University Press, Princeton, NJ.

Levine, P., Mouzakis, F. and Smith, R.P. (2003), 'Arms Export Controls and Emerging Domestic Producers', in Levine and Smith (2003), *Arms Trade Security and Conflict*, Routledge, London and New York.

Levine, P. and Smith, R.P. (1997), 'The Arms Trade', *Economic Policy*, Vol. 12, Issue 25.

—— (2000), 'Arms Export Controls and Proliferation', *Journal of Conflict Resolution*, Vol. 4, No. 6.

—— (eds) (2003), *Arms Trade Security and Conflict*, Routledge, London and New York.

Maggi, G. (1999), 'The Role of Multilateral Institutions in International Trade Cooperation', *The American Economic Review*, Vol. 89, No. 1.

Mastanduno, M. (1992), *Economic Containment: COCOM and the Politics of East-West Trade*, Cornell University Press, Ithaca, NY.

Ministry of Defence (2002), *Defence Industrial Policy*, Ministry of Defence Policy Paper No. 5.

Mouzakis, F. (2002), 'Domestic Procurement as an Alternative to Importing Arms', in Brauer and Dunne (eds) (2002), *Arming the South*, Palgrave, Basingstoke.

National Audit Office (NAO) (2004), 'Battlefield Helicopters', HC486, NAO.

Panofsky, W. (1990), 'Barriers to Negotiated Arms Control', in Kenneth Arrow et al. (eds), *Barriers to Conflict Resolution*, Norton, London.

Pierre, A.J. (ed.) (1997), *Cascade of Arms*, Brookings Institute, Washington, DC.

Sandler, T. (2003), 'Arms Trade, Arms Control and Security: Collective Action Issues', in Levine and Smith (2003), *Arms Trade Security and Conflict*, Routledge, London and New York.

Smith R.P. and Tasiran, A. (2005), 'The Demand for Arms Imports', *Journal of Peace Research*, Vol. 42, No. 2.

Smith, R.P. and Udis, B. (2001) 'New Challenges to Arms Export Control: Whither Wassenaar?', *The Nonproliferation Review*, Vol. 8, No. 2, reprinted in Levine and Smith (2003), *Arms Trade Security and Conflict*, Routledge, London and New York.

Spiegel, P. (2003), 'Air Tanker Contract Flies into Turbulence', *The Financial Times*, 3 November 2003.

Stockholm International Peace Research Institute (SIPRI) (2004), *Armaments, Disarmament and International Security*, SIPRI Yearbook, Oxford University Press, Oxford.

Written Answers to Questions, 8 July 2002, Foreign and Commonwealth Affairs, U.K. Parliament, <www.publications.parliament.uk/pa/cm200102/cmhansrd/vo020708/text/20708w01.htm>.

PART II
Exploration of Regimes

Chapter 3

The Wassenaar Arrangement: Transparency and Restraint through Trans-Governmental Cooperation?

Michael Lipson[1]
Assistant Professor, Concordia University, Montreal

Introduction

The Wassenaar Arrangement is the successor regime to the Coordinating Committee on Multilateral Export Control (COCOM), which coordinated western restrictions on trade with communist states during the Cold War.[2] Named for the Dutch town near The Hague which hosted the negotiations to establish the arrangement, the Wassenaar Arrangement (WA) is primarily a transparency regime, meant to encourage restraint in the export of conventional arms and dual-use goods and technologies (items with both civilian and military applications) through information sharing and consultation among exporting states. Notwithstanding its name, the WA is headquartered not in the Netherlands but in Vienna, where the government of Austria donated space, resources and diplomatic provisions for a small secretariat.

Although Wassenaar is widely criticized as a weak institution, the limited restrictions that it places on its participating states reflect the different interests and threat perceptions of its members. Founded by 33 states in 1996, the arrangement has recently seen a significant expansion of its participating members to 40 states, with the addition of Croatia, Estonia, Latvia, Lithuania, Malta, Slovenia and South Africa since 2004.[3] Of the 40 participating states, 29 are also members in all of the other multilateral export control regimes: the NPT Nuclear Exporters Committee, or Zangger Committee (ZAC); Nuclear Suppliers Group (NSG); Missile Technology Control Regime (MTCR); and Australia Group (AG).[4] Of the other 11, all except Croatia are members of at least two other export control regimes.[5] Most major arms exporters are Wassenaar participants.[6] The Wassenaar Arrangement has recently engaged in 'outreach' activities to China (Wassenaar Arrangement 2005b). However, China has not been invited to participate to date, because of concerns regarding both implementation of its national export controls and its exports to Iran and Pakistan (Grimmett 2004).[7]

Participating states such as France and Russia on the one hand, and the United States on the other, have very different views and interests in relation to arms exports. Participating states' views on dual-use trade are also divergent. Such differences have frustrated and delayed efforts within Wassenaar to agree on proposals to strengthen the Arrangement, most notably by requiring prior notification of 'undercuts' or exports to non-participating states of items for which licences had been denied by another participant. Wassenaar's reliance on participating states to implement controls at the national level also leads to variation in implementation. However, the participating states have agreed to enhance their information exchange and achieved consensus on non-binding statements standards for implementing national export controls on small arms and light weapons (SALW), shoulder-launched anti-aircraft missiles (man-portable air defence systems, or MANPADS), intangible software and technology, and export of non-listed items to countries under international embargo (Anthony and Bauer 2004, 746).

Thus, Wassenaar has accomplished more than frequently dismissive assessments of its performance would indicate, but less than might be hoped for. This chapter argues that assessments of Wassenaar's past effectiveness and future prospects depend to a significant extent on often implicit assumptions about what the regime can and should do. The following sections review Wassenaar's origins, principles, operational procedures, record and challenges of evaluating its effectiveness. The chapter then considers alternative theoretical perspectives on international cooperation, and their significance for the future of the Wassenaar Arrangement. The central argument of the chapter is that Wassenaar is often inappropriately evaluated against an implicit baseline of a COCOM-like intergovernmental organization with a small membership of like-minded states. Wassenaar is more appropriately understood as a basis of *trans-governmental* cooperation among diverse participants with overlapping but different interests. Understood in this way, the 'glass' – the WA and its prospects – appears half full rather than half empty.

Wassenaar's Origins[8]

When the Cold War ended, COCOM's rationale disappeared, and both European members and Russia pressed for its dissolution in the early 1990s. Russia argued that COCOM now impeded its integration into the international economy and political structure of the West. European states regarded COCOM as an anachronism, inappropriate to a post-Cold War world. Some, in particular France and Germany, resented COCOM, viewing it as an instrument for US control over European trade with Russia and Eastern Europe – through the veto established by the requirement of consensus for exceptions to COCOM restrictions (Lewis 2005; Wallander 1999, 184). Although the US attempted to adapt and preserve COCOM, it became clear that this would not be possible.

In the years since COCOM began operating in 1950, a system of multilateral export control regimes (MECR) had evolved to manage controls on the transfer of items related to nuclear, chemical and biological warfare, and missile delivery systems. The Zangger Committee, NSG, MTCR and AG – together with COCOM – formed a complementary set of control arrangements for the range of military-related goods and technologies traded internationally. COCOM's disbanding without a replacement would have meant that no multilateral regime would coordinate export controls of conventional arms or dual-use goods and technologies. Iraq's 1990 invasion of Kuwait highlighted the danger of uncontrolled arms build-ups by aggressive regional powers. And revelations after the 1991 Gulf War of the extent to which Iraq's nuclear programme had advanced in secret, coupled with belated recognition of the crucial contributions dual-use exports from western states had made to the Iraqi nuclear programme, constituted powerful reasons to maintain some means of international coordination of conventional arms and dual-use export controls.

While created as a successor to COCOM, Wassenaar had roots in other non-proliferation and arms trade-related policy initiatives of the early 1990s. In 1991, the UN General Assembly established a UN Register of Conventional Arms to promote transparency in the arms trade. At the July 1991 London Summit of the G7, members agreed to work towards common restrictions on arms transfers to 'countries and areas of particular concern', understood to refer to Iran, Iraq, Libya and North Korea (G7 1991). The George Bush administration promoted the 1991 Middle East Arms Control Initiative in meetings of the five permanent members of the UN Security Council (P-5). The P-5 worked towards agreements on common criteria for export restraint, and possible prior notification and consultation amongst themselves of prospective arms sales. However, a 1992 US decision to sell F-16 fighter jets to Taiwan prompted the Chinese to suspend their participation, and the talks were never resumed (Pierre 1997 377–80; Lewis 2005).

According to James A. Lewis: 'The arms transfer component of the Middle East initiative became, at the United Kingdom's suggestion, a proposal for a regime with global scope to prevent destabilizing arms transfers' (Lewis 2005). Elements of this proposal – including a set of agreed 'guidelines for conventional arms transfers' – eventually 'became a precedent for the UN Register of Conventional Arms, the Wassenaar Arrangement, and the European Code of Conduct' (Lewis 2005). Thus, the negotiations to establish Wassenaar drew on other post-Cold War initiatives as well as COCOM, and on states' experience of dual-use export control coordination in the Nuclear Suppliers Group, Missile Technology Control Regime, Australia Group and EU Community regime for dual-use export controls.

US recognition that COCOM's days were numbered led to consideration of various options. One option considered by the George Bush administration was 'to trade away the general exceptions procedure, essentially the US veto, in COCOM, for a strengthening of the other regimes, on the theory that COCOM was doomed anyway and that we might as well get something for it while we still had the leverage'.[9] This idea was dropped, and Bush was subsequently defeated in the 1992 election. The impetus for addressing COCOM's future in the new administration was provided at the April 1993 Vancouver Summit, where Russian President Boris

Yeltsin pushed for COCOM to be dismantled. Yeltsin argued that COCOM was an outdated vestige of the Cold War and interfered with Russia's integration into the international economy. In response, the Clinton administration developed a proposal that combined elements of COCOM procedures, the P-5 arms transfer talks, and the G7 negotiations on controlling industrial exports to so-called rogue states (Lewis 2005).

In mid-1993, the United States concluded that COCOM was no longer viable, and initiated diplomatic contacts with its allies on creating a successor.[10] The initial US proposal, presented to the UK, France and Germany in July, envisioned an arms and dual-use export control regime with COCOM-like procedures, with Russia as a member, targeting Iran, Iraq, Libya and North Korea. Britain, supported by Germany, questioned the need for a successor regime, but France supported some sort of replacement. A September 1993 NATO meeting endorsed the creation of a replacement for COCOM, but not along the lines proposed by the US.

Britain demanded COCOM's termination by a specified date as a condition of beginning negotiations for a successor. With support from other European members, the UK pushed for dissolution by 31 December 1993. A compromise termination date of 31 March 1994 was agreed to.[11] Export licensing decisions would be subject to 'national discretion' as of January 1994 (Grimmett 2004, 2). The formal decision to shut COCOM down and establish a successor regime including former COCOM targets as members was taken at a 16 November 1993 High Level Meeting of COCOM members in The Hague.[12]

According to a US official involved in the transition from COCOM to Wassenaar: 'We formally terminated COCOM on March 31, 1994, but delayed considerably longer than anticipated in getting the successor institution started. The US originally hoped for a seamless transition, with the new arrangement starting upon the termination of COCOM'.[13] Ultimately, two and a half years of difficult negotiations were required to establish what was known during the negotiations as the 'New Forum'. Initially, the COCOM members and cooperating countries (Austria, Finland, Ireland, New Zealand, Sweden and Switzerland) participated in the negotiations (Wassenaar Arrangement n.d.). Russia, along with Hungary, Poland and the Czech and Slovak Republics, was invited to participate in September 1995 after extended bilateral negotiations between the US and Russia over Russian arms exports to Iran.

While western European states viewed Russian participation in a COCOM successor as essential, the United States, and to a lesser extent Canada and Britain, took the view that Russia should be admitted only once its commitment and capacity to abide by the new regime's principles were established (Litavrin 1997, 107). According to Pyotr Litavrin: 'The central reason for America's cautious approach was its lack of confidence in Russia's national export control system' (Litavrin 1997, 108). In addition, the US was concerned about Russia's political stability and role as an arms supplier to Iran. Russian arms sales to Iran became the sticking point that held up Russian participation in the New Forum negotiations for 18 months. After bilateral negotiations between the US and Russia, Yeltsin committed in September 1994 that while Russia would fulfil existing contracts with Iran, it would not enter into any further agreements to sell Iran arms. The United States was still concerned about the implications for the regions of the existing contracts, and wanted a specified date by which Russian arms transfers to Iran would cease. These issues were resolved at the May 1995 Clinton–Yelstin Summit in Moscow, and a follow-on meeting in June between US Vice President Al Gore and Russian Prime Minister Victor Chernomyrdin. The US expressed its satisfaction that fulfilment of the existing contracts would not alter the regional military balance or introduce new technological capabilities into the region (Litavrin 1997, 109). With Russia committing in a confidential *aide memoire* to end its arms sales to Iran by the end of 1999, the path was cleared for Russia's admission to the New Forum (Broder 2000).

With Russia's participation arranged, 28 states announced a decision to establish the Wassenaar Arrangement in a 19 December 1995 declaration issued at the Peace Palace in The Hague. However, the inaugural plenary meeting in Vienna on 2–3 April 1996 – at which Argentina, Romania and South Korea joined as 'founding members' – deadlocked over Russian refusal to agree to undercut notification (Walkling 1996a) – that is, to notify participating states within 30–60 days of approving a licence for an export of a sensitive item equivalent to one denied by another member within the previous three years. The meeting was suspended pending resolution of the dispute, which threatened to kill the new regime before it became operational (Goldring 1996; Walkling 1996a). Facing a unified position from the other participating states, and not wanting to be blamed for the negotiations' failure, Russia ultimately accepted the consensus in favour of undercut notification at a reconvened plenary meeting in July (Walkling 1996b). With Bulgaria and Ukraine participating as founding members, the Wassenaar Arrangement became operational with 33 participating states. The control lists and information exchanges took effect on 1 November, and the first working plenary meeting was held in mid-December 1996.

The new regime, lacking the consensus on a shared threat that girded COCOM's demanding rules including vetoes of proposed exports, focused instead on the less onerous principles of transparency and restraint in transfers of arms and dual-use goods and technologies. In light of the extent to which the international community was caught by surprise by the extent of Iraq's conventional and unconventional arms build-ups, and by the Iraqi invasion of Kuwait, it was widely agreed that greater transparency among arms suppliers could make it possible to recognize the development of regionally destabilizing arms build-ups and to coordinate restraint among suppliers in response. COCOM, targeting the Soviet Union, had not controlled arms or dual-use exports to Iraq, both of which had been employed in Iraq's arms programmes prior to the invasion of Kuwait. While not formally targeting specific states, Wassenaar has operated on the understanding that Iran, Iraq (prior to the overthrow of Saddam Hussein's regime), Libya and North Korea were 'states of concern' regarding which export restraint would be practised.

The Initial Elements

The purposes and rules of the Wassenaar Arrangement are contained in the regime's founding document, the 'Initial Elements', which establishes the structure of the Arrangement's control lists and rules for information exchange.[14] According to the Initial Elements (IE), the purpose of the arrangement is 'to contribute to regional and international security and stability, by promoting transparency and greater responsibility in transfers of conventional arms and dual-use goods and technologies, thus preventing destabilising accumulations'. Wassenaar is to 'complement and reinforce, without duplication', other non-proliferation treaties and organizations, including the other multilateral export control regimes. Promoting cooperation to prevent arms build-ups in states or regions of concern to participating states is listed as an additional purpose. The IE also emphasize that the Arrangement is not targeted on any state and does not interfere with 'bona fide civil transactions' or the legitimate right to self-defence under Article 51 of the UN Charter. After the September 11 attacks, participating states amended the Initial Elements to add a fifth purpose: 'to prevent the acquisition of conventional arms and dual-use goods and technologies by terrorist groups and organizations, as well as by individual terrorists'.

Like COCOM, Wassenaar is an informal arrangement. Its rules and decisions constitute legally non-binding political commitments. The secretariat's role is limited to organizing meetings and facilitating communication between national representatives and points of contact. The secretariat has a staff of only about ten people. It is not an autonomous policy-making body. The Arrangement's decision-making body is the Plenary, consisting of representatives of all participating states, with a rotating chair.

Decisions are made by consensus of participating states. The implications of decision-making by consensus in Wassenaar, however, are very different than in COCOM. Consensus decision-making in COCOM formed the basis of a very restrictive system of controls. COCOM rules prohibited the export of dual-use items on its embargo list (International List I) or (except in limited quantities) a 'quantitative' list (International List II). However, in 1954 members established an exceptions procedure under which exceptions permitting export of controlled items could be made if all members consented (Mastanduno 1992, 88; Hardt and Tomlinson 1983). Coupled with broad export restrictions, the consensus requirement gave every member the power to veto others' proposed exports of controlled items. Unlike COCOM, Wassenaar does not have a veto provision. Because there are no formally stated restrictions on exports to any particular state, there can be no system for exceptions to such a rule. Although the US initially sought to retain the COCOM veto in the successor organization, there was intense opposition to this provision. The US also became concerned that with the larger membership and greater divergence of foreign policy interests in the 'New Forum', the US might face vetoes of its own arms exports to allies such as Taiwan and Israel (Lewis 2005). Although critics often point to the lack of a veto provision as a weakness of Wassenaar, a US export control official explained in 2000:

> One thing our Wassenaar partners have consistently made clear for the last seven years is that they will never submit to the kind of consensus arrangement for export approval – known as the 'veto' – that was found in COCOM … No other export control regime has a veto rule for export decisions and we would be sadly mistaken if we think we can get Wassenaar or any other export control regime to adopt such a constraint (United States Congress 2000).

Consensus decision-making has, however, blocked or delayed the adoption of proposed enhancements of Wassenaar such as prior notification of undercutting exports.

Although the IE state that Wassenaar 'will not be directed against any state or group of states' – critical to differentiating Wassenaar from COCOM – it was understood at the Arrangement's establishment that Iran, Iraq, Libya and North Korea were considered states of concern to participating states. In particular, US negotiators sought private assurance of an understanding that members would not sell arms to these four states. In December 2000, however, Russia abandoned the June 1995 Gore–Chernomyrdin agreement under which it had committed not to enter into new contracts for arms sales to Iran.[15] In addition to the four states of concern, at the 1996 and 1998 plenaries, participating states committed to support, respectively, UN Security Council Resolution 1076 calling for an end to the supply of arms and ammunition to Afghanistan, and the 1998 moratorium on the import, export and manufacture of light weapons by the Economic Community of West African States (ECOWAS).

The Initial Elements specify that Wassenaar is 'open, on a global and non-discriminatory basis, to prospective adherents that comply with the agreed criteria' set out in Appendix 4.[16] These criteria are:

- Whether it is a producer/exporter of arms or industrial equipment respectively;
- Whether it has taken the WA Control lists as a reference in its national export controls;
- Its non-proliferation policies and appropriate national policies, including:
    - Adherence to non-proliferation policies, control lists and, where applicable, guidelines of the Nuclear Suppliers Group, the Zangger Committee, the Missile Technology Control Regime and the Australia Group; and through adherence to the Nuclear Non-Proliferation Treaty, the Biological and Toxicological Weapons Convention, the Chemical Weapons Convention and (where applicable) START I, including the Lisbon Protocol;
    - Its adherence to fully effective export controls (Wassenaar Arrangement 2003a).

Decisions to admit new members are made by consensus. From Wassenaar's 1996 founding by 33 states, membership remained constant until Slovenia's admission at the 2004 plenary, followed by the admission of Croatia, Estonia, Latvia, Lithuania and Malta in the spring and summer of 2005, and South Africa's admission at the

December 2005 plenary bringing the number of participating states to 39 (Wassenaar Arrangement 2004, 2005a, 2005b). Outreach efforts continue.

Wassenaar maintains two lists of controlled items – a munitions list and a dual-use list.[17] The latter, consisting of approximately 1,000 items, is divided between a Basic (Tier 1) list and a Sensitive (Tier 2) list, which contains a subset of 'very sensitive' items (Danielsson 2005).[18] France and Russia have stated that they regard the lists as 'reference lists' for information sharing, but that participating states are not obligated to control every item on the lists in their national export control systems (Boese 2003a, 181).[19] The munitions list covers nearly 300 items with primarily military purposes, divided into 22 categories (Danielsson 2005). For purposes of information exchange on conventional arms, members agree to report on exports in eight categories of arms. These categories do not correspond precisely to the structure of the munitions list (Reinicke 1998, 184). The first seven categories – battle tanks; armoured combat vehicles (ACVs); large calibre artillery systems; fixed and variable-wing military aircraft (except most trainers) and unmanned aerial vehicles (UAVs); military and attack helicopters; warships; missiles and missile systems – are based on the UN Register of Conventional Arms. An eighth reporting category – small arms and light weapons (SALW), including man portable air defence systems (MANPADS) such as Stinger missiles – was added in 2003.[20] Participating states exchange aggregated information semi-annually, in April and October, on deliveries to non-participating states of items on the munitions list.

States also exchange aggregated licence denial information for items on the basic (Tier 1) dual-use list on a biannual basis. For sensitive (Tier 2) items, states are required to notify the secretariat of licence denials for exports to non-members within 60 (preferably 30) days of the denial. States also exchange aggregated information on transfers of Tier 2 items biannually. For items in the 'very sensitive' subset of Tier 2, states also agree to exercise 'extreme vigilance' through their national export control processes. Very sensitive items include stealth technology, high performance computers, advanced radar, advanced jet engine technology and submarine detection instruments (United States Mission to International Organizations in Vienna n.d.). The lists are reviewed at the discretion of participating states, and have been updated repeatedly.

Although Wassenaar, unlike the non-proliferation export control regimes, lacks a *prohibition* on undercutting (a 'no-undercut' rule), there is an informal norm against the practice, and it is apparently rare. It is estimated that only five or six instances occurred between 1996 and 2002 (Boese 2003a, 175; Washington Trade and Tariff Letter 2002b). Some regard Wassenaar's undercut *reporting* requirement as embodying a weak no-undercut rule (Lewis 2005). The existing requirement – that members notify all participating states 'preferably within 30 days, but no later than within 60 days' of approving a licence for an undercutting export on the dual-use list's Tier 2 'sensitive' annex – is intended to ensure that members have an opportunity to persuade the notifying state to reverse itself before the transfer takes place. If the export takes place less than 30 (or 60) days after the licence is granted, however, this opportunity will be lost (Jaffer 2002, 522).[21] To strengthen Wassenaar's no-undercut provision, the US has persistently urged members to commit to notify prior to granting an undercutting licence. The proposal has received substantial support, but has been blocked by Russian opposition (Washington Trade and Tariff Letter 2002b).

Wassenaar members conduct information exchanges twice a year – in April and October. The annual plenary meeting is held in December. The Plenary can also call *ad hoc* meetings. Three working groups perform specialized tasks. The control lists are reviewed in Experts Group (EG) meetings – usually in April and September – and EG Technical Working Group meetings, which propose changes for decision by the Plenary. The General Working Group (GWG), which usually meets in May and October, reviews policy issues relating to the working of the information exchanges and states' cooperation within the Arrangement. In preparation for the 2003 plenary, at which participating states conducted the second overall assessment of the Arrangement, a new process was developed involving task forces made up of subsets of the overall membership. Eleven such task forces, each addressing a specific issue such as control lists, arms brokering, small arms and light weapons, and MANPADS, developed recommendations for discussion in the GWG and at the Plenary. The 2003 plenary's impressive productivity (discussed below) may be attributable in part to this process (Anthony and Bauer 2004, 744–5).

A Licensing and Enforcement Officers Meeting (LEOM), sponsored by the GWG, meets annually – in the spring or summer – to discuss the implementation and enforcement of export controls, and sharing of intelligence to improve enforcement. The plenary chair also calls meetings of Vienna Points of Contact (VPOC) to facilitate ongoing communication between participating states and the Secretariat. According to a US official involved in the Wassenaar Arrangement's early operation, 'There is no need for weekly meetings, and countries make great effort to minimize the number of meetings'.[22] However, the official reported that the US representative to the Wassenaar Arrangement was in daily contact with the Secretariat, and communicated with representatives from other participating states several times a week, usually by phone.

Through such activities, states seek to identify and prevent further development of 'destabilizing accumulations' of arms. The underlying logic is that of cooperative security or 'preventive defence', a concept advanced by policymakers in the Clinton administration focusing on preventing the emergence of security threats through measures such as arms control, the development of early warning systems and preventive conflict intervention, and engagement and confidence building within institutional frameworks (Carter et al. 1992; Carter and Perry 1999). By sharing information, states can better identify destabilizing arms build-ups in progress, and impede them through coordinated efforts. This, it is hoped, can help prevent conflicts such as the 1991 Gulf War, by denying states of concern the capacity to commit aggression.

The Initial Elements do not define 'destabilizing accumulation', but the 1998 plenary meeting issued a nonbinding document titled, 'Elements for Objective Analysis and Advice Concerning Potentially Destabilising Accumulations of

Conventional Weapons' (Wassenaar Arrangement 1998a). The document specifies criteria to take into account in assessing the likely effects of arms and dual-use technology exports on regional stability. These include: the importing state's motivation in acquiring the item(s); implications for regional stability and balances of power; the importing state's security and defence posture; and effects of the export on the importing state's operational capabilities. In addition, a set of non-binding 'best practices' for export control enforcement were agreed upon at the December 2000 plenary meeting.

Developments since Wassenaar's Establishment

At the time of Wassenaar's establishment, US Under Secretary of State Lynn Davis, the leading advocate of the organization's creation, described it as 'just an initial international framework that will need to be elaborated and defined more fully' (United States Department of State 1996). This statement reflected disappointment by the US at the relatively limited commitments that emerged from the lengthy negotiations establishing Wassenaar, as well as hope that the Arrangement could be progressively strengthened over time (Yerkey 1996). For the first few years of the regime's operation, proposals to deepen cooperation in Wassenaar made relatively little headway. Recently, however, substantial progress has been made, which some have pronounced a 'major breakthrough' (Anthony and Bauer 2004, 745). At the 2003 plenary, the Initial Elements were amended to incorporate a new reporting category, and participating states agreed on non-binding standards for regulating non-listed items, arms brokering and shoulder-held anti-aircraft missiles. Having deepened their cooperation, participating states broadened its scope by admitting six new members in the next two years, with outreach to additional non-members continuing.

Annual plenary meetings between 1996 and 2002 saw incremental changes to WA. The first two years of the regime's operation were taken up largely with defining the procedures and methods of the WA's operation. At the December 1996 plenary, members agreed not to sell arms or ammunition to parties to the conflict in Afghanistan, and in 1997 endorsed and agreed to support the Economic Community of West African States' (ECOWAS) moratorium on the import, export and manufacture of light weapons in West Africa.

A head of secretariat was not appointed until 1998 due to a deadlock over competing American and German candidates, eventually resolved by agreement on an Italian head. The plenary chair, Staffan Sohlman, served as acting head of secretariat in the interim. The information exchanges also had a rocky start. Only 30 of 33 states submitted data on their arms transfers at the first data exchange in September 1996, and only half of the members reported on their dual-use transfers to non-members (Walkling 1997). Reporting was significantly improved by the second information exchange in March 1997 (Arms Control Today 1997). Discussions on internal rules and procedures continued through 1997 (Anthony and Zanders 1998,

375). At the 1998 plenary meeting, members agreed to controls on encryption with keys of greater than 64 bits while removing controls on weaker encryption, eliminated controls on widely available civilian telecommunications equipment, and adopted non-binding criteria to identify 'destabilizing accumulations' of conventional arms (Markoff 1998; Wassenaar Arrangement 1998b).

In accordance with the Initial Elements, the first overall assessment of the Wassenaar Arrangement was conducted in 1999. Many proposals were discussed in the GWG meetings, and over 50 were considered at the December plenary (Anthony 2000, 672). However, aside from minor changes to the lists and information exchanges, consensus was not achieved to adopt these proposals. Some of the proposals rejected in 1999 were adopted in later years, however.

In 2000, participating states agreed to adopt harmonized criteria for regulation on the export of MANPADS, marking 'the first time the WA agreed to harmonized export controls on any class of weapons' (United States Department of State 2004). Wassenaar's MANPADS guidelines were subsequently adopted by the Organisation for Security and Cooperation in Europe (OSCE). WA members also adopted non-binding lists of 'best practices' for export control enforcement, for implementing the standard of 'extreme vigilance' regarding Tier 2 items specified in the Initial Elements, and for disposal of surplus military equipment. At the 2001 plenary, just weeks after the September 11 terrorist attacks, members amended the initial elements to make it a purpose of the WA to 'prevent the acquisition of conventional arms and dual-use goods and technologies by terrorist groups and organisations, as well as by individual terrorists'. The 2001 plenary also further modified the control lists, and adopted a 'Statement of Understanding on Intangible Transfers of Software and Technology', agreeing to maintain national controls on software and technology that can be transferred electronically.

At the 2002 plenary, Russia blocked proposals to add small arms and light weapons (SALW) as a new reporting category, to require prior notification of undercuts (10 days in advance of licence approval), and to add a 'catch-all' clause requiring exporters to apply for licences for items not included in export control lists when the exporter knows or is informed that such items may be used for military purposes (Washington Trade and Tariff Letter 2002b). However, members did adopt a paper on 'best practices' for regulating exports of SALW and a 'Statement of Understanding on Arms Brokerage'. They also agreed to relax controls on computers (but tighten controls on radiation-hardened computer chips) and to expand the reporting category for ships to cover displacements of 150 (versus 750) tonnes, and those armed with torpedoes with ranges of 25 km (Boese 2003b). They also agreed, in the wake of a November al Qaeda attack on an Israeli Boeing 757 in Kenya, to consider strengthening WA MANPADS guidelines.

In 2003, participating states undertook the second overall assessment of the regime, and decided to continue the practice at four-year intervals. As noted above, the 2003 plenary marked a major advance in the Wassenaar Arrangement's development (Anthony and Bauer 2004, 745–6). Several major initiatives that had previously been stymied were approved. In particular, Russia relented on its earlier opposition to addition of an SALW reporting category (including MANPADS) and a 'catch-all' clause. Participating states agreed on a 'Statement of Understanding on Control of Non-Listed Dual-Use Items', which applies a catch-all rule to exports of non-listed dual-use items to destinations under UN or regional arms embargos.[23] For exports to such destinations, exporters must apply to national licensing authorities for an export licence, subjecting the sale to export control scrutiny (Wassenaar Arrangement 2003b). WA also strengthened its MANPADS guidelines, requiring that export decisions be approved at senior levels, that design features to prevent unauthorized use be incorporated into newly manufactured missiles, and that members take steps to dismantle excess missiles and help others to do so (Boese 2004). Members also approved a paper on 'Elements for Effective Legislation on Arms Brokering', agreeing to regulate arms brokers through national licensing systems. And the WA published a 'List of Advisory Questions for Industry', identifying 'red flags' that should alert exporters to potential illicit activity about which export control authorities should be notified. However, Russia continued to block prior notification of undercuts (Washington Trade and Tariff Letter 2004). Nonetheless, the 2003 plenary marked a major advance for Wassenaar.

Building on the progress in 2003, WA maintained the system of task forces developed in the 2003 assessment (Anthony and Bauer 2005, 706). The focus in 2004 was on exports of interest to terrorists, and the control lists were amended to tighten controls on such items. Further modifications (regarding jamming equipment and unmanned aerial vehicles) were made in 2005. In addition to admitting new states, a major focus since 2003 has been 'outreach' – to non-members, to industry, and to other export control regimes. The secretariat and the Japanese permanent mission to international organizations in Vienna co-hosted an outreach seminar to non-member states in October 2004 and an industry outreach seminar in October 2005. Individual members also conducted outreach activities. In 2005, the regime published an 'indicative list of end-use assurances' required by participating states for approval of licences.

Evaluating Wassenaar

Evaluating Wassenaar's effectiveness is complicated by several factors. First, the Arrangement's purpose is ultimately, by identifying and interrupting destabilizing accumulations of arms, to prevent armed conflicts from arising in the first place. Its ultimate success, then, is measured in non-events. The difficulty of identifying conflicts that could have emerged but did not is compounded by the fact that, because export control regimes function alongside other non-proliferation and arms trade-related activities, 'it is difficult to attribute accomplishments exclusively to the regimes' (United States General Accounting Office 2002, 7). Wade Boese notes:

> Wassenaar's impact on the global arms trade is difficult to measure. The annual overall value of the global arms trade has ebbed and flowed over the past six years with several countries buying large amounts of weaponry. Moreover, members' exchanges of

information on their exports and denials are confidential among Wassenaar members, making it nearly impossible for outsiders to determine whether members are acting with more restraint or foregoing sales since the arrangement's establishment (Boese 2003a, 176).

A 2002 study of non-proliferation export control regimes by the US Congress's General Accounting Office (GAO) determined that, 'Neither the US government, member governments in the regimes whom [the report's authors] contacted, nor the regimes have established explicit criteria for assessing the regimes' effectiveness' (United States General Accounting Office 2002, 26). While the report's criticisms applied to the NSG, AG and MTCR as well as Wassenaar, it stated that 'several government officials and industry representatives noted that the mission, obligations and political commitment of the Wassenaar Arrangement are not as clear as those of the other regimes. Thus, assessing the effectiveness of this regime would be "especially problematic" (United States General Accounting Office 2002, 26).

Nonetheless, it is possible, at least to some extent, to evaluate participating states' compliance with their commitments in the WA. As noted above, reporting of arms transfers was initially far short of the requirements in the Initial Elements, but improved significantly in WA's first year. However, the 2002 GAO Report found that participating states report dual-use licence denials on time (within 60 days after denial for tier 2 items, and every six months for Tier 1 items) 'only about 36 [per cent] of the time' (United States General Accounting Office 2002, 14). Further, the report found that members sometimes take as long as a year or more to implement agreed changes to control lists, producing variation in export control enforcement across participating states (United States General Accounting Office 2002).

Despite a collective commitment at the 1998 plenary to 'maximum restraint' to arms sales to war-torn regions, Russia exported military aircraft and equipment to Ethiopia, and Bulgaria approved exports of tanks to Ethiopia and Uganda (Bonner 1998). In 2000, Russia abandoned its 1995 commitment to end arms sales to Iran, though it promised to sell only 'defensive' weapons (Grimmett 2005, 59). However, undercutting exports have reportedly been rare (Boese 2003a, 175). And while sales inconsistent with participating states' commitments such as the above examples are relatively easily identifiable, it is more difficult to measure Wassenaar's successes. A US official involved in Wassenaar's early operation expresses confidence 'that there have been some sales that have not taken place because of the existence of Wassenaar, but it would be really difficult to measure to what extent its existence deters irresponsible sales'.[24] Similarly, the 2002 GAO report describes a former head of the Wassenaar Secretariat as judging 'that the situation would be worse without the Arrangement' (United States General Accounting Office 2002, 8). In a 2002 assessment, Cassady Craft documented significant procedural, substantive and information exchange-related cooperation – distinguishing '88 cooperative events' – in Wassenaar's first six years of operation (Craft 2002).[25] And the 2003 plenary saw, in the words of the plenary chair, 'some of the most significant progress' in the Arrangement's short history (Boese 2004).

Much of the criticism of the WA stems from its procedural rules, and especially their differences from COCOM. Wassenaar does not require states to deny any specific items to any particular targets, leaving export licensing decisions to national discretion. Wassenaar also lacks COCOM's 'veto'. The lack of a requirement of prior notification of undercutting exports undermines participating states' ability to persuade others to forego undercuts. And participating states' divergent threat perceptions, coupled with consensus decision-making, have made efforts to strengthen Wassenaar slow and arduous.

There have been occasional calls from some in the United States to recreate a COCOM-like arrangement. The 1999 Report of the House Select Committee on US National Security and Military/Commercial Concerns with the People's Republic of China (known as the Cox Report) recommended that the US seek to 'establish new binding international controls on technology transfers that threaten international peace and US national security' (United States Congress 1999, 168). Also in 1999, the US Congress commissioned a study group on multilateral export controls to 'develop the framework for a new, effective COCOM-like agreement that would regulate certain militarily useful goods and technologies on a multilateral basis' (Study Group on Enhancing Multilateral Export Controls for US National Security 2001, 45 note 1). However, no serious attempt to create a post-Cold War COCOM-like regime has been undertaken. Instead, the US has focused on strengthening Wassenaar, achieving incremental successes.

Wassenaar was established with a large membership holding diverse interests and views of states of concern, no provision for enforcement, and little in the way of binding requirements on the participating states. This approach is considered as perverse by those who regard binding rules and enforcement as keys to the effectiveness of multilateral organizations (Downs et al. 1997). However, Wassenaar's design – focusing on transparency, consultation and capacity-building – exemplifies the 'managerial' approach to securing compliance with international regimes (Chayes and Chayes 1998).[26] Thus, one's assessment of the WA depends largely on the baseline employed.

Wassenaar as Trans-Governmental Network: The Virtues and Limits of Informal Cooperation and 'Soft Law'

An alternative perspective on the Wassenaar Arrangement is to regard it as the framework for a network of government officials with export control responsibilities.[27] The distinguished international legal scholar Anne-Marie Slaughter has recently argued that such 'trans-governmental' networks are the sinews of a pragmatic twenty-first century international order (Slaughter 2004). Facing collective problems requiring coordination among states, government officials with specialized responsibilities – such as export control – network with their functional counterparts in other governments, developing common standards and practices, which are then implemented through national political systems. States respond to the governance challenges of globalization by disaggregating into functional components and agencies, which form networks with their foreign counterparts. These 'government networks', according to Slaughter, marry the coercive regulatory power of states to the flexibility and adaptability of the network form.[28] They can achieve coordinated responses to collective action problems without the international bureaucracy and sovereignty constraints associated with treaties and formal intergovernmental organizations. Slaughter regards them as forming a 'disaggregated' world order.

The Wassenaar Arrangement is a framework for the creation and strengthening of a trans-governmental network of export control officials addressing conventional arms and dual-use technologies. It illustrates Slaughter's observation that, 'Many international organizations are primarily convening structures for networks of government officials' (Slaughter 2004, 22). Within the organizational framework of the Wassenaar Arrangement, distinct but related networks operate within the plenary and working groups.

Trans-governmental networks operate in their areas of specialization somewhat autonomously of national political leadership (Keohane and Nye 1974, 43–4). Otherwise, trans-governmental relations would be indistinguishable from intergovernmental diplomacy. WA Plenary, General Working Group and Expert Group meetings are attended by officials of different levels of seniority. At plenary meetings, participating states are represented by senior officials (equivalent to US Under Secretary or Assistant Secretary rank). General Working Group meetings consist of mid-level officials, and Experts Group meetings are comprised of technical experts (Export Practitioner 1998). These officials reach agreements on technical and procedural standards with relatively little direct involvement by the highest levels of their governments.

Slaughter distinguishes three types of trans-governmental network: information networks, enforcement networks, and harmonization networks. Wassenaar's information exchange, as well as related activity in the Experts Group and GWG, constitutes an information network. Enforcement networks, 'focuse[d] primarily on enhancing cooperation among national regulators to enforce existing national laws and rules' (Slaughter 2004, 55), are exemplified by meetings of licensing and enforcement officials in Wassenaar's LEOM. And the EG, GWG and Plenary also act as harmonization networks when they make changes that are incorporated into national control lists, and agree on policies such as a catch-all clause and restrictions on MANPADS that harmonize national export control regulations. The system of task forces developed during the 2003 assessment process establishes smaller, more specialized networks as well. Government networks, according to Slaughter, 'coexist and increasingly interact with networks of nongovernmental actors, both from the private and nonprofit sectors' (Slaughter 2004, 132). Wassenaar exhibits such contact in its outreach to industry – such as the October 2005 outreach seminar – and contacts with nongovernmental export control policy organizations such as the Centre for International Trade and Security (CITS) from the US, the Centre for International Security Trade Control (CISTEC) in Japan and the Moscow Centre on Export Controls.[29]

Trans-governmental networks do not operate in the same way as formal multilateral agreements and organizations. International organizations facilitate international cooperation within centralized structures, by reducing transaction costs, pooling costs and risks, and exercising delegated authority (Abbott and Snidal 1998). They often possess a degree of independence, acting autonomously on the basis of authority arising from their perceived impartiality, expertise, and embodiment of shared social purpose (Abbott and Snidal 1998; Barnett and Finnemore 2004). Formal international agreements operate on the basis of different configurations of binding obligations, precise rules, and delegated authority to adjudicate and interpret (Abbott et al. 2000). Agreements characterized by high levels along all three dimensions are 'hard law'. Measured against these baselines, Wassenaar falls short.

Criticisms of Wassenaar as insufficiently centralized and independent and not resting on 'hard law' neglect the virtues of informality and the power of soft law. According to Charles Lipson, informal agreements such as the Wassenaar Arrangement are attractive to states when flexibility, speed and a low public profile are desired (Lipson 1991). Similarly, Abbott and Snidal claim that states will prefer 'soft law' – characterized by low levels of legal obligation, precision and delegation of authority – when sovereignty costs and uncertainty are high (Abbott and Snidal 2000, 444). Trans-governmental networks facilitate cooperation on the basis of soft law (Slaughter 2004, 178–81). Thus, Abbott and Snidal note, the Wassenaar Arrangement 'illustrates the use of soft legalization to facilitate compromise' (Abbott and Snidal 2000, 445).[30]

'Soft legalization' makes agreements possible under circumstances that might otherwise cause negotiations to fail – a large number of states, divergent preferences, varying levels of consensus across different sub-issues, and varying levels of state capacity (Abbott and Snidal 2000, 444–5). Once established, they shape national regulations by establishing models that, while non-binding, provide focal points for cooperation. States seeking to enhance domestic capacity and develop internationally compatible systems will often copy models perceived as successful or promoted by organizations that are prominent in the relevant issue area. Organization theorists refer to the resulting convergence in policies and procedures as 'mimetic isomorphism' (DiMaggio and Powell 1983). Thus, Wassenaar has specialized in 'soft law in the form of principles, guidelines, codes, standards, and best practices' (Slaughter 2004, 179). Soft law allows the creation of loose frameworks that can be strengthened over time (Abbott and Snidal 2000, 446–7). And they provide contexts of ongoing interaction within which norms can be established and participants socialized.

In January 1996, US Under Secretary of State Lynn Davis described the Wassenaar Arrangement as an 'initial international framework' to build on (United States Department of State 1996). Three years later, a US official with responsibilities related to Wassenaar argued that, rather than decrying the lack of binding and restrictive rules in the Arrangement, 'I would say that we should look on it as a venue to promote better/best practices'.[31] Cooperation within Wassenaar has reflected this view of the Arrangement as a forum for developing common standards and enhancing cooperation. Since 1996, Wassenaar members have developed four sets of 'best practices' (for surplus military equipment disposal, implementing 'extreme vigilance' regarding exports of Tier-2 very sensitive items, effective enforcement, and regulating SALW Exports). In addition, they have adopted 'Statements of Understanding' regarding intangible technology, arms brokerage and non-listed dual-use items (catch-all), and lists of 'Elements' for identifying destabilizing accumulations and for arms brokerage legislation. Members have also released lists of standard end-use assurances and 'red flag' questions for industry.[32] At the 2003 plenary, several of these (the criteria for identifying destabilizing accumulations, statement of understanding on intangibles, SALW best practices, elements for MANPADS control, and catch-all clause) were combined with the Initial Elements and renamed the 'Guidelines and Procedures, including the Initial Elements'. Although other measures such as prior notification of undercuts remain unrealized – despite significant support – due to opposition by states such as Russia, this record is consistent with the claim that '[b]ecause even soft legal agreements commit states to characteristic forms of discourse and procedure, soft law provides a way of achieving compromise over time' (Abbott and Snidal 2000, 446).

Proposals and Prospects

A number of proposals have been offered regarding Wassenaar's future. In a 2001 review for the US Congress's study group on multilateral export controls, Frank Cevasco provided an overview and assessment of ten alternatives, grouped in three overall categories of replacing, modifying or augmenting the WA (Cevasco 2001). Cevasco's alternatives entailing Wassenaar's replacement were: (1) recreate a 'COCOM clone'; (2) establish a multilevel regime consisting of a more restrictive core group, and subordinate levels consisting of states with weaker commitments to transfer controls; (3) create a cluster' of small, highly specialized regimes focusing on particular categories of the current control lists; (4) create a merged regime, incorporating the other MECRs within an integrated organization; and (5) a narrowed focus on the most threatening states, employing export controls, disruption and interdiction.

Options for modifying Wassenaar include: (6) creating 'focus groups' within Wassenaar consisting of key suppliers of specific categories of controlled goods; (7) replacing consensus decision-making with qualified majority voting; (8) incorporation of features of the EU dual-use regime, including denial notification, a no-undercut rule, and a catch-all rule; and (9) transferring responsibility for controlling items on WA lists to other MECRs. Finally, a tenth option would establish a parallel and smaller regime of like-minded states that would function more efficiently by excluding recalcitrant WA members.

Cevasco identifies numbers (5), (6), (7) and (10) as the most feasible and promising alternatives (Cevasco 2001, 57). The subsequently established Proliferation Security Initiative partially embodies alternative (5), and the system of task forces developed in the 2003 WA assessment largely implements number (6).

The Centre for International Trade and Security, an influential NGO in the export control field, has championed a merged regime, employing majority or qualified majority decision-making, incorporating the existing MECRs (NSG, MTCR, AG, WA) as working groups within a larger framework (Gahlaut et al. 2004; Joyner 2004). However, political support for this proposal has not been forthcoming to date. Similarly, little support exists for creation of a 'COCOM clone', which is widely viewed as politically unfeasible in the absence of the Cold War political–military consensus that animated COCOM (Cevasco 2001, 36).

Another option with seemingly little political impetus behind it is Wolfgang Reinicke's innovative proposal for industry self-regulation of dual-use exports through a mixed public–private regulatory organization, an Automated Technology Transfer Registry (Reinicke 1998, 173–217). Based on models in use in securities regulation and financial crimes, the ATTR would integrate information (including content, destination, recipient and end-use) that dual-use exporters would be required to submit. Using artificial intelligence, the registry would flag exports exhibiting problematic indicators for review by national export control authorities. The system would emphasize 'disclosure' over 'denial', trading off relaxed restrictions on dual-use exports for more extensive reporting by industry enabling improved identification of genuinely destabilizing dual-use trades.

Finally, the option of a parallel regime resembles an effort during the negotiations to establish Wassenaar to have a 'small group' consisting of Britain, France, Germany, Italy, Russia and the United States provide leadership for Wassenaar through deeper cooperation among prominent states. This effort failed because members of the small group – France, Germany and Russia – were more resistant to stringent restraints than states such as Norway, the Netherlands and Japan that were excluded (Lewis 2005). Although a small group centred on the participants in the 2000 Framework Agreement Concerning Measures to Facilitate the Restructuring and Operation of the European Defence Industry would exclude Russia (and include Spain and Sweden), it is not clear any such effort would be more successful than the original WA small group (Cevasco 2001, 51). Jaffer (2002) recommends a bilateral approach to key western states.

More plausible enhancements, at least in the short term, would include US proposals within Wassenaar for prior notification of undercuts, and reporting on specific transfers rather than aggregated data (Grimmett 2004, 6). European participating states have expressed concern that consultations on arms sales should be strengthened before further enhancements are made to the dual-use procedures (Washington Trade and Tariff Letter 2002a). Given Russian opposition to prior notification of undercuts (Washington Trade and Tariff Letter 2004), a fallback option may be to seek a limited no-undercut rule for cruise missiles and related technologies covered by Wassenaar (Bolkcom and Squassoni 2002, 5). Henry Sokolski has also suggested that Wassenaar members employ national catch-all regulations and their participation in the other MECRs to substitute for a Wassenaar no-undercut rule. Participating states should, he recommends, identify WA-listed items with chemical, biological or nuclear applications, and prevent their export to 'projects of concern' under domestic catch-all regulations. States denying such licences would then:

> notify all other nations in the relevant control regime (whether it be the NSG, AG, or MTCR) not to undercut its denial of this export. In this fashion, the no-undercut rules of the other MECRs could be extended to some of the most critical of Wassenaar listed items without creating a new export regime or new agreed lists (Sokolski 2000, 3).

Such proposals, however, constitute patches on the underlying problem: the divergent threat perceptions and national interests of Wassenaar member states. For the Arrangement to become a more centralized and authoritative entity would require a significant convergence of members' foreign policy views (Lewis 2005). As Smith and Udis note:

> In the case of the WA, concerted commitment by the major arms producers would be required – particularly the United States, the United Kingdom, and France – in order to change the structure of payoffs (putting more weight on long-term security consequences); develop an effective monitoring capability; and infuse the arrangement with more credibility and autonomy (Smith and Udis 2001, 90).

The different foreign policy views of leading Wassenaar members inhibit such a development. The shared threat that enabled COCOM's effectiveness is gone. And the level of consensus that exists among MECR participants regarding unconventional weapons and ballistic missiles is lacking with regard to the items Wassenaar covers. The possession and transfer of WA-listed items are considered legitimate, and not inherently dangerous. Accordingly, it is significantly more difficult to reach consensus on meaningful restrictions on their transfer. The area in which Wassenaar has been able to achieve its most significant cooperation – MANPADS – illustrates the point, reflecting participating states' shared sense of threat from possible terrorist acquisition of MANPADS. However, similar consensus does not exist on other weapons systems or the dual-use list.

Given the political unfeasibility of deeper cooperation of the type achieved in COCOM – or even in the other MECRs – the most promising avenues for strengthening COCOM are those that accept and build on its basic nature as a framework for trans-governmental networking. These include pre-licence notification of undercuts, more specific arms transfer reporting, capacity-building and more intensive ongoing consultation. Trans-governmental networks have been criticized for lacking both democratic accountability and the capacity to overcome power asymmetries and conflicting interests (Gilpin 2001, 400; Anderson 2005). However, as military and intelligence coordination through a trans-governmental network in the Proliferation Security Initiative (through Plenary and Operational Experts Group meetings) illustrates, states are turning to governmental networks even in areas directly related to national security (Lehrman 2004). And, as Wassenaar's recent record suggests, participants in trans-governmental networks can progressively deepen and expand their cooperation, even amidst national differences.

References

Abbott, K.W., Keohane, R.O., Moravcsik, A., Slaughter, A.M. and Snidal, D. (2000), 'The Concept of Legalization', *International Organization*, Vol. 54, No. 3.

Abbott, K.W. and Snidal, D. (1998), 'Why States Act through Formal International Organizations', *Journal of Conflict Resolution*, Vol. 42, No. 1.

—— (2000), 'Hard and Soft Law in International Governance', *International Organization*, Vol. 54, No. 3.

Anderson, K. (2005), 'Squaring the Circle? Reconciling Sovereignty and Global Governance through Global Government Networks', *Harvard Law Review*, Vol. 118, No. 4.

Anthony, I. (2000), 'Appendix 11A. Multilateral Weapon and Technology Export Controls', in *SIPRI Yearbook 2000: Armaments, Disarmament, and International Security*, Oxford University Press, New York.

Anthony, I. and Bauer, S. (2004), 'Transfer Controls and Destruction Programmes', in *SIPRI Yearbook 2004: Armaments, Disarmament, and International Security*, Oxford University Press, New York.

—— (2005), 'Transfer Controls', in *SIPRI Yearbook 2005: Armaments, Disarmament, and International Security*, Oxford University Press, New York.

Anthony, I. and Zanders, J.P. (1998), 'Multilateral Security-Related Export Controls', in *SIPRI Yearbook 1998: Armaments, Disarmament, and International Security*, Oxford University Press, New York.

Arms Control Today (1997), 'Wassenaar Members Review Data Exchange [News Brief]', *Arms Control Today*, Vol. 27, No. 3.

Barnett, M. and Finnemore, M. (2004), *Rules for the World: International Organizations in Global Politics*, Cornell University Press, Ithaca, NY.

Boese, W. (2003a), 'The Wassenaar Arrangement', in T. Gabelnick and R. Stohl (eds), *Challenging Conventional Wisdom: Debunking the Myths and Exposing the Risks of Arms Export Reform*, Federation of American Scientists/Center for Defense Information, Washington, DC.

—— (2003b), 'Wassenaar Members Adopt Small Arms Initiative', *Arms Control Today*, Vol. 33, No. 1.

—— (2004), 'Wassenaar Endorses Steps to Deny Terrorists Arms', *Arms Control Today*, Vol. 34, No. 1.

Bolkcom, C. and Squassoni, S. (2002), 'Cruise Missile Proliferation', CRS Report RS21252, Government Printing Office, Washington, DC.

Bonner, R. (1998), 'New Weapons Sales to African Nations Cause Concern at Arms-Control Conference', *New York Times*, 6 December 1998.

Broder, J.M. (2000), 'Russia Ending Deal on Arms Negotiated by Gore', *New York Times*, 23 November 2000.

Carter, A.B. and Perry, W.J. (1999), *Preventive Defence: A New Security Strategy for America*, Brookings Institute, Washington, DC.

Carter, A.B., Perry, W.J. and Steinbruner, J.D. (1992), *A New Concept of Cooperative Security*, Brookings Occasional Paper, Brookings Institute, Washington, DC.

Centre for Non-Proliferation Studies (2006), 'The Wassenaar Arrangement on Export Controls for Conventional Arms and Dual-Use Goods and Technologies (Successor to COCOM)', *Inventory of International Non-proliferation Organizations & Regimes*, <http://cns.miis.edu/pubs/inven/pdfs/wass.pdf>.

Cevasco, F.M. (2001), 'Survey and Assessment: Alternative Multilateral Export Control Structures', Working Paper No. 3, CSIS/Stimson Centre Study Group on Enhancing Multilateral Export Controls for US National Security, <www.stimson.org/exportcontrol/pdf/paper3.pdf>.

Chayes, A. and Chayes, A.H. (1998), *The New Sovereignty: Compliance with International Regulatory Agreements*, Harvard University Press, Cambridge, MA.

Craft, C. (2002), 'New Challenges in Multilateral Efforts to Control the Conventional Weapons Trade', *The Monitor*, Vol. 8, No. 2.

Danielsson, S. (2005), 'Address to 7th Annual International Export Control Conference, Stockholm, Sweden', 20 September 2005, <http://www.exportcontrol.org/library/conferences/1379/009_-_Update_on_Wassenaar_Arrangement_-_Amb.pdf>.

DiMaggio, P. and Powell, W. (1983), 'The Iron Cage Revisited: Institutional Isomorphism and Collective Rationality in Organizational Fields', *American Sociological Review*, Vol. 48.

Downs, G.W., Rocke, D.M., and Barsoom, P.N. (1997), 'Managing the Evolution of Multilateralism', *International Organization*, Vol. 52, No. 2.

Dursht, K.A. (1997), 'From Containment to Cooperation: Collective Action and the Wassenaar Arrangement', *Cardozo Law Review*, Vol. 19, No. 3.

Export Practitioner (1998), 'What is the Wassenaar Arrangement?', *Export Practitioner Online*, Vol. 12, No. 9.

G7 (1991), 'Declaration on Conventional Arms Transfers and NBC Non-Proliferation', 16 July 1991, <www.g8.utoronto.ca/summit/1991london/arms.html>.

Gahlaut, S., Beck, M., Jones, S. and Joyner, D. (2004), *Roadmap to Reform: Creating a New Multilateral Export Control Regime*, Centre for International Trade and Security, Athens, GA.

Gilpin, R.L. (2001), *Global Political Economy: Understanding the International Economic Order*, Princeton University Press, Princeton, NJ.

Goldman, C.A. and Pollack, J.D. (1997), *Engaging China in the International Export Control Process: Options for US Policy*, RAND Documented Briefing DB-197, RAND, Santa Monica.

Goldring, N.J. (1996), 'Wassenaar Arrangement in Limbo', *BASIC Reports*, 52, 13 May 1996.

Grimmett, R.F. (2004), 'Military Technology and Conventional Weapons Export Controls: The Wassenaar Arrangement', CRS Report for Congress RF20517, Congressional Research Service, Washington, DC, 21 May 2004.

—— (2005), 'The Wassenaar Arrangement', in A.F. Woolf, 'Arms Control and Non-Proliferation Activities: A Catalog of Recent Events', CRS Report for

Congress RL30033, Congressional Research Service, Washington, DC, 7 January 2005.

Hardt, J.P. and Tomlinson, K.S. (1983), 'Appendix 5A: COCOM's Operating Procedures and an Assessment of its Effectiveness', in A.S. Becker (ed.), *Economic Relations with the USSR: Issues for the Western Alliance*, Lexington Books, Lexington, MA.

Jaffer, J. (2002), 'Strengthening the Wassenaar Export Control Regime', *Chicago Journal of International Law*, Vol. 3, No. 2.

Joyner, D.H. (2004), 'Restructuring the Multilateral Export Control Regime System', *Journal of Conflict & Security Law*, Vol. 9, No. 2.

Keck, M.E. and Sikkink, K. (1998), *Activists beyond Borders: Advocacy Networks in International Politics*, Cornell University Press, Ithaca, NY.

Keohane, R.O. and Nye, J.S. Jr. (1974), 'Trans-governmental Relations and International Organizations', *World Politics*, Vol. 27, No. 1.

Khripunov, I. (2003), 'Export Control Assistance to Russia and Other FSU States', in R.J. Einhorn and M.J. Flournoy (eds), *Protecting Against the Spread of Nuclear, Biological, and Chemical Weapons: An Action Agenda for the Global Partnership, Vol. 2: The Challenges*, Centre for Strategic and International Studies, Washington, DC.

Lehrman, T.D. (2004), 'Rethinking Interdiction: The Future of the Proliferation Security Initiative', *The Nonproliferation Review*, Vol. 11, No. 2.

Lewis, J.A. (2005), 'Looking Back: Multilateral Arms Transfer Restraint: The Limits of Cooperation', *Arms Control Today*, Vol. 35, No. 9.

Lipson, C. (1991), 'Why Are Some International Agreements Informal?', *International Organization*, Vol. 45, No. 4.

Lipson, M. (1999), 'The Reincarnation of COCOM: Explaining Post-Cold War Export Control Cooperation', *The Nonproliferation Review*, Vol. 6, No.2.

—— (2004), 'Transaction Cost Estimation and International Regimes: Of Crystal Balls and Sheriff's Posses', *International Studies Review*, Vol. 6, No. 1.

—— (2005–2006), 'Trans-governmental Networks and Non-Proliferation: International Security and the Future of Global Governance', *International Journal*, Vol. 61, No. 1.

Litavrin, P.G. (1997), 'Russia, the Wassenaar Arrangement, and the Creation of International Restraints on Arms Transfers', in A.J. Pierre and D.V. Trenin (eds), *Russia in the World Arms Trade*, Carnegie Endowment for International Peace, Washington, DC.

Markoff, J. (1998), 'International Group Reaches Agreement on Encryption', *New York Times*, 4 December 1998.

Mastanduno, M. (1992), *Economic Containment: COCOM and the Politics of East-West Trade*, Cornell University Press, Ithaca, NY.

Pierre, A.J. (1997), 'Toward an International Regime for Conventional Arms Sales', in A.J. Pierre (ed.), *Cascade of Arms: Managing Conventional Weapons Proliferation*, Brookings, Washington, DC.

Raustiala, K. and Slaughter, A.M. (2002), 'International Law, International Relations and Compliance', in W. Carlsnaes, T. Risse and B.A. Simmons (eds), *Handbook of International Relations*, Sage, Thousand Oaks, CA.

Reinicke, W.H. (1998), *Global Public Policy: Governing without Government?*, Brookings, Washington, DC.

Slaughter, A.M. (2004), *A New World Order*, Princeton University Press, Princeton, NJ.

Smith, R. and Udis, B. (2001), 'New Challenges to Arms Export Control: Whither Wassenaar?', *The Nonproliferation Review*, Vol. 8, No. 2.

Sokolski, H. (2000), 'A More Transparent, Less Intrusive, Market Approach to Export Controls', Presented to the CSIS Control Regime Working Group, November 2000, <www.npecweb.org/Reports/Presentation001115AMoreTransparentExportControls.pdf>.

Study Group on Enhancing Multilateral Export Controls for US National Security (2001), 'Final Report', Henry L. Stimson Centre, Washington, DC, <www.stimson.org/exportcontrol/pdf/finalreport.pdf>.

US Congress (1999), 'House Select Committee on US National Security and Military/Commercial Concerns with the People's Republic of China [Cox Report]', Government Printing Office, Washington, DC.

—— (2000), 'The Wassenaar Arrangement: Testimony of Under Secretary of Commerce for Export Administration William Reinsch before the Senate Governmental Affairs Committee, 12 April 2000', <www.fas.org/spp/starwars/congress/2000_h/00041200_reinsch.htm>.

US Department of State, Bureau of Non-proliferation (2004), 'Fact Sheet: Wassenaar Arrangement on Export Controls for Conventional Arms and Dual-Use Goods and Technologies, March 22, 2004', <www.state.gov/t/np/rls/fs/30957.htm>.

US Department of State, Office of the Spokesman (1996), 'The Wassenaar Arrangement', Address by Under Secretary of State for Arms Control and International Security Affairs Lynn E. Davis to the Carnegie Endowment for International Peace, Washington, DC, January 23, 1996, <http://dosfan.lib.uic.edu/ERC/arms/arms_briefing/960123arms_briefing.html>.

US General Accounting Office (2002), 'Non-proliferation: Strategy Needed to Strengthen Multilateral Export Control Regimes', GAO-03-43, Government Printing Office, Washington, DC.

US Mission to International Organizations in Vienna (n.d.), 'Questions & Answers: Some Basics about The Wassenaar Arrangement', <www.usun-vienna.rpo.at/_index.php?cmd=cmdFrontendSpeechesAndRelatedDocumentsDetail&speechid=101>.

Walkling, S. (1996a), 'Wassenaar Regime Plenary Meeting Adjourns Following Disagreements', *Arms Control Today*, Vol. 26, No. 3.

—— (1996b), 'Wassenaar Members Resolve Most Differences During July Plenary', *Arms Control Today*, Vol. 26, No. 5.

—— (1997), 'Wassenaar Members End Plenary: First Data Exchange Falls Short', *Arms Control Today*, Vol. 26, No. 10.

Wallander, C. (1999), *Mortal Friends, Best Enemies: German-Russian Cooperation After the Cold War*, Cornell University Press, Ithaca, NY.

Washington Trade and Tariff Letter (2002a), 'Europeans Want to Tie Arms Controls to Dual-Use Controls', *Washington Trade and Tariff Letter*, Vol. 2, No. 20.

—— (2002b), 'Russia Again Foils Effort to Tighten Wassenaar Controls', *Washington Trade and Tariff Letter*, Vol. 22, No. 50.

—— (2004), 'US Fails Again to Get Wassenaar to Adopt "No-Undercut" Policy', *Washington Trade and Tariff Letter*, Vol. 24, No. 50.

Wassenaar Arrangement (1998a), 'Elements for Objective Analysis and Advice Concerning Potentially Destabilising Accumulations of Conventional Weapons', This is a paper approved by the Wassenaar Plenary. It is available at: <http://www.wassenaar.org/docs/criteria.html#paper>.

—— (1998b), 'Public Statement – 3 December 1998', <www.wassenaar.org/publicdocuments/public031298.html>.

—— (2003a), 'Purposes, Guidelines, and Procedures, including the Initial Elements', <www.wassenaar.org/2003Plenary/initial_elements2003.htm>.

—— (2003b), 'Statement of Understanding on Control of Non-Listed Dual-Use Items', <w.wassenaar.org/guidelines/index.html#Statement_of_Understanding>.

—— (2004), 'Public Statement, 2004 Plenary Meeting of the Wassenaar Arrangement on Export Controls for Conventional Arms and Dual-Use Goods and Technologies', <www.wassenaar.org/publicdocuments/docs/Elements for Public Statement.doc>.

—— (2005a), 'Public Statement, 2005 Plenary Meeting of the Wassenaar Arrangement on Export Controls for Conventional Arms and Dual-Use Goods and Technologies, Vienna, 14 December 2005', <www.wassenaar.org/publicdocuments/public131205.html>.

—— (2005b), 'Statement by the Plenary Chair of the Wassenaar Arrangement, Vienna, 29 June 2005', <www.wassenaar.org/publicdocuments/2005_newstates.html>.

—— (n.d.), 'Genesis of the Wassenaar Arrangement', <www.wassenaar.org/publicdocuments/history.html>.

Yerkey, G.G. (1996), 'US Welcomes New Export Regime But Says It Falls Short of US Goals', *International Trade Reporter*, Vol. 13, No. 1.

Notes

1. The author thanks Jonathan Bujeau for research assistance. All errors and shortcomings are the responsibility of the author.
2. The standard work on COCOM is Mastanduno (1992).
3. Cyprus has applied for admission to Wassenaar (Anthony and Bauer 2005, 713). The current participating states are: Argentina, Australia, Austria, Belgium, Bulgaria, Canada, Croatia, the Czech Republic, Denmark, Estonia, Finland, France, Germany, Greece, Hungary, Ireland, Italy, Japan, Latvia, Lithuania, Luxembourg, Malta, the Netherlands, New Zealand, Norway, Poland, Portugal, the Republic of Korea, Romania,

the Russian Federation, Slovenia, Slovakia, South Africa, Spain, Sweden, Switzerland, Turkey, Ukraine, United Kingdom and the United States.

4. The European Union's Community regime for dual-use technology export controls and EU Code of Conduct on Arms Exports are excluded here because they are only open to EU members. All EU members except Cyprus participate in Wassenaar, as do acceding countries Bulgaria and Romania, and candidate countries Croatia and Turkey.
5. Croatia joined the NSG in 2005. Estonia, Latvia, Lithuania and Malta participate in the NSG and Australia Group. Romania, Slovakia and Slovenia participate in the Zangger Committee, NSG and Australia Group. New Zealand participates in all the regimes except the Zangger Committee. Russia and South Africa participate in all except the Australia Group.
6. In 2001 WA members 'account[ed] for about 94 percent of annual arms exports' (Cevasco 2001, 55). Boese (2003b) listed Belarus, Brazil, China, Israel and South Africa as non-participating major arms exporters. (South Africa was admitted at the 2005 Plenary.) All of these states have been the subject of outreach efforts (Anthony and Bauer 2004, 745; 2005, 706). Israel participated in a 2004 WA Outreach Seminar, but its status as an NPT non-signatory complicates prospects for its membership. Belarus has reportedly considered applying for Wassenaar membership (Khripunov 2003, 143).
7. During the negotiations to replace COCOM, contacts occurred between China and participating states. However, '[a]bsent a signal that the United States would agree, no one pushed for China to join' (Lewis 2005, 48, note 6). According to a 1997 RAND briefing, the US kept China informed (Goldman and Pollack 1997, 33).
8. This section draws upon Lipson (1999; 2004).
9. Author's interview with former US government official, Washington, DC, 14 January 1999.
10. This paragraph is based on Lewis (2005).
11. Author's interview with former US government official, Washington DC, 15 January 1999.
12. The 17 COCOM members were the members of NATO, except Iceland, together with Japan and Australia.
13. Personal communication (email) with author, US government official involved in Wassenaar Arrangement, 17 May 1999.
14. At the 2003 Plenary, the Initial Elements were integrated with additional initiatives agreed by the participating states and renamed the 'Purposes, Guidelines, & Procedures, including the Initial Elements' (Wassenaar Arrangement 2003a).
15. Russia justified this action on grounds that the agreement had been confidential and was abrogated by its release to the US press (Broder 2000).
16. The WA usually refers to 'participating states' rather than 'members'. However, some public documents do use the term 'member' (i.e. Wassenaar Arrangement n.d.).
17. The munitions list is adapted from COCOM's. The dual-use list takes the place of COCOM's International Industrial List. Items formerly on COCOM's Atomic Energy Control List are controlled through the NSG.
18. According to Lewis (2005), the dual-use lists are subdivided this way as a vestige of failed efforts by the US to obtain agreement on prior review – notifying and consulting participating states in advance of transferring a controlled item. Facing resistance, the US proposed restricting prior review to Tier 2 only, and then only to the very sensitive

subset. These proposals were not adopted.

19. According to Boese (2003a), Italy does not control certain listed firearms.
20. The WA adopted guidelines on MANPADS in 2000 and SALW in 2003. SALW, including MANPADS, was adopted as a reporting category of the munitions list in 2003. States shared information about SALW prior to the addition of the new category.
21. There is also the danger that a participating state could take advantage of others' denial notifications to identify potential customers, and then seek undercutting contracts.
22. Personal communication with the author, 17 May 1999.
23. Specifically, it applies to destinations under binding UN arms embargo, or under a regional arms embargo if the latter is binding on a Wassenaar member or the member has voluntarily committed to respect it.
24. Personal communication with the author, 17 May 1999.
25. Some of these 'events' – such as agreements to decontrol items, or the 1996 agreements not to specify targets of the regime and to leave export licensing decisions to national authorities – might be regarded by critics as failures more than successful cooperation.
26. Craft (2002) applies the managerial-enforcement distinction to Wassenaar. For a review of this literature, see Raustiala and Slaughter (2002).
27. Elsewhere, I apply this argument to the overall system of MECRs (Lipson 2005–2006).
28. I adopt Keck and Sikkink's (1998, 8) definition of networks as 'forms of organization characterized by voluntary, reciprocal, and horizontal patterns of communication and exchange'. Networks are widely thought to be relatively more effective than traditional hierarchies under globalization.
29. All three organizations work closely with national export control agencies. CITS, organizationally part of the University of Georgia, is technically a state actor.
30. Abbott and Snidal cite Dursht (1997) on this point.
31. Personal communication with the author, 17 May 1999.
32. All are available at the 'Public Documents' section of the WA website: <www.wassenaar.org/publicdocuments/index.html>.

Chapter 4

Emptying the Haunted Air: The Current and Future Missile Control Regime

Scott Jones
Senior Research Associate,
Centre for International Trade and Security,
University of Georgia

> Each will have his personal Rocket … each Rocket will know its intended and hunt him … through our World, shining and pointed in the sky at his back, his guardian executioner rushing in, *rushing closer*. …
>
> Thomas Pynchon, *Gravity's Rainbow*

Introduction

On 9 December 2002, a ship operated by a North Korean crew carrying 12 disassembled Scud missiles bound for Yemen was boarded and seized by Spanish and United States military forces in the Arabian Sea (Ricks and Slevin 2002). While the United States had the authority to stop and search the ship, it did not have the authority to seize the vessel, which was later released to the Yemeni government. In response, White House press secretary Ari Fleischer remarked: 'The US inability to prevent the North Korean Scud transfer to Yemen demonstrates a need to improve international regimes against missile proliferation. One thing that this does underscore is the need to take a look [at] – and we will do so with friends and others around the world – whether or not the international regimes that deal with missile proliferation need a second look' (Global Security Newswire 2002). The Yemeni Scuds case represents some of the more salient challenges confronting contemporary missile non-proliferation efforts, undertakings that have traditionally centred upon the Missile Technology Control Regime (MTCR).

Arguably since the inception the International Code of Conduct Against Ballistic Missile Proliferation (ICOC), the MTCR has served as the only international (multilateral) effort to curb missile proliferation.[1] As such, it has been vested with powers and responsibilities beyond its rather modest objectives and institutional design.[2] The establishment of the ICOC – and, in part, the US decision to deploy a National Missile Defence (NMD) system – strongly suggests the inadequacy of the MTCR. Nevertheless, this is not to suggest the 'failure' or, in and of itself, the inadequacy of the MTCR. On the contrary, the MTCR can be duly credited for curtailing several national ballistic programmes and serving, in the absence of a formal prohibitive norm, as the *de facto* standard against missile proliferation.[3] Notwithstanding these more positive attributes, like the other multilateral export control arrangements, the MTCR faces institutional and external challenges to its own long-term viability.

Despite recent alternative missile control efforts, such as the Russian-proposed Global Control System (GCS) and the UN Panel of Experts, and the absence of credible demand-side arms control efforts, the MTCR is still the control standard for missile non-proliferation norms and practices.[4] Unlike these various efforts, the MTCR covers *all* unmanned delivery systems – which include cruise missiles and unmanned aerial vehicles (UAVs) – within a specified performance parameter, the unique challenges these systems pose to the MTCR's effectiveness notwithstanding (Gormley and Speier 2003; see also US GAO 2003). As the international default, the MTCR provides the template for current and future initiatives to stem missile proliferation. To serve in this capacity, however, fundamental adaptations will have to be made to the scope and practices of the MTCR.

This chapter begins by examining the founding and evolution of the MTCR, with particular emphasis on its institutional development and the prominent US engineering and leadership role. Second, we review the internal and external challenges to regime viability in light of the changing nature of the missile proliferation threat. Lastly, we conclude by assessing how effective the MTCR is perceived to be considering the compatibility of members' interests, the degree of export control harmonization and institutional outcomes.

MTCR Origins and Evolution

Initiated by US concerns regarding the proliferation of space launch capabilities and prompted by a series of events in the late 1970s and early 1980s, including South Korea's 1978 ballistic missile test and India's July 1980 SLV-3 tests, the United States and its G7 allies began negotiation on a missile control consortium, negotiations which culminated in the establishment on 16 April 1987 of the Missile Technology Control Regime (MTCR) and the release of its Guidelines.[5] The concept of missile proliferation was first conceived and implemented unilaterally by the United States (see Cooper 2001, 15–20).[6] Until this point, weapons of mass destruction (WMD) and delivery means were issues confined to arms control and disarmament negotiations between the United States and the Soviet Union.[7] The concern that other states – particularly in the developing world – could wed the growing availability of ballistic missile technology with nuclear weapons prompted US-led efforts to coordinate supply-side controls.[8]

The rudiments of the MTCR were enunciated in National Security Decision Directive 70 (NSDD-70) of 30 November 1982.[9] NSDD-70 instructed the relevant

US executive agencies to implement appropriate methods to restrain the spread of nuclear-capable ballistic and cruise missiles. In addition to mandating the immediate implementation of stringent unilateral export controls on missile-related military and dual-use equipment and technology, NSDD-70 also called for simultaneously trying to multilateralize this effort among key western supplier countries, which was successfully accomplished in 1987 (Ozga 1994).

When the first official meeting of the MTCR was convened in 1987, delegates were unanimous in their belief that the principal goal of the organization was best characterized as inhibitory and not as a comprehensive solution to missile proliferation. Other means, such as diplomacy, sanctions, and sundry incentives, were to complement the rather basic, but by no means uncomplicated, instrument of trade controls inherent in the guidelines and control lists.

The Guidelines establish the basis of coordination of export control policies and appropriate procedures in the field of transfers of missile technologies and equipment.[10] The Guidelines emphasize that they are not designed to impede national space programmes for international cooperation in such programmes as long as such programmes could not contribute to delivery systems (other than manned aircraft) for such weapons. The Guidelines, including the Annex, form the basis for controlling transfers to any destination beyond the member-state government's jurisdiction or control of all delivery systems (other than manned aircraft) capable of delivering weapons of mass destruction, and of equipment and technology relevant to missiles whose performance in terms of payload and range exceeds stated parameters.

The Guidelines are implemented in accordance with the national legislation of each member state. The Annex contains 20 item groups divided into two categories. Category I (items 1 and 2) are the items of greatest sensitivity. Category I items include complete systems and major subsystems capable of carrying a payload of 500 kg over a range of at least 300 km, and specifically designed production facilities for such systems.[11] Category II items include other missile defence elements not tightly restricted but requiring case-by-case review including missile-related components such as propellants, avionics equipment and other items used for the production of Category I systems. The regime prohibits the transfer of Category I production facilities; and a 'no undercut' rule prohibits members from exporting anything already denied by another member. Countermeasures to ballistic and cruise missile defence are not covered. Restrictions cover 'transfers to any destination beyond the Government's jurisdiction or control'. If, for example, a system remains under US jurisdiction and control, it is not covered by MTCR.

Category I hardware and technology 'regardless of their purpose' are subject to 'strong presumption to deny' transfers. Category I transfers are 'authorized only on rare occasions and where the government: 1) obtains binding government to government undertakings involving the assurances from the recipient government … and, 2) assumes responsibility for taking all steps necessary to ensure the item is put only to its stated end use'.

Several levels of rules apply to these items:

- *Absolute prohibition (until further notice)* on the transfer of Category I complete production facilities or the technology for such facilities. It obviously does not make sense to have a non-proliferation regime that allows the creation of new suppliers.
- *Strong presumption to deny transfers* of Category I items. This strong presumption of denial also applies to missiles of any range or payload, or any MTCR-controlled item, for which the purpose is deemed to be the delivery of nuclear, biological or chemical payloads. Transfers of Category I items may be made. But they are to be 'rare' and may only be made if there are 1) binding government-to-government assurances with respect to the end-use and end-user and 2) supplier and not just recipient responsibility for the end-use.
- *Case-by-case review* of export applications for all controlled items.
- *No-undercut provision* according to which MTCR partners will respect each others' export denials or consult before undercutting a denial.
- *Information exchanges* to enforce these rules.
- *Catch-all provisions*, observed by most partner governments, under which export reviews will be required for missile-related transfers, whether or not on the MTCR control list, to any destination engaged in Category I programmes.[12]

Recent MTCR Developments

During the August 2002 meeting in Warsaw, parties to the MTCR decided on greater clarity in the definitions of 'range' and 'payload'. Members agreed that the current range of 300 km would be the distance achieved at 'range maximizing' capability. The definition of payload was expanded to include the cover support structures and countermeasures. The new definitions were in response to a controversy over the ambiguity of both range and payload during the late 1990s. At that time, the United Kingdom and France sold *Black Shaheen* cruise missiles, which have a maximum capable range of 500 km, to the United Arab Emirates. Both countries, which are members, argued that the sale was not in violation because the missiles' range was below 300 km when flying at sea level.

Meeting in Buenos Aires in late September 2003, members of the MTCR agreed to add catch-all provisions to the regime's guidelines. Catch-all provisions furnish a legal basis to control items that are not identified in the MTCR annex or national control lists. Such a circumstance would occur if the member state believes that an item is bound for a restricted missile programme, specifically a Category I missile; that is, those exceeding the regime's 300 km and 500 kg range and payload thresholds. Thus, for example, an export licence would be required for *any* trade with an organization involved in producing a Category I missile, such as a Pakistani entity known to be engaged in producing the Ghauri I missile or an Iranian entity supporting the production of the Shahab 3 missile. Before reaching consensus on making catch-all provisions a part of the regime's guidelines, 30 of the 33 member states had already incorporated such measures into their own national control systems. Theoretically, making catch-all regime-wide broadens the effectiveness of this important supply-side control measure.

Also agreed upon in Buenos Aires were restrictions on the transfer of so-called intangible technology, which might include the sending of missile blueprints via email or facsimile. As with catch-all provisions, many of the MTCR member states had already incorporated controls on intangible technology transfers into their own national control regulations. These controls will now become an MTCR-wide requirement. Both the catch-all and intangible technology transfer controls reflect the regime's vigorous attention of late to stanching the flow of equipment and technology integral to either developing a Category I missile or qualitatively improving its performance. Such attention is warranted because missile proliferators have found it difficult to transfer complete missile systems and have turned to transferring dual-use equipment and technology, much of which comprise the critical components of complete missile systems.

In the absence of a missile non-proliferation treaty, the MTCR has been a useful tool in countering the proliferation of missile components, technologies and materials by establishing international norms against missile technology sales. The existence of the MTCR and US sanctions based partly on them has provided a basis for US diplomatic–political efforts to constrain questionable exports from countries such as China and Russia. It has positively impacted export control practices of several European nations and others, likely preventing the 'best teams' from transferring systems and technologies. Although difficult to measure, the growth in the relative sophistication of the missile threat to the United States and its friends and allies from rogue or irresponsible nations has probably been slowed.

As a consequence of the MTCR, proliferators have been forced to indigenize their missile programmes – increasing the difficulties of their programmes and the unreliability of their missiles. Indeed, the greatest source of expanding missile capabilities, especially in relative sophistication and range, has been from countries not party to the MTCR, such as North Korea, which, to date, has been limited to providing systems based on Scud technology (the so-called 'Scud barrier'). Still, the MTCR has not proven to be a panacea. The regime suffers from leakage of technology, inconsistent interpretations of the guidelines, and from the growing problem of secondary and tertiary proliferation. It is important to stress, however, that the MTCR is only one of several 'non-proliferation' tools the United States can use to counter missile export activities.

The current trend is toward a *de facto* multilateral missile non-proliferation standard observed even by some non-members of the MTCR, such as the recent EU-led Hague Code of Conduct on Missile Proliferation and the Russian effort to create a Global Control System (GCS).[13] Some non-member interdictions of transfers violated UN sanctions against Iraq and should have been blocked even in the absence of MTCR. However, the UN missile sanctions against Iraq are based on the technical structure of the MTCR.

Internal and External Challenges

The continuing ability of the MTCR to stem missile proliferation is compromised by a host of internal and external challenges. This section itemizes both the external and internal obstructions. The subsequent section concludes with an examination of options for strengthening the MTCR.

External

The threat of ballistic missile proliferation has been dramatically highlighted over the past few years by a growing number of countries that have tested short-to-intermediate-range ballistic missiles. These include India's Agni-1 and Agni-2; Pakistan's Ghauri-1, Ghauri-2 and Shaheen; North Korea's Taepo Dong-I; China's Dong Feng-31 ICBM; and Iran's Shahab-3.[14] Anxiety over North Korea's much anticipated launch test of the Taepo-Dong-II has caused intense diplomatic and military manoeuvring (Agence France Presse 1999; Struck 1999; Mufson 1999). While the Berlin talks have led to an announced test suspension by Pyongyang, the key elements of North Korean missile programmes, including the DPRK's continued development and sales, remain unaddressed. Missile acquisition and developments efforts are also occurring in other regions of tension and instability, such as the Middle East, the Gulf and South Asia. For example, Iran is developing the Shahab-4, Pakistan is moving ahead with the Shaheen-II, and Syria reportedly is acquiring Chinese M-9 missiles via Pakistan and North Korea (Jones and McDonough 1998; Lackey 1999; Aneja 1999).

Ongoing transfers of missile systems and related technologies to other regions, in particular the highly contentious Gulf region and the Middle East, remain a serious proliferation concern. China and North Korea have over the years been charged with willingly supplying missiles, missile components and relevant technologies to Third World customers. While China has pledged to abide by the MTCR guidelines since 1992 (and indeed Beijing's records in this regard have improved noticeably in recent years), there remain allegations that Chinese missile components and technology continue to be transferred to such countries as Pakistan and Iran. A recently released US intelligence report charges that China may have transferred medium-range missiles to Pakistan (National Intelligence Council 2001; Landay 1999). Beijing has also had to contend with allegations that it has provided assistance to Iran designed to improve the latter's anti-ship missiles, thus violating a Chinese pledge to the United States not to engage in such activities (*The Times of India* 1999b).

North Korea also serves as a source of missile proliferation and is reported to have played a prominent role in Pakistan's missile development (Bermudez 1998, 16–17). Indian authorities have recently intercepted a North Korean ship at *Kandla* port heading for Pakistan, with 177 crates of blueprints, manuals and machine tools for Scud missiles (Reuters 2003). Pyongyang's missile assistance and transfers to Iran are also a matter of concern.

The spread of ballistic missiles around the world was greatly facilitated by the export in the 1970s and 1980s of Scud-B missiles from the former Soviet Union. With an increasing number of countries abiding by the MTCR, the number of potential missile suppliers has declined dramatically. Of the principal missile exporters, only North Korea has not agreed to comply. Moreover, additional countries have learned to copy, modify, extend the range of, and produce their own missiles, and a small number have developed long-range systems, often in conjunction with space-launch programmes and foreign technical assistance. For example, western countries assisted India's space launch vehicle programme in its early stages, and that provided the basis for its missile programme. Indeed, India's missile programme traces its origins to the US-produced Scout Sounding Rocket (Weiss 2001). Western firms, especially in Europe, provided technology for Argentina's Condor II missile programme, which was based on the US Pershing II (Scheffran and Karp 1992, 239–40). Nevertheless, the majority of ballistic missile proliferation involves Scud or Scud-derived materials and technology.[15]

Even so, MTCR constraints have slowed the acquisition by developing countries of technologies associated with more advanced missiles – those having ranges in excess of 1,000 km or guidance errors of less than roughly 0.3 per cent of their range. Given the complex set of technologies and expertise used in advanced aircraft, especially high-performance jet engines, it remains virtually impossible for developing countries to acquire these systems without assistance. However, no internationally binding restrictions limit trade in combat aircraft, and such arms transfers continue to be used as an instrument of foreign policy. Moreover, over capacity in western defence industries, and the economic difficulties facing newly independent Soviet republics and eastern European states, provide great incentive to develop arms export markets.

Secondary Suppliers In 1987, only six states (the United States, United Kingdom, Russia, China, France and Israel) produced missiles with ranges over 1,000 km. In 2002, eight produced such missiles, the additions being India and Pakistan. Also in 1987, the Treaty on the Elimination of Intermediate-Range and Shorter-Range Missiles (the INF Treaty) required elimination of all Soviet and American longer-range intermediate nuclear force (LRINF) missiles with ranges between 1,000 and 5,500 km, as well as shorter-range intermediate nuclear force (SRINF) missiles with ranges between 500 and 1,000 km.

Traditional export control mechanisms, such as the MTCR, presume a limited number of suppliers, a clear distinction between military and civilian technologies, and a foreign dependence with regard to components, technical know-how and manufacturing technology. However, one of the phenomenal technological developments over the past two decades has been the increasing number of countries that have acquired an indigenous capability to develop missile delivery systems.

Today, a dozen or more non-western countries either already possess short- or medium-range missile systems or have the capability to develop them. Most of them are not MTCR members; some, like North Korea, are active suppliers. Although the most sophisticated ballistic missiles with longer ranges are still difficult to acquire, low-end missiles and the requisite technologies reverse-engineered from the Soviet Scud series are widely available. Denial strategies that rely prominently on export controls will be less effective in stemming the proliferation of missile delivery systems since many of the emerging supplier states do not subscribe to non-proliferation.

Competing Control Initiatives In contrast to global norms against nuclear, chemical or biological weapons activity, strong norms against missile possession, development and testing do not exist. The international community strongly condemned nuclear tests by China, France, India and Pakistan in the period 1995–8, with some states imposing trade and aid sanctions against them. Yet in 1998 and 1999, missile tests by India, Pakistan and Iran faced far less criticism. Neither the UN General Assembly nor the Security Council passed resolutions condemning these tests. Further, none of these states encountered major aid or trade sanctions (instead incurring only minor US export control sanctions). Eventually, however, three instruments were introduced to address growing concern over missile proliferation: United Nations (UN) initiatives,[16] the Russian-proposed Global Control System (GSK)[17] and the MTCR-initiated Code of Conduct (ICOC), or Hague Code of Conduct.

Of the three, only the International Code of Conduct received a truly international response. Where the MTCR relies on technological criteria to guide policy among a select group of states, the Hague Code of Conduct tries to elevate a single, consistent set of principles to guide all countries in efforts to halt ballistic missile proliferation. The undertaking is all about building moral norms, rules of the road that everyone will accept. Completed in 2002, the Hague Code of Conduct is not a treaty for signature but a text to which states subscribe, pledging cooperation: to prevent and to curb the proliferation of ballistic missile systems capable of delivering weapons of mass destruction; to exercise the 'maximum possible restraint' over their own ballistic missile procurement; not to 'contribute to, support or assist' any ballistic missile programme in countries violating international obligations; and to implement transparency 'to increase confidence and to promote non-proliferation'.[18]

With 119 subscribing states to date, the ICOC is the most important effort to correct the greatest shortcoming of the MTCR: its lack of a unifying normative principle to guide all action against the spread of ballistic missiles (Karp 2005). With its focus on collective ideals, this European initiative represents perhaps the last surviving initiative of universalist arms control and disarmament from the 1990s. Nevertheless, the ICOC's provisions are vague, lack enforcement capabilities, and do not address cruise missiles or UAVs. Furthermore, the competitive nature of parallel groups undermines the *de facto* norm-setting missile proliferation body, the MTCR.

Competing Export Control Objectives Export control objectives sometimes conflict with other non-proliferation goals. For example, the Bush administration's desire for missile defence cooperation with regional friends and allies continues to be complicated by MTCR restrictions. National Security Presidential Directive 23 (NSPD-23) attempted to de-conflict these two objectives through presidential fiat: 'The goal of the Missile Technology Control Regime (MTCR) is to help reduce the global missile threat by curbing the flow of missiles and related technology to proliferators. The MTCR and missile defences play complementary roles in countering the global missile threat. The United States intends to implement the MTCR in a manner that does not impede missile defense cooperation with friends and allies'. NSPD-23 also ordered the Secretaries of State and Defence to review US commitments under the MTCR in relation to the transfer of missile defence technology, a review which should have been completed by mid-2003.[19] Instead, it appears that internal reviews of the NSPD continue within the departments, and discussions have not yet reached the interagency level. Balancing missile defence cooperation with non-proliferation goals will continue to vex future US administrations.[20]

Internal

Consensus Rules and Growing Membership The MTCR has expanded nearly five-fold since 1987. Some have argued that membership expansion increases the representational value of the MTCR and nominally broadens the international norm against missile proliferation. Others fear, however, that adding new members with disparate security interests will make it more difficult for the MTCR to reach consensus on addressing emerging challenges, in particular, the need to control new underlying technologies that will enable the growth of missile proliferation in the next two decades.

MTCR membership criteria, although they have never been officially announced, include like-mindedness and effective export controls (Speier 1997, 6–7). Since 1987, the MTCR has expanded to include 34 countries considered important for controlling missile technology, nearly half of which are not major suppliers of missile systems (see Table 4.1). In addition, a number of other countries (that is, China, Israel and Romania) have made unilateral statements of their intention to adhere to the MTCR Guidelines, with China formally expressing its intent to join the regime in 2004.[21] However, unilateral adoption of export control measures based on MTCR guidelines and lists is not tantamount to actual 'adherent' status, as member states have independent policies for the determination of an official adherence. For example, the United States recognizes adherent states only after a bilateral accord has been reached.

Table 4.1 MTCR Membership

Year	Total members	Members
1987	7	Canada, (West) Germany, France, Italy, Japan, UK, US
1990	13	Spain, Belgium, Luxembourg, Netherlands, Australia, Denmark
1991	18	Norway, New Zealand, Austria, Sweden, Finland
1992	22	Portugal, Switzerland, Ireland, Greece
1993	25	Iceland, Argentina, Hungary
1995	28	Russia, South Africa, Brazil
1997	29	Turkey
1998	32	Czech Republic, Poland, Ukraine
2001	33	South Korea
2004	34	Bulgaria

At its inception, the regime's informal membership criteria emphasized like-mindedness, effective export control laws and enforcement, and a strong non-proliferation track record and counted only exporters as members. As the MTCR has expanded to 34 members, however, its standards have eased, allowing countries to be admitted which are not completely like-minded, do not completely share the same non-proliferation ideals as the original members, and are not even exporters. These have included EU and NATO members such as Norway and Iceland, but also former Soviet republics such as Russia and Ukraine.[22]

Rather than the more standardized criteria of the past, admission of new members to the MTCR today has become a bargaining process involving political and commercial trade-offs and side payments. So, whether or not China, for example, joins the organization is going to depend largely on what demands the current members and Beijing bring to any accession negotiation and the prospects that they can be realized or surrendered (Zaborsky 2004).

Although one of the principal objectives of the regimes is to coordinate or harmonize national policies, it is clear that some countries are not implementing and enforcing export controls in a manner consistent with their non-proliferation objectives. Aside from the United States and some of the larger supplier states, for instance, few countries are actually imposing civil or criminal penalties for export control violations. This suggests that enforcement is lacking. Indeed, various studies of national export control systems continue to show that wide discrepancies among the control systems of regime member countries persist (see, for example, Beck, Cupitt, Gahlaut and Jones 2003).

Inadequate Information Sharing Information sharing is critical to effective multilateral control efforts. Despite extensive efforts aimed at developing information-sharing networks, MTCR members are not sharing information fully or efficiently. A recent study by the US General Accounting Office (GAO) drew attention in particular to the failure of some states to pool information about denials of export licence applications (US GAO 2002).[23] The GAO found, for example, that 65 per cent of members have never reported export denials (ibid., 12). Many countries provide pre-licence consultations that result in *de facto* denials. These, too, are also almost never reported to other regime members.[24] The failure to share information, or to share it in a timely manner, undercuts the ability of members to assess patterns in technology trading or acquisition and detect activities of proliferation concern. Efforts to strengthen information sharing, including proposals that would have member states report on export approvals, have met with resistance from a few regime members (US GAO 2002,14). The consensus rules cited above have allowed resistance from a determined minority to stall badly needed reforms in this area.

Outmoded Technological Parameters While the initial focus of the regime was on controlling the proliferation of nuclear-capable systems, its purview was expanded to include missiles for the delivery of chemical or biological weapons (CBW) in 1993. MTCR members have nominally agreed to exercise the most stringent control over what are referred to as Category I systems, or MTCR-class. The technical means – predicated as they are on the physical laws governing ballistic missiles – to determine this category, however, are inadequate for controlling many unmanned systems,[25] such as cruise and loitering missiles and unmanned aerial vehicles (UAVs).[26] Moreover, the underlying technology of cruise missile and UAV systems is nearly identical with that of manned systems and therefore ubiquitous.[27] For example, more than 80 countries today have cruise missiles of some kind. Eighteen of these countries manufacture cruise missiles domestically. The remaining 62 countries import these weapons (International Institute for Strategic Studies, various).

While the MTCR has been relatively effective in limiting the spread and sophistication of ballistic missiles, its ability to control more precisely the proliferation of unmanned systems is insufficient.[28] Although most cruise missile sales to date have been of relatively short-range anti-ship systems, it is clear that ranges are increasing. Moreover, the ease with which anti-ship systems can be converted to the land-attack role suggests that land attack cruise missile (LACM) inventories could readily increase. The land-attack-capable Taiwanese Hsiung Feng II, for example, which has been offered for export, is effectively a reverse-engineered US Harpoon anti-ship cruise missile (ASCM). The relative simplicity of cruise missile technology, and the increasing availability of technologies such as global positioning system (GPS) mean that an increasing number of countries are acquiring the ability to develop land-attack cruise missiles. Category I type controls will be further outstripped by growth in air vehicle types and applications. As a result of the inflexibility of current MTCR controls, proliferators can purposely design systems to circumvent Category I controls, such as the Indo-Russian 'Brahmos' supersonic anti-ship cruise missile (ASCM) (see Eschel 2005).

Abandoned Arms Control Initiative Originally, the regime required all new members to eliminate any missile or missile development programmes that exceeded the limits of the regime. This restriction, however, did not apply to the originating seven countries. The MTCR was founded in 1987 by the original Group of Seven (G7) partners. Between 1989 and 1993, 16 additional governments were added, all treaty allies of, or linked in security terms to, the original seven. Four additional governments were added in the 1993–5 period – Argentina, Brazil, South Africa and Russia. This was a 'new class' of governments, each having previously engaged in missile activities against which the MTCR had been directed (Mistry 2003a; Speier 2001). Their incorporation helped in some ways, but also presented new problems. They were admitted only after the existing members were satisfied that their objectionable activities – Argentina's *Condor* programme being an example – had been discontinued. But with Brazil's admission in 1995, the MTCR for the first time accepted a new member that was continuing a programme against which the regime had been directed, and even allowed that Brazilian programme to be eligible for assistance. Brazil was developing a space-launch vehicle (called the VLS) capable, in a surface-to-surface mode, of delivering a 500 kg payload to a range of 10,000 km – a true ICBM capability. Within a month of Brazil's admission, South Korea said it would seek membership in order to be able to develop a longer-range missile (Nazarkin 1998).

The regime's terms state that it is not 'designed to impede national space programmes … as long as such programmes could not contribute to delivery systems for weapons of mass destruction'. MTCR members are expected to take special precautions in such transfers, however, since the technology used in space launch vehicles (SLVs) is virtually identical to that used in ballistic missiles (Zaborsky 2003).

Conclusion

On 14 December 2001, the United States provided formal notification of its withdrawal from the Anti-Ballistic Missile (ABM) Treaty. The US action was designed to remove treaty and other procedural obstacles to implementing a system of national missile defence (NMD). The urgency to pursue such systems was predicated on a ballistic missile threat assessment strongly suggesting the increased likelihood of a strike on the US homeland.[29] In the process of realizing NMD, the Bush administration was careful to articulate its support for the Missile Technology Control Regime (MTCR), arguing that the MTCR was a critical component to the overall non-proliferation regime and served to complement NMD as a countermeasure to actual and future missile proliferation.[30] Both NMD and withdrawal from the ABM Treaty imply the relatively altered nature of the missile proliferation threat, a threat the MTCR was designed to curtail. Furthermore, both issues intimate that supplementary measures to the MTCR are required in order to address more ably the missile proliferation threat.

Much of the current debate over the effectiveness of the MTCR is premised on a *relative* missile proliferation threat perception and, principally, on an unexamined battery of performative expectations. In the case of the former, intelligence estimates themselves have proliferated since the mid-1990s – arguably having been politicized in the process[31] – thereby problematizing any assessment of the state of international missile proliferation. In the case of the latter, *universal* criteria for assessing MTCR effectiveness are absent.[32] On this last point, it is important to note that the relatively modest function of the MTCR has been unofficially empowered beyond its scope and domain, becoming – by default – the primary bulwark against missile proliferation.[33] As noted above, the alternative missile control initiatives are insufficient insofar as they do not address cruise missiles and UAVs. Instead, they should be viewed as part of a larger multilateral dialogue on the proliferation of WMD delivery means.[34]

With respect to the actual missile proliferation threat, the MTCR can be credited with greatly delimiting the spread of ballistic missile systems. Even with an increase in the number of suppliers outside of the regime, the number of ICBM and IRBM producing or holding states has decreased (see Table 4.2), owing in large measure to supplier-side restraint and the prohibitive norm enshrined in 'Category 1' or 'MTCR-class' systems transfers.[35] The results, however, are less sanguine regarding cruise missiles (Gormley 2003).

Table 4.2 Missile/Unmanned Delivery Vehicle Proliferation Trends: 1987 vs 2003[36]

Threat	Status (1987 vs 2005)	Trends
ICBM (>5,500 km)	57% decrease	↓
IRBM (3,000–5500 km)	97% decrease	↓
MRBM (1,000–3,000 km)	3 new national programmes (7 nations total vs 4 then)	↑
SRBM (<1,000 km)	Up, but declining as Scud inventories age	↓
Number of nations with ballistic missile programmes of concern	Fewer, less advanced (11 in mid-1980s, 7 today)	↓
Cruise Missiles (ASCM and LACM)	Inventories of and production capability for both anti-ship and land-attack cruise missiles increase	↑
Unmanned Aerial Vehicles (UAVs)	As with cruise missiles, UAV proliferation and production capabilities increasing	↑

ASCM: Anti-Ship Cruise Missile
ICBM: Intercontinental Ballistic Missile
IRBM: Intermediate-Range Ballistic Missile
LACM: Land-Attack Cruise Missile
MRBM: Medium-Range Ballistic Missile
SRBM: Short-Range Ballistic Missile

The state of missile proliferation today is, by default, commentary on the effectiveness of the MTCR. While some praise the regime's cogency, crediting all manner of agency to the regime, others criticize its exclusivity and failure to address missile proliferation between non-members.[37] In either case, the MTCR is the only enduring international missile non-proliferation standard. As such, it is enlisted to make any number of points about the state of missile proliferation, points which are largely incidental to the basic function of the regime.

Unlike a treaty-based regime, the MTCR is, at its core, simply an association of states seeking to coordinate their export licensing practices relevant to missile technology. In this sense, it acts as a supplier cartel, with all the inherent advantages and problems associated with that type of arrangement. It is this lack of a more formal international legal standing that, to a large extent, drives both praise and criticism of the regime. Its erstwhile legitimacy or image problems, however, are slowly receding.[38] The interest of China, for example, Libya and nine other countries in joining the regime illustrates the global shift in attitudes toward a mechanism previously dismissed as a poorly disguised cartel (Zabrosky 2004, 20–26).

With renewed interest in the MTCR, expressed by the new queue of applicants, a fundamental re-examination of the regime's mandate and scope are necessary. Beyond the institutional and technical issues relevant to the operation of the regime under new constraints, a more basic, substantive question must be addressed: what do we expect the MTCR to do? As noted, the MTCR is nothing more than the sum of national export control systems, coordinated by a mutually agreed upon control list, exporting guidelines and information sharing means. There is little, for example, the regime can do to prohibit North Korean missile sales to Iran. The traditional means of policing such scenarios have resided outside the MTCR.[39]

Because there are extra-MTCR efforts – NMD, GCS, the HCOC and UN Panel of Experts – to stem missile proliferation, the MTCR is not adversely affected or undermined. Although not by design, the emerging international missile non-proliferation architecture evinces a rudimentary division of labour, with the MTCR at its core. Nevertheless, to serve as the international 'linchpin' of international missile non-proliferation, the MTCR will have to modify its structure and rules (Van Diepen 2004). This will involve developing rules and procedures appropriate to an increasingly diverse membership and adapting the guidelines to keep pace with new delivery vehicle technologies, such as UAVs.[40] With respect to procedural modifications, decisions on some issues could be decided by majority or qualified majority vote instead of consensus. Only the most crucial decisions should require a unanimous vote. Only on rare occasions, and only on issues that are non-negotiable, should individual member states be able to bring the work of the MTCR to a standstill.

Perhaps most critically, the essential effectiveness of the MTCR resides in, as noted, the members' respective export control systems. To that extent, regime efficacy is solely dependent upon a relatively uniform approach to implementation amongst the membership. This uniformity may prove elusive with increased membership, especially in the absence a MTCR-level enforcement mechanism. The US interest in missile defence cooperation and the Russian and European interest in exporting sub-Category I cruise missiles are cases in point (see, for example, Graham 2003; Svitak and Ratnam 2003). Widening interpretations of the guidelines amongst an increasingly disparate membership is the central issue to be addressed in reforming the MTCR. A viable reform effort, moreover, will be one based upon cooperation rather than coordination.[41]

To achieve cooperation, among very disparate states with divergent interests, a contract-like agreement may work better than what exists today. Such agreements usually include some type of bargain in which there are direct exchanges between the parties involved. The MTCR began as a mechanism for strong coordination on the export behaviour of the founding supplier states. However, over time, the MTCR has transformed into a cooperation arrangement, where the fundamental security objectives of the regime have broadened in order to accommodate new members. In essence, the regime began admitting non-exporting members and/or members seeking bargains and side-payments. Thus the goals of the regime have changed with changing membership, yet its internal decision rules have lagged behind, giving rise to questions about its current and future effectiveness. This situation should, at least in theory, give rise to new rules or organizing principles.

A completely informal setting is no longer suitable for a regime with mixed membership and static rules. The conditions for membership will need to be precise, coherent, and clearly stated. Binding dozens of diverse members into some informal and generalist arrangement will not make much of a difference in terms of fighting proliferation. The regime of this type will have to be based on a formal agreement, not necessarily as detailed and comprehensive as a treaty, but with clearly determined obligations of the parties. At a minimum, it should clearly define 'violation' to avoid different interpretations of members' behaviour. Ironically, in the current rules structure, meaningful structural reform of the MTCR would require either dissolution of the regime or unanimous consent. In either case, the rules must be changed in order to address the coordination versus cooperation problématique.

References

Agence France Presse (1999), 'S. Korean Defense Minister Seeks Support for Missile Test Halt', *Inside China Today*, 27 August 1999.

Ahlström, C. (2004), 'Arrows for India? Technology Transfers for Missile Defense and the MTCR', *Journal of Conflict & Security Law*, Vol. 9, No. 1 .

Aneja, A. (1999), 'Pakistan Begins Work on Shaheen-II', *The Hindu*, 27 September 1999.

Beck, M., Cupitt, R.T., Gahlaut, S. and Jones, S. (eds) (2003), *To Supply or To Deny: Comparing Non-proliferation Export Controls in Five Key Countries*, Kluwer Law International, New York.

Bermudez, J. (1998), 'A Silent Partner', *Jane's Defence Weekly*, 20 May 1998.

—— (1999), 'A History of Ballistic Missile Development in the DPRK', Occasional Paper No. 2, Centre for Non-Proliferation Studies, Monterrey Institute of International Studies, Monterrey, CA.

Bolkcom, C. and Squassoni, S. (2002), *CRS Report for Congress: Cruise Missile Proliferation*, Congressional Research Service/CRS, Foreign Affairs, Defense, and Trade Division, CRS21252, 3 July 2002, Washington, DC.

Bowen, W.Q. (1996), 'Brazil's Accession to the MTCR', *The Nonproliferation Review*, spring–summer 1996.

—— (1997), 'US Policy on Ballistic Missile Proliferation: The MTCR's First Decade (1987–1997)', *The Nonproliferation Review*, Fall 1997.

—— (2000), *The Politics of Ballistic Missile Nonproliferation*, St Martin's Press, New York.

Centre for Non-Proliferation Studies (2000), 'North Korea: A Second Taepo-dong Test?', Monitoring Proliferation Threat Project, Centre for Non-Proliferation Studies, University of Georgia.

Chellaney, B. (1994), 'An Indian Critique of US Export Controls', *Orbis*, Vol. 25, Summer 1994.

Chengappa, R. (1999), 'Boom for Boom', *India Today*, 26 April 1999.

Cirincione, J. (2000), 'Assessing the Ballistic Missile Threat', Testimony of Joseph Cirincione, Director of the Non-proliferation Programme of the Carnegie Endowment for International Peace, before the Senate Sub-Committee on International Security, Proliferation, and Federal Services, February 2000.

Cooper, D.A. (2001). 'The United States and the Evolution of International Supply-Side Missile Non-Proliferation Controls', in *Missile Proliferation and Defenses: Problems and Prospects*, Occasional Paper No. 7, Centre for Non-Proliferation Studies, May 2001.

Cupitt, R.T. and Khripunov, I. (1997), 'New Strategies for the Nuclear Suppliers Group (NSG)', *Comparative Strategy*, Vol. 16, No. 3, July–September 1997.

Dobbs, M. (2002), 'How Politics Help Define the Threat', *Washington Post*, 14 January 2002.

Eschel, T. (2005), 'Paris Air Show: Israel Extends Missile Offerings within MTCR Limits', *Aerospace Daily and Defense Report*, 14 June 2005.

French Ministry of Defence (2000), 'Maîtrise des Armements, Désarmement, et Non-proliferation: L'Action de la France, Ministère de la Défense', La Documentation Française, Paris.

Gahlaut, S. and Zaborsky, V. (2004), 'Do Export Control Regimes Have Members They Really Need?', *Comparative Strategy*, Vol. 23, No. 1, January/February/March 2004.

Global Security Newswire (2002), 'North Korea: Yemen Expects Fast Return of Scuds Shipment', 12 December 2002.

Gormley, D.M. (1998), 'Hedging Against the Cruise Missile Threat', *Survival*, April 1998.

—— (2003), 'New Developments in Unmanned Air Vehicles and Land-Attack Cruise Missiles', in *SIPRI Yearbook 2003: Armaments, Disarmament and International Security*, Oxford University Press, Oxford.

Gormley, D.M. and Speier, R. (2003), 'Controlling Unmanned Air Vehicles: New Challenges', Paper Commissioned by the Non-Proliferation Education Centre, 19 March 2003, <www.npec-web.org/projects/uavs.pdf>.

Graham, B. (2003), 'US Controls Hamper Foreign Role in Missile Defense', *Washington Post*, 19 October 2003.

Grospeaud, M. (2001), 'Le MTCR Face a La Proliferation des Missiles', Occassional Paper, No. 26, Institut d'Etudes de Sécurité.

Hindustan Times (1999), 'Agni-II Joins Nation's Missile Showcase', 12 April 1999.

International Institute for Strategic Studies (various), *The Military Balance*, Oxford University Press, London.

Isby, D. (1998), 'Barriers to Proliferation and Pathways to Transfer: Building Ballistic Missile Capabilities Under MTCR', in Commission to Assess the Ballistic Missile Threat to the United States, Appendix III, Unclassified Working Papers, July 1998.

Jones, R.W. and McDonough, M.G. (1998), 'Missile Proliferation, 1995–97', with Toby Dalton and Gregory Koblentz, *Tracking Nuclear Proliferation: A Guide in Maps and Charts, 1998*, Carnegie Endowment for International Peace, Washington, DC.

Jones, S. and Zaborsky, V. (eds) (1997), 'Missile Proliferation and MTCR: The Nth Member and Other Challenges', Occasional Paper, Centre for International Trade and Security, June 1997.

Joshi, M. (1998), 'Deadly Option', *India Today*, 4 May 1998.

Karp, A. (1996), *Ballistic Missile Proliferation: The Politics and Technics*, Oxford University Press, Oxford.

—— (2000), 'The Spread of Ballistic Missile Missiles and the Transformation of Global Security', *The Nonproliferation Review*, Spring–Summer 2000.

—— (2005), 'Going Ballistic? Reversing Missile Proliferation', *Arms Control Today*, June 2005.

Kugler, M. (2003), 'International Missile Defense Cooperation and the MTCR', Presentation to the Non-Proliferation Policy Education Centre, 30 June 2003, <www.npec-web.org/projects/kugler.pdf>.

Lackey, S. (1999), 'A Dangerous Race in a Multi-Axial World: The Missile Club in the Middle East', *Al-Wasat*, FBIS translation, 30 August 1999.

Landay, J.S. (1999), 'Missile Issues Put Chill on US–China Thaw', *The Christian Science Monitor*, 17 September 1999.

Mistry, D. (1997). 'Ballistic Missile Proliferation and the MTCR: A Ten-Year Review', *Contemporary Security Policy*, Vol. 18, No. 2.

—— (2003a), *Containing Missile Proliferation: Strategic Technology, Security Regimes, and International Cooperation in Arms Control*, University of Washington Press, Seattle, WA.

—— (2003b), 'Beyond the MTCR: Building a Comprehensive Regime to Contain Ballistic Missile Proliferation', *International Security*, Vol. 27, No. 4.

Mufson, S. (1999), 'Korean Missiles Push US Defense Plans', *Washington Post*, 5 September 1999.

Myers, S.L. (1998). 'Missile Test by North Korea: Dark Omen for Washington', *New York Times*, 1 September 1998.

National Intelligence Council (2001), 'Foreign Missile Developments and the Ballistic Missile Threat to the United States through 2015', National Intelligence Council Report.

Nazarkin, Y. (1998), 'Nonproliferation of Missile Technology', Conference of the PfP Consortium of Defense Academies and Security Studies Institutes, 'Networking the Security Community in the Information Age', October 1998, <www.isn.ethz.ch/3isf/Online_Publications/WS5/WS_5D/Nazarkin2.htm>.

Ozga, D. (1994), 'A Chronology of the Missile Technology Control Regime', *The Nonproliferation Review*, Vol. 1, No. 2.

Reuters (2003), 'North Korea Plans to Sell Missiles to Iran', 6 August 2003.

Ricks, T. and Slevin, P. (2002), 'Spain and U.S. Seize N. Korean Missiles', *Washington Post*, 11 December 2002.

Rodan, S. and O'Sullivan, A. (1998), 'Iran Test-Fires Shahab-3 Missile', *Jerusalem Post*, 24 July 1998.

Sadeh, S. (1999), 'Israel Said To Be Testing Missiles In Lebanon', *Ha'aretz*, June 1999.

Scheffran, J. and Karp, A. (1992), 'National Implementation of the MTCR: The US and German Experiences', in H.G. Brauch, H. van der Graaf, J. Grin and W. Smit (eds), *Controlling the Development and Spread of Military Technology*, VU University Press, Amsterdam.

Smith, M. (2001), 'The MTCR and the Future of Ballistic Missile Non-Proliferation', *Disarmament Diplomacy*, February 2001.

—— (2003), 'Pros and Cons of the MTCR', *Bulletin*, No. 21, International Network of Engineers and Scientists against Proliferation, April 2003, <www.inesap.org/bulletin21/bul21art23.htm>.

Speier, R. (1997), 'Russia, Ukraine, and the Nth Member Problem', in S. Jones and V. Zaborsky (eds), 'Missile Proliferation and MTCR: The Nth Member and Other Challenges', Occasional Paper, Centre for International Trade and Security, June 1997.

—— (2001), 'How Effective Is the Missile Technology Control Regime?', Nonproliferation Brief 4 (7), Carnegie Endowment for International Peace, 12 April 2001.

—— (2004), 'Complementary or Competitive? Missile Controls vs Missile Defense', *Arms Control Today*, June 2004, <www.armscontrol.org/act/2004_06/Speier.asp>.

Struck, D. (1999), 'US, N. Korea to Hold Talks on Missile Test', *Washington Post*, 27 August 1999.

Svitak, A. and Ratnam, G. (2003), 'Missile Defense vs Non-Proliferation: White House Policy Tests International Limits', *Defense News*, 14 July 2003.

Thielman, G. (2003), 'Rumsfeld Reprise? The Missile Report That Foretold the Iraq Intelligence Controversy', *Arms Control Today*, Vol. 33, No. 6.

Times of India (1999a), 'China Tests New Mobile Missile', 1 September 1999.

—— (1999b), 'China Denies Missiles Deal with Iran', 31 August 1999.

United Nations (2002), *The Issue of Missiles in All Its Aspects: Report of the Secretary-General*, A/57/229, 23 July 2002, <http://projects.sipri.se/expcon/UNSG-missile.pdf>.

US General Accounting Office (1996), 'Foreign Missile Threats: Analytical Soundness of Certain National Intelligence Estimates', GAO/NSIAD 96-25, August 1996.

—— (2002), 'Nonproliferation: Strategy Needed to Strengthen Multilateral Export Controls', Report to Congressional Committees, GAO 03-43, October 2002.

—— (2003), 'Nonproliferation: Improvements Needed to Better Control Technology Exports for Cruise Missiles and Unmanned Aerial Vehicles', GAO 04-175, November 2003.

Van Diepen, Vann (2004), 'Controlling the Spread of Ballistic Missiles', Statement by Vann Van Diepen, Director, Office of Chemical, Biological, and Missile Non-Proliferation, US Department of State, Arms Control Association and Embassy of Argentina Press Briefing, 23 November 2004, <www.armscontrol.org/events/20041123_ballistic_missiles_transcript.asp>.

Weiss, K. (2001), 'The Limits of Missile Diplomacy: Missile Proliferation, Diplomacy, and Defense', *World Affairs*, Vol. 163, No. 3.

Yuan, J.-D. (2000), 'The MTCR and Missile Proliferation: Moving Toward the Next Phase', International Security Research and Outreach Programme, International Security Bureau, Department of Foreign Affairs and International Trade, May 2000.

Zaborsky, V. (2003), 'Missile Proliferation Risks of International Space Cooperation', *World Affairs*, Vol. 165, No. 4.

—— (2004), 'Does China Belong in the Missile Technology Control Regime?', *Arms Control Today*, Vol. 34, No. 8.

Notes

1. The ICOC, or Hague Code of Conduct, Code is a schedule of 'a set of principles, commitments, confidence-building measures and incentives' designed to create a common concept of what is termed 'responsible missile behaviour', to be implemented via a multilateral instrument open to all states. Interestingly, the ICOC is viewed as a completely independent undertaking *vis-à-vis* the MTCR. It is, however, a direct extension of the MTCR, having been discussed, initiated and sponsored by MTCR members. While the ICOC was approved at the 2002 Ottawa Plenary, efforts to construct a demand-side missile non-proliferation vehicle date back to French discussions in 1991. The Office of the President of the French Republic released its 1991 'Plan for Arms Control and Disarmament' in which France recognizes the role of the MTCR in arms control, but points out that the current regime is only a step towards a more general agreement. France calls for a broader agreement with geographic enlargement, increased control, universal applicability to all members, establishment of rules for international cooperation for civilian use of space, and prevention of technology leakage from

civilian to military projects. France proposes the development of confidence-building measures, including the establishment of a 'code of good conduct' and a mechanism for the notification of space launches. See Ozga (1994). See also French Ministry of Defence (2000).

2. Noted missile proliferation analyst Aaron Karp observes: 'With so much potentially at stake from missile proliferation, it is all the more ironic that its restraint rests on something so modest as the MTCR' (Karp 2000).
3. With respect to the MTCR's relative success, even a cursory review of the literature covering the MTCR suggests the near-consensus acceptance of the view that in the MTCR's first decade, Argentina, Brazil, Egypt, Iraq, Libya, South Africa, South Korea, Syria and Taiwan were thwarted from advancing their missile ambitions.
4. On 4 October 2000 Iran introduced a resolution on missiles to the 55th session of the UN First Committee. The resolution emphasizes the 'need for a comprehensive approach towards missiles, in a balanced and non-discriminatory manner, as a contribution to international peace and security'. The resulting UN Panel of Government Experts met to establish such a comprehensive approach. The exercise, however, collapsed with recognition of the impossibility of drafting a consensus report: <www.reachingcriticalwill.org/political/missiles/missilesindex.html>. The Russian- proposed Global Control System (GCS) for the non-proliferation of missiles and missile technology would be, were it realized, a universal transparency regime for launches of ballistic missiles and space delivery vehicles, including, as a component, a multilateral advance notification regime for planned launches of such missiles, as suggested by several states on various occasions: <www.fas.org/nuke/control/mtcr/news/GSC_content.htm>.
5. American concern intensified primarily because of the progress that several countries were making in developing and producing their own rockets. This centred on the activities of five principal countries, including Israel, Libya, South Korea, Taiwan and India. American concern was exacerbated by each country's simultaneous pursuit of civilian and suspected military nuclear programmes. In short, Washington became anxious about the potential role ballistic missiles might play as delivery vehicles for nuclear weapons in the developing world. The use of ballistic missiles by both sides during the Iran–Iraq War, as well as the use of Scuds in the Afghani and the later Yemeni civil wars, also underscored this proliferation concern. See: Bowen (1997, 22–3).
6. Cooper notes that the US attempted to instil Coordinating Committee for Multilateral Export Control (COCOM)-like controls in the MTCR's infrastructure, an initiative universally rejected by the member countries.
7. In the 1950s and 1960s few restrictions were placed on the transfer of nuclear and space technology between states. From the early 1960s onwards the US transferred technical data on sounding rockets and space launch vehicles (the equivalent of short-range and intermediate-range missiles respectively) as well as complete sounding rockets to other NATO members, and to Argentina, Brazil, India, South Korea, Mexico, Pakistan and Taiwan. The former Soviet Union and West European states undertook similar technology transfers. In addition to their space-technology transfers, both superpowers exported short-range ballistic missiles. Washington transferred 120 km range Lance missiles to its North Atlantic Treaty Organization (NATO) allies, and supplied 40 km range Honest John artillery rockets to South Korea and Taiwan, while Moscow supplied Scud missiles to its Warsaw Pact allies and to clients in the Middle East. It should be noted that Washington and Moscow also aided longer-range missile programmes of their close allies. Washington assisted missile projects in Britain and France, and has

actually transferred a strategic missile – the Trident – to the UK. Moscow supplied assistance to Chinese ballistic missile programmes in the 1950s. For more information on early missile transfers, see Scheffran and Karp (1992, 238–40).

8. In the period 1978–81, four events that illustrated the potential of non-industrialized nations to build missiles greatly increased concerns in US policymaking circles about the growing availability of and interest in rocket technology. These events included South Korea's 1978 test of a surface-to-surface missile; Iraq's bid to purchase rocket stages from Italy, discovered in 1979; India's launch of a satellite in 1980; and a German firm's unsuccessful test of a rocket stage in Libya in 1981. See Karp (1996).
9. The Nixon administration's decision to sell production licences of a Delta space launch vehicle to Japan was denounced in Congress as a sacrifice of US technology; the ensuing debate in Congress eventually led to the promulgation of a revised export control policy: National Security Decision Memorandum (NSDM) 187. This Congressional act drastically reduced US cooperation with foreign rocket programmes in order to protect US commercial interests in space launch services and to shield the Space Shuttle project. In the mid-1970s, the US also began limiting missile sales; for example, it denied Israeli requests made after the 1973 Yom Kippur war for the 1,000 km range Pershing I missile, and instead supplied Israel with the 120 km range Lance missile. See Mistry (1997).
10. Specifically, the Guidelines outline the goal of the regime: 'to limit the risks of proliferation of weapons of mass destruction (that is, nuclear, chemical and biological weapons), by controlling transfers that could make a contribution to delivery systems (other than manned aircraft) for such weapons'.
11. The 300 km range limit correlates to the distances, in a majority of strategic theatres of conflict, where nuclear missile use might be considered. This range was also considered to be a convenient, workable and achievable parameter around which international export controls could be established. The 500 kg payload limit recognizes that emerging nuclear states are likely initially to develop relatively crude nuclear weapons. At the 2002 MTCR plenary in Warsaw, the definition of payload was expanded to cover support structures and countermeasures, as well as the warhead itself.
12. Regime members agreed during the 2004 Buenos Aires plenary meeting to make the inclusion of catch-all provisions into national export control regulations a regime-wide requirement.
13. At the October 2000 MTCR Helsinki summit, a draft of a new initiative, Code of Conduct Against Missile Proliferation, was introduced. In July 2000, the European Union (EU), the principal architect of the initiative, adopted a 'Common Position on the Fight Against Ballistic Missile Proliferation' that called for the universal adoption of the new Code of Conduct at a UN Conference in 2002. The 33 nation MTCR, in its plenary session on 24–28 September 2001 in Ottawa, Canada, revisited the idea and augmented the original draft text of the Code of Conduct. Approximately a hundred nations convened in Paris in February and in Madrid in June 2002 to discuss strengths and weaknesses of the Code of Conduct. In their final meeting in The Hague, Netherlands, on 25 November 2002, 92 countries became formal signatories of the International Code of Conduct Against Ballistic Missile Proliferation. The document requires the signatory states to prepare an annual report on their programmes and to signal any upcoming missile tests. However, the Code of Conduct is not legally binding, and it has at least two other serious deficiencies. First, key non-MTCR member states – China, India, Pakistan, Iraq and Iran – have opted to stay outside the framework.

Second, developing a mechanism of space-related incentives to forgo ballistic missile programmes is extremely divisive.

14. For select coverage, see Joshi (1998); Chengappa (1999); *Hindustan Times* (1999); Myers (1998); *Times of India* (1999a); Centre for Nonproliferation Studies (2000); Rodan and O'Sullivan (1998).
15. The continued viability of the so-called 'Scud Barrier' is a subject of considerable debate. See Smith (2003), see also Isby (1998).
16. In accordance with General Assembly Resolution 55/33 of 20 November 2000, the UN Secretary-General was requested to prepare a report on the issue of Missiles in all its aspects. A group of government experts was established to help prepare the report, including representatives from 23 states. The report, which was presented in July 2002, underlined the concern of states about a number of missile-related developments (UN 2002).
17. In June 1999, Russia proposed a Global Control System (GSK – from Russian *global'naya sistema kontrolya*) at the G8 summit at Cologne, Germany. Later it shaped a more detailed form during two international conferences arranged for governmental representatives by the Russian Ministry of Foreign Affairs, held in Moscow in March 2000 and February 2001. The genealogy of GSK is rooted in 1992, when then Russian President Boris Yeltsin, in his speech given at the UN Security Council on 29 January, proposed a Global System for Protecting the International Community Against Missile Attack. However, by 2001 the idea of the Global Control System had modified into something unique, which would involve the MTCR as well as various existing notification and confidence building measures. Contrary to the 1992 GSK proposal, the GSK does not contain any military enforcement measures. The GSK called for the establishment of an international non-strategic missile defence system, possibly operated by multilateral military contingents. At the same time, initially the GSK proposed only non-military enforcement measures, although its vagueness permitted the inclusion of military options in some other categories. To date, the effort was faltered, becoming a point of departure for missile control discussions rather than an end point. See <www.fas.org/nuke/control/mtcr/news/GSC_content.htm>.
18. The text is available on the website of the Austrian Ministry of Foreign Affairs at <www.bmaa.gv.at/up-media/114_HCOC.pdf>.
19. For an unofficial copy of the text of NSPD-23, see <www.fas.org/irp/offdocs/nspd/nspd-23.htm>. See also Speier (2004).
20. During the first term, the Bush administration had undertaken extensive legal contortions to justify cooperation on the Israeli Arrow (missile defence) programme. See Kugler (2003).
21. Author interview with Ambassor Mariusz Handzlik, MTCR Chairman, 2002–2003, April 2004.
22. At the regime level, there is always the issue of the inevitable trade-off between increased membership and regime efficacy in terms of the agenda, agreement and enforcement issues which would have to be worked out among member states. See, for example, Cupitt and Khripunov (1997, 305–17); Ozga (1994, 68) and Bowen (1996, 86–91). A more recent study is Gahlaut and Zaborsky (2004, 19).
23. The GAO found that the failure to share information on approvals prevents regime members from determining whether undercutting was taking place (US GAO, 2004).
24. *De facto* denials refers to the practice in several countries whereby informal consultations between the exporters and the licensing officials help exporters decide whether they

should even bother to apply for a particular export licence. Officials may indicate that a licence for a particular export to an end-user is likely to be denied, discouraging the exporter from even applying. Several regime members have low rates of denial, according to their official statistics, because of such pre-screening. Absent the pre-screening data, fellow members may grant a licence for the same item.

25. A recent GAO study, for example, highlighted the technical and policy challenge posed by briskly evolving unmanned aerial technologies: 'Distinctions between cruise missiles and UAVs are becoming blurred as the militaries of many nations, in particular the United States, add missiles to traditional reconnaissance UAVs and develop UAVs dedicated to combat missions' (US GAO, 2003). Similarly, a Congressional Research Service (CRS) report notes: 'In contrast to ballistic missile proliferation, cruise missiles present a particular challenge for monitoring and control because they exploit technology that is well understood and well established in the civil aviation industry. Missile airframes, navigation systems, jet engines, satellite maps, and mission planning computers and software all can be purchased on the commercial market. Cruise missile technology "hides in plain sight" – making it difficult to identify a military programme. At the same time, commercial availability generally means relatively low-cost weapons for many nations and, potentially, non-state actors' (Bolkcom and Squassoni 2002, 2; see pp. 3–4 for more information about the MTCR).
26. The flexibility of cruise missiles to trade off payload and range configurations makes agreement on how to calculate capabilities difficult. Moreover, overlapping military and civilian technology increases pressure to allow technology exports. Ballistic missiles do have a civilian counterpart technology – space launch vehicles – but the technologies are not nearly as ubiquitous as they are for UAV technologies in the aircraft industry. See Gormley and Speier (2003); Gormley (1998); and Bolkcom and Squassoni (2002).
27. There is no universally accepted definition of cruise missiles, but they can be categorized as unmanned aerial vehicles (UAVs) that are a) continually powered by an air-breathing or rocket engine; b) generally guided for their entire flight; c) weaponized; and d) generally optimized for one-way missions. This contrasts with weaponized UAVs such as the Predator, that can perform multiple missions, but they are treated similarly under the MTCR.
28. The Wassenaar Arrangement picks up the lower range of the capability spectrum with respect to cruise missile and UAV systems. Wassenaar, which supersedes Cold-War COCOM (Coordinating Committee) export controls, specifically regulates UAVs and UAV technology designed for military purposes. Thus, exports of cruise missiles with ranges shorter than 300 km that can carry warheads weighing less than 500 kg that are not destined for countries with WMD programmes are subject to restrictions under Wassenaar. However, Wassenaar includes exceptions, as does the MTCR, for technologies and components intended for manned aircraft.
29. The missile threat to the US is based on a series of seemingly contradictory intelligence and task force reports dating back to the early 1990s. The most recent survey, the 1998 'Report of the Commission to Assess the Ballistic Missile Threat to the United States' (or the 'Rumsfeld Report') warns: 'The newer ballistic missile-equipped nations [North Korea, Iran and Iraq] … would be able to inflict major destruction on the US within about five years of a decision to acquire such a capability (10 years in the case of Iraq). During several of those years, the US might not be aware that such a decision had been made'. While National Intelligence Estimate (NIE) on the subject, 'Foreign Missile Developments and the Ballistic Missile Threat to the United States Through 2015', was

released in 1999, it merely confirmed the conclusions of the Rumsfeld Report that the ballistic threat was growing at an alarming rate. An informative survey of the various ballistic missile reports is found in Thielman (2003). See also US GAO (1996).

30. In National Security Presidential Directive (NSPD) 23, President Bush outlined the rationale behind and nature of NMD cooperation with US allies. In so doing, the administration seeks to preserve, to the extent allowable, the present scope and domain of the MTCR: 'The goal of the Missile Technology Control Regime (MTCR) is to help reduce the global missile threat by curbing the flow of missiles and related technology to proliferators. The MTCR and missile defenses play complementary roles in countering the global missile threat. The United States intends to implement the MTCR in a manner that does not impede missile defense cooperation with friends and allies' (National Security Presidential Directive-23, 16 December 2002). A copy is available on the Federation of American Scientists website: <www.fas.org/irp/offdocs/nspd/nspd-23.htm>.

31. The US intelligence community had been judged harshly by elements of Congress for the alleged sanguinity of its past assessments of foreign ballistic missile developments. Yet, an attempt to get a more forward-leaning professional assessment on missiles by appointing a commission chaired by former CIA director Robert Gates did not succeed in fundamentally altering previous intelligence judgments that the ballistic missile threat to the United States was not immediate. After passing a new law, which broke with the congressional tradition of naming commission members proportionately between the parties, the Republican majority did succeed in appointing a new commission under Rumsfeld and naming six of its nine members. See Dobbs (2002). Making similar observations, noted missile proliferation analyst, Mark Smith observed: 'Despite the fact that the political impact of ballistic missiles is a considerable distance ahead of technological realities, the strategic implications of proliferation are far-reaching, not least in terms of the impact as a driver of US plans for ballistic missile defense (BMD)'.

32. A survey of the literature addressing the MTCR reveals the absence of any methodical attempt to assess regime effectiveness. The collective thinking regarding MTCR 'successes' points to curtailment of the Argentine, Brazilian, Egyptian, South African, South Korean and Taiwanese missile programmes. Liabilities include both institutional flaws (for example, decision-making procedures and lack of enforcement mechanisms) and the growth of secondary proliferation (for example, North Korean serial missile proliferation). Representative studies of the MTCR include: Bowen (2000); Mistry (2003a); Weiss (2001); Yuan (2000); Ozga (1994, 66–93).

33. The MTCR was designed to curb, not end, missile proliferation. Aaron Karp notes: 'With so much potentially at stake from missile proliferation, it is all the more ironic that its restraint rests on something so modest as the MTCR' (Karp 2000, 115).

34. Aaron Karp notes of the various missile non-proliferation efforts: 'The MTCR, the Hague Code of Conduct, and to a lesser extent the UN Panel of Government Experts dominate multilateral activity (on missile non-proliferation). Although the three are often described as different approaches to a common goal, they actually aim toward distinct objectives. They are based on very different and largely incompatible assumptions. That their divergences have been overlooked is possible only because their progress has been so uneven. None of the three ever claimed to be a comprehensive solution to the global spread of ballistic missiles. Indeed, they are increasingly overburdened by specific missile challenges. Even so, collectively they constitute one of the most

sophisticated international dialogues on arms control and disarmament in the world today' (Karp 2005).

35. 'MTCR-class' has become a term of art regarding missile exports. Israel, for example, has cited MTCR constraints as its reason for not supplying India with the Arrow II theatre missile defence interceptor. See: Ahlström (2004, 103–25).
36. This chart was adapted from Joseph Cirincione's work on assessing the ballistic missile threat. See Cirincione (2000).
37. A representative reading list would include: Bowen (2000); Mistry (2003a); Grospeaud (2001); Jones and Zabrosky (1997); Mistry (2003b); Smith (2001); Speier (2001); Weiss (2001).
38. The various multilateral export control regimes became part and parcel Non-Aligned Movement (NAM) politics in the early 1990s. For example, Brahma Chellaney contends, 'The non-proliferation policies of Western powers are founded on a strategy of preventing Third World development of technologies that might impinge on the Western powers' military and economic interests' (see Chellaney 1994).
39. US MTCR-based missile sanctions, for example, are codified into the Iran Non-Proliferation Act of 2000.
40. Procedural changes may include, for example, a modified voting process. Currently, all decisions within the MTCR are made on a consensus basis. This practice was not so problematic when the members of the regimes were few in number. However, the significant growth in membership in recent years, along with the MTCR decision to co-opt members whose perspectives on security differ from those of the longstanding members, poses a serious functional problem.
41. If the goal is coordination, then the arrangement should be worked out among states with similar political, economic and technological interests. They do not require a treaty, because they can work together quite well in an informal setting. That is, for instance, what we witnessed in the early years of the MTCR. The regime was established by a group of like-minded nations concerned about the spread of missile technologies. Those nations (that is, the G 7) did not require broad bargains to be struck, nor side-payments made, because they had roughly similar interests and objectives. See Jones and Zaborsky (1997).

Chapter 5

CBW Export Controls: Towards Regime Integration?

Alexander Kelle
Lecturer, Queen's University, Belfast

Introduction

Even after a cursory look at the debate on export controls in general and those aimed at chemical and biological dual-use materials, technologies and services in particular, one cannot avoid the impression that much of that debate is dominated by either rhetoric or ignorance (Roberts 1995). The rhetoric is provided by fundamental and dogmatic critics of these controls, many of which are to be found in the Non-Aligned Movement (NAM) and who equal export controls with a strategy of export denial. Their criticism, however, has not been substantiated with figures as to how big a trade volume has been denied to them. Even the enumeration of a set of instances, in which exports were denied and end-uses were very obviously and unambiguously peaceful, has not been forthcoming from the camp of dogmatic export control critics. This – as well as the fact that most of the states who are accused of withholding essential technologies and material from developing states are trading states who have an interest in free, and not restricted trade – very much nurtures the suspicion that export controls are either misunderstood or misrepresented when they are portrayed primarily as a means to implement a strategy of export denial. This rhetoric has led many export control proponents to ignore these criticisms as outlandish and politically motivated, rather than based in fact. This perception, in turn, has prompted the mantra-like reiteration of the well-known western position that export controls are a mere manifestation of the non-transfer norms (see below) contained in the nuclear weapons control regime and the chemical and biological weapons prohibition regimes. As a result, a constructive debate on chemical and biological weapons-related export controls has been taking place only to a limited extent.

Such a constructive debate might usefully start with an explication of the functions that export controls on dual-use goods, technologies and services serve. Their primary goal is to ensure the civil application of exported commodities and services and to deter recipients from using them in military programmes. In order to fulfil this function domestically, that is in the supplying state, export control measures have to be capable of identifying illegal exports and of threatening the potential exporter with a level of punishment that exceeds any gain from such an illegal export. Although export controls on dual-use goods and equipment pursued in isolation from other non-proliferation measures cannot prevent the acquisition of WMD by a determined proliferant, they can slow down the procurement process and increase the proliferant's costs. When coordinated among supplier states, export controls provide a level playing field for potential suppliers in different states, thereby greatly increasing the hurdles for a proliferant. Harmonized export controls – such as in the Australia Group – make it more difficult to play one supplier against the other, since the individual exporters do not have to face comparative disadvantages because of unequal export control guidelines (Müller et al. 1993; Roberts 1998).

Export controls are but one part of the more comprehensive control (in the case of nuclear weapons) or prohibition regimes (in the case of chemical and biological weapons). As there are a number of different understandings and usages of the term 'regime' in the academic literature (Hasenclever, Mayer and Rittberger 1997), let alone in the political arena, it is necessary to briefly outline its usage in this chapter: international regimes are an issue area specific subset of international institutions 'around which actor expectations converge in a given issue area' (Krasner 1982, 185). International regimes display a four-part structure, consisting of principles, norms, rules and procedures. As Krasner has summarized:

> Principles are beliefs of fact, causation, and rectitude. Norms are standards of behaviour defined in terms of rights and obligations. Rules are specific prescriptions or proscriptions for actions. Decision-making procedures are prevailing practices for making and implementing collective choice (Krasner 1982, 186).

Understood in this way, international regimes shape expectations, prescribe roles, guide behaviour and thus create an order in a particular issue area among actors on the international level (Müller 1993).

In the issue areas of chemical and biological weapon prohibition, the core underlying principle is that the use of chemical and biological weapons (CBW) constitutes an abhorrent act of warfare and, as such, has to be prohibited. Since the late nineteenth century this principle has found its way into a number of international treaties which culminated in the Biological and Toxins Weapons Convention (BTWC) 1972 and the Chemical Weapons Convention (CWC) 1993. Both BTWC and CWC form the central pillars of the two prohibition regimes, which will be discussed in detail in the third part of this chapter. The preceding section will analyse the activities of the Australia Group in the area of chemical and biological export controls. The final part of the chapter will summarize the state of play and assess prospects for a higher degree of regime integration as regards the non-transfer norms contained in the two regimes and the Australia Group's functions.

Chemical and Biological Weapons Export Controls and the Australia Group

The Australia Group (AG) was founded in 1985, following an Australian initiative. The AG's original purpose was to harmonize national controls on the trade in dual-use chemical warfare agents. It was created in response to the rapid proliferation of chemical weapons, their repeated use in the Iran–Iraq war, and the limited progress in negotiations on the CWC (Robinson 1992; Smithson 1997). The AG consisted originally of 15 states[1] plus the European Union (EU) in an observer role. However, even among these states, the harmonization and deepening cooperation on expanded export controls was not uncontroversial, as some EU member states questioned whether the cooperation among AG participants was in conformity with other obligations they had already undertaken, most notably EU membership, where one of the founding treaties, the Rome Treaty, in its Article 223 gives exclusive authority to member states in matters of defence (Robinson 1992, 159). Despite these initial worries, the AG continuously expanded both its membership and the range of goods and technologies covered by its harmonized controls.

Membership of the Group has more than doubled from the 15 founding members. While initial growth in membership was restricted geographically to Europe, with the addition of Argentina in 1993 and South Korea in 1996, the AG expanded into the Americas and Asia. The latest member Ukraine, which took part in AG proceedings for the first time in April 2005, brings current AG membership to 39 states plus the European Union (Australia Group 2005). Initially, the AG met bi-annually, but later moved to an annual meeting schedule. It is noteworthy that the AG is not an international organization in the formal sense. It does not have a budget, standing bureaucracy or permanent office buildings. Rather, the Australian embassy in Paris acts as contact point, providing secretarial services for the annual meetings.

> The Australia Group is an informal arrangement. Participants do not undertake any legally binding obligations: the effectiveness of the cooperation between participants depends solely on their commitment to CBW nonproliferation goals and on the effectiveness of measures implemented nationally which aim at preventing the spread of chemical and biological weapons (Australia Group, 2000).

In 1990 AG participants agreed to expand their controls to cover biological weapon agents and toxins, as well as dual-use equipment necessary for their production. In 1992 control lists were agreed upon which covered 18 bacteria, four rickettsiae, 25 viruses and 14 toxins. In addition, dual-use equipment like fermenters, centrifuges, aerosol chambers and filter and freeze-drying equipment with certain technical specifications were subjected to controls (Robinson 1992). The following year, the AG agreed on a so-called no-undercut policy which relies on 'procedures for ensuring that denials of an export of a listed item for CBW non-proliferation reasons by one member would be respected by all other members' (Australia Group 1993). The meeting in October 1995 reflected the increased risk of terrorists acquiring chemical and biological weapons, as evidenced by the Aum Shinrikyo sarin gas attack in the Tokyo subway system earlier that year – a topic the AG would return to a few years later in the aftermath of the anthrax mailings in the United States in the autumn of 2001. In addition to the growing terrorist threat continuous reviews and updates of the AG's procedures, guidelines and control lists were necessitated by advances in science and technology and changes in the international regulatory environment

(Australia Group 2001). Thus the AG had to bring its controls on the transfer of chemical mixtures in line with the parameters agreed upon by the Organization for the Prohibition of Chemical Weapons (OPCW) member states during the 5th session of the Conference of State Parties in 2000.

Australia Group controls made a quantum leap in 2002 when its participants agreed on a new set of measures which went considerably beyond those previously agreed upon. First of all, the AG adopted 'formal guidelines governing the licensing of sensitive chemical and biological items' which included a so-called 'catch-all' provision, supplementing the exclusively list-based approach pursued before (Australia Group 2002). These guidelines were subsequently made publicly available (Australia Group 2004). In addition, the AG agreed to control 'for the first time, the intangible transfer of information and knowledge which could be used for chemical and biological weapons purposes'. The group furthermore agreed to tighten controls on certain equipment, such as fermenters, for which the volume threshold at which controls would be started to apply was lowered from 100 to 20 litres, and to add more toxins to its control list (Australia Group 2002).

Overall, two decades of efforts to control sensitive biological and chemical items in order to prevent their use in chemical and biological weapons programmes of either states or sub-state groups, such as terrorist organizations, has resulted in the formulation of export control guidelines, to which all AG participants adhere, and a set of six control lists covering dual-use chemical manufacturing facilities and equipment and related technology, chemical weapons precursors, dual-use biological equipment and related technology, biological agents, animal pathogens and plant pathogens (all lists available at <www.australiagroup.net>). From the point of view of critics of the AG's activities in the chemical realm, it is not only the controls on manufacturing equipment that they regard as contravening the letter and spirit of the CWC but also the fact that 24 of the 63 precursors on the AG list are not listed on any of the CWC's three schedules on chemicals. This gives the appearance that the AG chemical weapons precursor control list covers a wider area than the CWC schedules and, one could argue, in conjunction with its application to CWC state parties, runs counter to Article XI of the CWC (see below).

The Chemical and Biological Weapons Prohibition Regimes

The Chemical Weapons Prohibition Regime

Regime Structure[2] As already mentioned above, the principles of an international regime are the shared beliefs of regime participants about the issue area which they want to regulate through the regime. In the case of the chemical weapons prohibition regime, the belief that the use of chemical weapons constitutes an abhorrent act of warfare – sometimes referred to as chemical weapon taboo (Price 1997) – is the central regime principle. It leads to the central regime goal: in the words of the preamble of the CWC, 'for the sake of all mankind, to exclude completely the possibility of the use of chemical weapons'. The second regime principle reflects the recognition that the peaceful uses of chemistry are a legitimate undertaking. However, as peaceful uses of chemistry cannot be taken for granted, two additional principles have been agreed upon: first, defences against the threat or use of chemical weapons are a legitimate undertaking, and secondly the acknowledgement that regime compliance by state parties needs to be verified. Finally, due to the nature and speed of scientific and technological advances in chemistry and the life sciences more generally, state parties share an understanding of the dynamic character of the issue area that the chemical weapon prohibition regime is set up to regulate.

The regime norms are derived from these five principles. They are to guide state behaviour in the issue area and thereby lead to the achievement of the regime goals. From the recognition that the use of chemical weapons constitutes an abhorrent act of warfare, a couple of core regime norms follow: first of all, states which possess chemical weapons have to destroy their stockpiles completely (the disarmament norm). State parties who do not possess chemical weapons commit themselves not to acquire them (the non-acquisition norm). All state parties agree never to use chemical weapons (the non-use norm) and – central to the argument of this chapter – not to transfer materials or technology that will aid a third party in chemical weapon production (the non-transfer norm).

The verification principle in turn has lead state parties to submit information related to chemical weapons and chemical industry (the declaration norm) to the OPCW. Likewise, state parties allow the OPCW's secretariat to perform on-site inspections (the inspection norm) of the accuracy of the declarations, the progress of CW destruction, and other obligations they have undertaken.

The principle that civilian applications of chemistry are legitimate informs the CWC's cooperation norm, which prescribes that the implementation of the Convention must not impede the civilian applications and free trade in chemicals for purposes not prohibited under the CWC. In cases of the threat or use of chemical weapons against a state party to the CWC, the provision of assistance to be provided by those in a position to do so has been included in the text of the CWC (the assistance norm). The consultation norm takes on two different forms in the chemical weapons prohibition regime: firstly, CWC state parties commit themselves to consultation in case of problems in implementing the treaty. Secondly, in the context of the Australia Group, of which only some CWC members are participating, states have agreed to consult one another in case of a transfer request which threatens to contribute to the proliferation of chemical and biological weapons. Furthermore, the internalization norm requires state parties to the CWC to translate the stipulations contained in the Convention into their national legal systems. Lastly, but not least, state parties are under an obligation to keep the regime current with respect to developments in science and technology (S&T) of relevance to the regime (the adaptation norm).

The rules and procedures of the chemical weapons control regime are so numerous that discussion of these rules and procedures is well beyond the scope of this chapter. However, some of the rules and procedures that relate to the non-transfer norm will be addressed in subsequent sections.

CWC Transfer System and Australia Group Controls In the final stages of negotiating the CWC, the then ambassador of Australia to the Conference on Disarmament, Ambassador O'Sullivan made a statement in August 1992 on behalf of the Australia Group, according to which its members would review its activities in the field of export controls 'with the aim of removing such measures for the benefit of State Parties to the Convention acting in full compliance with their obligations under the Convention' (Conference on Disarmament 1992). As Feakes (2001, 47) has pointed out, this statement was not greeted with universal optimism by NAM members. However, in the end it proved useful in securing the approval of the CWC's text.

Non-transfer-related regulations are contained in a number of Articles of the Convention. According to Article I (1), 'each State Party to this Convention undertakes never under any circumstances: (a) To … transfer, directly or indirectly, chemical weapons to anyone'. Following Article VI (2), '[e]ach State Party shall adopt the necessary measures to ensure that toxic chemicals and their precursors are only … transferred … for purposes not prohibited' under the CWC. In addition, Article XI (2) tasks state parties in section (e) to 'undertake to review their existing national regulations in the field of trade in chemicals in order to render them consistent with the objective and purpose of this Convention'.

More detailed transfer guidelines are found in the Verification Annex, Parts VI, VII and VIII. Part VI contains the 'Regime for Schedule 1 Chemicals and Related Facilities', according to which 'a State Party may transfer Schedule 1 chemicals outside its territory only to another State Party and only for research, medical, pharmaceutical or protective purposes. Chemicals transferred shall not be retransferred to a third State'.

In Part VII of the Verification Annex, the regime for Schedule 2 chemicals and related facilities is spelled out. Section C on 'Transfers to States Not Party to this Convention' stipulates that Schedule 2 chemicals shall only be transferred to or received from state parties. This obligation has taken effect three years after entry into force of the CWC, that is, in the spring of 2000. During the interim three-year period, each state party had to require an end-user certificate for transfers of Schedule 2 chemicals to states not party to the CWC. Such end-user certificates had to state: that the transferred chemicals will only be used for purposes not prohibited under the CWC; that they will not be retransferred; their types and quantities; their end-use(s); and the name(s) and address(es) of the end-user(s).

Similarly, Part VIII of the Verification Annex contains the regime for Schedule 3 chemicals and related facilities. It states that when transferring Schedule 3 chemicals to states not party to the CWC, each state party shall adopt the necessary measures to ensure that the transferred chemicals shall only be used for purposes not prohibited under the CWC. A requirement – comparable to the one for Schedule 2 chemicals – exists for demanding an end-user certificate from the recipient state. Five years after the CWC's entry into force – that is, in April 2002 – the Conference of State Parties (CSP) had to consider the question of whether to establish other measures regarding transfers of Schedule 3 chemicals to states not party to the CWC. Although Feakes notes a correlation between the number of new accessions to the CWC in 2000 and the enactment of trade restrictions for Schedule 2 chemicals (Feakes 2001, 51), this did not seem to provide a big enough incentive for CWC state parties to restrict trade in Schedule 3 chemicals. Rather, reflecting many state parties interest in the chemical trade, April 2002 came and went without any additional trade-restricting measures being agreed upon.

A similar pattern of behaviour could be observed in relation to the transfers to non-state parties of mixtures containing Schedule 2 chemicals. A decision had to be reached on this matter because of the above-mentioned trade restrictions taking effect three years after the CWC's entry into force. According to the decision reached at the 5th session of the CSP in May 2000, transfers to non-state parties are permitted firstly, if the products contain 1 per cent or less of a Schedule 2A or 2A chemical; secondly, if the products contain 10 per cent or less of a Schedule 2B chemical or; thirdly, if products are identified as consumer goods packaged for retail sale for personal use or packaged for individual use (OPCW 2000).

The continued dissatisfaction of some NAM states with the export controls of the Australia Group applied to CWC member states was brought to the fore during the 3rd Session of the Conference of State Parties of the OPCW in November 1998. During this meeting of CWC state parties, Iran, Cuba and Pakistan submitted a draft resolution in which the Conference was asked to emphasize that the CWC 'has not envisaged any export control restriction in chemical trade between State Parties for peaceful purposes', that 'the OPCW should be seen as the sole responsible body to verify the compliance of the State Parties with their obligations undertaken under the Convention' and that CWC state parties 'should abide by the provisions of the Convention and abolish existing export control regimes against state parties in order to render their national regulations … consistent with the obligations undertaken in accordance with the Article XI of the Convention' (Iran, Cuba and Pakistan 1998). The draft resolution went on to request that state parties complete their review of national regulations so as to render them consistent with the above quoted stipulation of Article XI of the CWC. Predictably, this resolution was not adopted by the CSP. Instead, the OPCW's Executive Council was tasked to deal with the matter. Thus, form this point onwards export controls were explicitly on the Council's agenda, but no discernible action has been taken by that body. However, it has to be assumed that this trilateral initiative has been the motivator behind the Australian, Canadian, Swedish and US national papers that were presented to the 4th CSP session in outlining their respective national implementation mechanisms of Article XI including the review of their national export control regulations (Australia 1999; Canada 1999; Sweden 1999; United States of America 1999). Somewhat surprisingly NAM critics received some backing for their position from the Director-General of the OPCW's Technical Secretariat in his opening statement to the 5th Session of the CSP:

> As more states join the CWC, and as their chemical producers support it, the arguments originally advanced for the maintenance of restrictions outside a credible reliable international legal framework become increasingly redundant. Given this fact, the continuing existence of export controls by some State Parties against others is hard to understand and very difficult to justify.[3]

The First CWC Review Conference in April and May 2003 then witnessed another replay of the by now decades-old debate about whether the Australia Group violates the stipulations of the CWC and should be abolished without delay – or whether the AG represents an important instrument for CWC state parties to fulfil their non-proliferation obligations stemming from the Convention. The distribution of roles in this almost ritualistic exchange of arguments was entirely predictable: Brazil, India, Iran, Malaysia (on behalf of the NAM and China) and Pakistan criticized the AG; the United Kingdom and the US, among others, defended the need for its continued existence. Given the hardened fronts in this debate, the Review Document is confined to a reiteration of text contained in the CWC, urging the EU to 'continue its facilitation efforts to reach early agreement on the issue of the full implementation of Article XI' (OPCW 2003).

The Biological Weapons Prohibition Regime

Regime Structure[4] Four regime principles of the biological weapons prohibition regime, which are very similar to the ones identified earlier for the chemical weapons prohibition regime, can be identified. The first is related to the conviction of regime participants that the use of biological weapon agents constitutes an abhorrent act of warfare and is therefore prohibited. It was first expressed in the 1925 Geneva Protocol and later reiterated in the Biological and Toxins Weapons Convention (BTWC) preamble, in which BTWC state parties confirm their determination, 'for the sake of all mankind, to exclude completely the possibility of bacteriological (biological) agents and toxins being used as weapons, [c]onvinced that such use would be repugnant to the conscience of mankind'.

According to the second principle, on which the biological weapons control regime is based, peaceful uses of the biosciences are a legitimate undertaking. The wording of the prohibitions contained in Article I of the BTWC reflect this peaceful uses principle. Accordingly:

> Each State Party to this Convention undertakes never in any circumstances to develop, produce, stockpile or otherwise acquire or retain: (1) Microbial or other biological agents, or toxins whatever their origin or method of production, of types and in quantities that have no justification for prophylactic, protective or other peaceful purposes.

This so-called general purpose criterion makes it clear not only that peaceful uses of the biosciences are legitimate undertakings for state parties to the BTWC, but makes them such even if they involve pathogenic organisms or toxins in quantities and for purposes other than use as weapons.

The third regime principle expresses the assumption of states subscribing to the regime that defences against the threat or use of biological and toxin weapons are permitted, which is also expressed in the above quote from Article I of the Convention. This principle is rooted in the belief that the peaceful uses of biosciences cannot be taken for granted – be it for the lacking universality in membership or for a state party cheating on the obligations it has assumed. However, while this underlying belief has led, in both the nuclear non-proliferation regime and the chemical weapons control regime, to the manifestation of yet another principle, the verification principle, this has not materialized in the biological weapons context. Neither the 1925 Geneva Protocol nor the BTWC makes explicit reference to such a principle. The final principle underlying the BTWC control regime is the complementarity principle which is clearly stated in preambular paragraphs 2 to 4 of the BTWC: the 1925 Geneva Protocol and the BTWC complement one another.

Central to the biological weapons control regime is the non-use norm, which is explicitly spelled out in the 1925 Geneva Protocol and implicitly contained in Article I of the BTWC. Although this article of the Convention makes explicit reference only to the non-acquisition norm, it can be inferred from it that non-use is prohibited as well. The disarmament norm is contained in Article II of the BTWC. It requires that all state parties either destroy or divert to peaceful purposes all agents, toxins, equipment and means of delivery related to their biological weapons holdings within nine months after entry into force of the BTWC.

The non-transfer norm is contained in Article III of the BTWC, according to which state parties forswear to 'transfer to any recipient whatsoever, directly or indirectly, and not in any way to assist, encourage, or induce' any actor to acquire any of the items specified in Article I of the BTWC. The non-transfer norm is additionally strengthened through Article IV of the BTWC which calls for national implementation measures (internalization norm) to put the basic obligations under the Convention into effect. It is these two normative guideposts that members of the Australia Group regard as the legal basis for their activities.

In addition, the cooperation norm is spelled out in Article X of the BTWC, representing, from the point of view of many BTWC state parties (mostly from the developing world), the flip side of the non-acquisition and non-transfer norms. The assistance norm is contained in Article VII. It stipulates that state parties will come to each other's assistance in case of the use or threat of biological or toxic weapons against one of them. The consultation norm is spelled out in Article V of the BTWC, in which state parties agree to 'consult one another and to cooperate in solving any problems which may arise in relation to the objective of, or in the application of the provisions of, the Convention'.

Efforts to Strengthen the Regime What is clearly absent from the above enumeration of regime principles and norms is the existence of the verification principle and its corresponding declaration and inspection norms. This shortcoming in the regime structure was recognized by BTWC state parties and led the Third BTWC Review Conference in 1991 to establish a Group of Governmental Experts to identify and assess potential verification measures from a scientific and technical viewpoint (VEREX). Only when the report of that group was discussed during a Special Conference of the State Parties to the BTWC in September 1994, did the question of trade restrictions and export controls take centre stage (Special Conference 1994). It became apparent that several BTWC state parties were not too supportive of the idea of establishing a verification system for the BTWC. A group of developing countries

– which seemed to be more concerned about the financial burden of a verification system and questions of national sovereignty than of a neighbouring state secretly developing biological weapons – successfully managed to include in the mandate of a new Ad Hoc Group the task to negotiate measures to strengthen the implementation of Article X of the BTWC, that is, the cooperation norm of the regime. Thus, in light of the special interests of BTWC member states, the Ad Hoc Group, was tasked to consider, *inter alia*, 'specific measures designed to ensure effective and full implementation of Article X, which also avoid any restrictions incompatible with the obligations undertaken under the Convention' (Special Conference 1994).

Negotiations of the Ad Hoc Group started in January 1995 and progressed until July 2001, when the overall approach taken in the negotiations up to that point was rejected by the US administration and the draft Protocol text decreed for parties to reduce rather than increase security against biological weapons. The negotiations proceeded in four phases (Toth 1999): during the first phase which lasted until mid-1997, potential elements of a compliance protocol were identified. From mid-1997, negotiations were based on a rolling text, which was developed further during the negotiating sessions of the Ad Hoc Group. During the third phase in 1999, the formal structure of the protocol was negotiated and in the fourth phase, compromise language on the less controversial issues under negotiation was integrated in the rolling text. In order to create additional momentum for the Ad Hoc Group to enter into an end-game during which also the more controversial issues could be tackled, the chairman of the Ad Hoc Group developed a compromise text which he presented to delegations in spring of 2001 (Pearson, Dando and Sims 2001).

The July 2001 session of the Ad Hoc Group was scheduled to have a debate of the compromise text submitted by the Ad Hoc Group chairperson. While some delegations were criticizing specific elements of the document presented by Ambassador Toth, the US delegate, Ambassador Donald Mahley, concluded in his remarks:

> that the Chairman's text was not an adequate basis for completing the Protocol, that it could not be made an adequate base for further negotiation and, furthermore, that the whole conceptual framework on which the negotiations had been conducted, would have to be changed (quoted in Dando 2002, 175).

This conclusion was based on the assessment that the protocol 'would threaten national security and commercial proprietary information; and it would threaten the dual-use export control regime of the Australia Group' (Rosenberg 2001). This effectively ended the Ad Hoc deliberations. The so-called 'new process' which was initiated after the collapse of Ad Hoc negotiations does not address the non-transfer norm or its relation to the cooperation norm.

Non-Transfer and Cooperation Provisions in the Compliance Protocol and Australia Group Controls[5] With respect to strengthening the implementation of the norms expressed in both Article III (non-transfer) and X (cooperation) of the BTWC, a relatively small number of working papers were submitted by state parties participating in the Ad Hoc Group, which then found their way into the rolling text for the BTWC Compliance Protocol. As Littlewood points out, one has 'to understand that the debate in the Ad Hoc Group was a proxy discussion about the existence of the Australia Group and the perception of broken promises from the final stages of the negotiations on the CWC' (Littlewood 2005, 139).

Thus, it does not come as a surprise that when measures to enhance the implementation of Article III were discussed in some detail during the March 1997 session of the Ad Hoc Group, India introduced a working paper (India 1997a), proposing a number of far-reaching measures to strengthen the non-transfer norm, which amounted to nothing less than abrogating the present export control practice. They included a substantial transfer of national sovereignty to a future BTWC organization, which would have been empowered to decide on all biological weapons-related transfers. Under the scheme proposed by India, the BTWC organization and not the individual member state would have been the central decision-making organ. Following from that, if national export controls would become obsolete, so would harmonized national controls, that is, those of the Australia Group.

A more moderate approach to strengthening Article III of the BTWC was presented by Austria and New Zealand. In their working paper (Austria and New Zealand 1997), the two Australia Group members advocated to include in the future protocol an obligation for each state party to declare annually 'the national legal measures it has adopted in order to implement Article III of the BTWC' and to 'report to the Organization on an annual basis on its administrative and other related national implementation measures with regard to Article III of the BTWC to ensure that transfers of agents, toxins, and equipment are only authorized in compliance with the provisions of the Convention'. If such measures were implemented, not only would the decision-making power continue to reside with the state parties, but the declarations would also be limited to national measures. Harmonized measures, such as the ones of the Australia Group, would not be touched upon and, consequently, state parties would not be obliged to become more transparent to states outside this group.

As these positions were well known and did not change over the course of the Ad Hoc Group negotiations, it does not come as a surprise that only about a dozen of more than 450 working papers submitted to the group were dealing with the strengthening of the BTWC's Article III.[6] Littlewood reports that the politicized nature of Australia Group export controls even spilled over into other areas of the Ad Hoc Group's work and that 'negotiation on this issue was avoided because every debate on it soured the relationship between delegations on all other subjects' (Littlewood 2005, 147). This led to a situation where the portion of the rolling text dealing with the strengthening of the BTWC's Article III was still heavily bracketed even in May 2001, indicating still prevailing major disagreements among negotiating parties (Ad Hoc Group 2001a, 73–8).

The compromise proposal on the BTWC's Article III contained in the composite text presented by the chairperson of the negotiations (Ad Hoc Group 2001b, 396–400) foresaw, first, the revision and – if necessary – amendment of national legislation to regulate transfers of dual-use biological weapons agents, equipment and technology by state parties in order to bring national measures in line with the protocol. Secondly, it contained transfer guidelines, including specific measures which may be taken by state parties. In other words, adoption of the measures was not mandatory, but left to the discretion of individual states. The same applies to the notification of transfers and consultations among state parties on the implementation of these provisions. In sum, the proposed text contained hardly any legally binding obligations. Rather, one has to think of these stipulations as suggestions for best practice, which, as Littlewood has noted (2005, 154) conferred some legitimacy to the Australia Group's activities.

Thinking the Unthinkable? Prospects for Regime Integration

This chapter started with the assertion that much of the controversy over chemical and biological weapons export controls is fuelled by either rhetoric or disinterest, an assessment originally provided by Roberts a decade ago. As the debates in the context of both the CWC and the BTWC protocol negotiations since then have shown, this verdict holds true largely today. Some NAM states are still demanding the immediate cessation of 'parallel' export control regimes, that is the Australia Group, and instead advocate reliance on the transfer mechanisms, such as those provided by the CWC or which would have been provided for under the BTWC protocol had negotiations been concluded successfully. Likewise, apart from a somewhat higher degree of transparency – achieved in part by the establishment of a website and the publication of some key documents, such as the transfer guidelines – AG members continue to regard a fundamental rethink of their approach to export controls which could result in a move away from harmonized national export controls as something akin to heresy. This does not bode well for the integration of AG export controls into any of the two chemical and biological weapons prohibition regimes.

For any attempt at integration to stand a chance of succeeding, it will have to separate the harmonization function from the information or intelligence sharing function, because the assessment of Roberts of the biological weapons prohibition regime remains valid, that is, '[s]o long as proliferation is a concern of such scope and immediacy, and so long as the BTWC remains a weakly implemented regime, the functions of the AG cannot readily be transferred to the BTWC with any sense of optimism that the basic purposes and objectives of the treaty would be well served' (Roberts 1998, 247).

The same applies to the chemical weapons prohibition regime. Neither of the two regimes provides a regulatory framework which is conducive to sharing sensitive intelligence data, although a potential proliferator could be a regime member. Although the CWC contains a challenge investigation procedure to address concerns of non-compliance, up to date this procedure has not been invoked, neither on the basis of procurement activities, nor on the basis of other available information. This clearly shows that some state parties who claim to have information on potential violations of other regime members are reluctant to use this information to trigger a challenge inspection. This unwillingness to share such information with as large a group of countries as there are regime members in either of the chemical or biological weapons prohibition regimes can be expected to remain a defining feature of export control policies.

Still there are differences as to the prospects for and the degree to which regime integration with a view to the export control harmonization function of the AG might take place and would actually make sense. These are largely due, first of all, to the different states of development of the chemical and biological weapons prohibition regimes. As the biological weapons prohibition regime currently does not have any of the organizational structures or mechanisms available that are contained in its chemical weapons counterpart, there is very little to consolidate AG biological weapon-related controls with. The CWC, in contrast, has an implementing organization at its disposal, which the BTWC does not. Furthermore, there are precise rules and procedures to guide state action available in the chemical weapons context, which again are missing in the biological weapons realm. As has been noted above, in the initial stages of CWC implementation, 70 to 80 per cent of import and export data reported by state parties did not match, pointing to considerable implementation problems on the national level. So long as this ratio will not have been at least reversed, and more than three quarter of all data sets on exports and imports match one another, it is inconceivable that AG participants would consider merging their control efforts with the transfer mechanism established under the CWC. One obvious issue that would have to be tackled relates to the fact that AG control lists and CWC schedules overlap, but are not identical. Given the scientific and technical expertise assembled in the OPCW's Scientific Advisory Board (SAB), this would be the obvious subsidiary body to consider the matter – together with experts and representatives from AG participants and other interested state parties. Article XV, paragraphs 4 and 5 provide a simplified amendment procedure which would be applicable for changes in the CWC's three schedules.

Somewhat more problematic is the integration of the AG list on dual-use chemical manufacturing facilities and equipment and related technology. Although licensing the export of such items and technology is well within the purview of the CWC's general purpose criterion, no comparable list of items to be controlled exists within the CWC context. The addition of a new schedule to the CWC, however, is very unlikely to fall under the simplified amendment procedure of Article XV and would instead have to go through an amendment conference. Alternatively, the Conference of State Parties could take a decision that state parities are expected to licence such dual-use equipment in order to be in compliance with the obligation undertaken in Article I, paragraph 1(d) of the CWC, that is, the stipulation, not to 'assist … in any way, anyone to engage in any activity prohibited to a State Party under this Convention'. Such a decision, of course, would not carry the legal weight of a formal amendment, which would have to be ratified by CWC state parties.

These different stages of regime development are, at least partially, a reflection of the differences in the substance matter which is to be prevented from being misused for proliferation purposes. In the chemical weapons context, there are a number of past chemical weapons programmes on which the control efforts could be based, whereas in the biological weapons area, the composition of Australia Group control lists is largely informed by the 'intrinsic risk posed by a particular pathogen or toxin, rather than knowledge that it had been sought for proliferation purposes' (Mathews 2004, 3). In contrast to chemical warfare agents, pathogens and toxins occur in the natural environment which also makes it more difficult for export controls to restrain the proliferation of chemical and biological weapons. In addition, as reflected by the continuous additions to the AG biological weapons-related control lists, the revolution in the life sciences and advances in biomedical research make the biological weapons area a highly dynamic one. In contrast, chemical warfare agents and their precursors are well known and technological surprises which would necessitate additions to control lists for licensing purposes are therefore less likely.

One of the key issues surrounding AG export controls as they relate to the chemical and biological weapons prohibition regimes is the question of transparency or the lack thereof, even if only so perceived. As noted above, four AG participants submitted national papers to the OPCW concerning the review of their national implementation of CWC Article XI, some of which contained information on the actual denials of transfers. It should not be too difficult for all states participating in the AG to provide this kind of information on a regular basis. Such a step is not required by any of the declarations foreseen in the CWC, but it might serve to underscore the point made by the AG that export controls do not restrict legitimate trade, but rather enable it. A higher degree of transparency which shows that these licensing requirements are applied in a fair manner can in turn be expected to contribute to the robustness of the chemical weapon prohibition regime. Thus, it would be a small investment for AG participants to make, upon which they could, at a later stage and if the political will to do so materializes, build further integrating AG controls into the chemical weapons prohibition regime. With respect to the biological weapons prohibition regime, suitable structures for a perhaps future merger with AG licensing requirements would have to be created in the first place. After the abandonment of the Ad Hoc Group negotiations and the current minimalist approach to 'strengthening' the BTWC, it is very likely that AG biological weapons-related export controls will remain the only available 'multilateral' export control mechanism for the foreseeable future.

References

Ad Hoc Group (2001a), 'Procedural Report of the Ad Hoc Group of State Parties to the Convention on the Prohibition of the Development, Production and Stockpiling of Bacteriological (Biological) and Toxin Weapons and on Their Destruction', BTWC/AD HOC GROUP/56-1, 18 May 2001, <www.opbw.org>.

—— (2001b), 'Appendices [to Ad Hoc Group 2001a]', BTWC/AD HOC GROUP/56-2, 18 May 2001, <www.opbw.org>.

Australia (1999), 'Chemical Weapons Convention (CWC) Implementation Adjustment of Australian Export and Import Licensing Measures', C-IV/NAT.5, 17 June 1999, <www.opcw.org/html/global/c_series/csp4/civ_nat5.html>.

Australia Group (1993), 'Press Release: Australia Group Meeting', AG/Jun93/Press/Chair/10, <www.australiagroup.net/en/releases/ninety_three.htm>.

—— (2000), 'Background Paper. Export Licensing Measures on Materials Used in the Manufacture of Chemical and Biological Weapons', AG/May00/Press/Chair/18, <www.australiagroup.net/en/releases/background.htm>.

—— (2001), 'Press Release: Australia Group Meeting', AG/Oct01/Press/Chair/24, <www.australiagroup.net/en/releases/2001.htm>.

—— (2002), 'Press Release: Australia Group Meeting', <www.australiagroup.net/en/releases/press_2002_06.htm>.

—— (2004), 'Guidelines for Transfer of Sensitive Chemical or Biological Items', <www.australiagroup.net/en/guidelines.html>.

—— (2005), 'Media Release: 2005 Australia Group Plenary', <www.australiagroup.net/en/releases/press_2005.htm>.

Austria and New Zealand (1997), 'Working Paper by Austria and New Zealand', BTWC/AD HOC GROUP/WP.142, 14 March 1997, <www.opbw.org>.

Brazil (1996), 'Working Paper Submitted by Brazil: Article X Implementation in A BTWC Compliance Regime: Aspects of a Cooperative Approach', BTWC/AD HOC GROUP/WP.104 17, September 1996, <www.opbw.org>.

Canada (1999), 'Canadian Review Under Article Xl Paragraph 2(e): Canada's Export and Import Controls on CWC Chemicals and Precursors', C-IV/NAT.4, 15 June 1999, <www.opcw.org/html/global/c_series/csp4/civ_nat4.html>.

Conference on Disarmament (1992), 'Chemical Weapons: Final Records (PV) 1992 Session', CD/PV659, 10 August 1992.

Cuba (1995a), 'Working Paper Submitted by Cuba: Some Elements Associated to the Promotion of Science and Technology with Peaceful Aims within the Framework of the BTWC', BTWC/AD HOC GROUP/WP.4, 28 November 1995, <http://www.opbw.org>.

—— (1995b), 'Working Paper Submitted by Cuba: Rights and Obligations of the State Parties to the BTWC within the Framework of the Economic and Technological Development and in the Field of International Cooperation and Assistance, BTWC/AD HOC GROUP/WP.5, 28 November 1995, <www.opbw.org>.

Dando, M.R. (2002), *Preventing Biological Warfare: The Failure of American Leadership*, Palgrave, Basingstoke.

Fahmy, N. (1996), 'Export Control Regimes: A Critique', in J. Brown (ed), *Arms Control in a Multi-Polar World*, VU University Press, Amsterdam.

Feakes, D. (2001), 'Export Controls, Chemical Trade, and the CWC', in J. Tucker (ed.), *The Chemical Weapons Convention: Implementation Challenges and Solutions*, Monterrey Institute of International Studies, Monterrey, CA.

Hasenclever, A., Mayer, P. and Rittberger, V. (1997), *Theories of International Regimes*, Cambridge University Press, Cambridge.

India (1997a), 'Working Paper by India: Guidelines to Ensure Compliance with Obligations under Article III of the Convention on the Prohibition of the Development, Production and Stockpiling of Bacteriological (Biological) and Toxin Weapons and on Their Destruction (BTWC)', BTWC/AD HOC GROUP/WP.126, 5 March 1997, <www.opbw.org>.

—— (1997b), 'Working Paper by India: Measures to Strengthen Implementation of Article X of the BTWC', BTWC/AD HOC GROUP/WP.131, 10 March 1997, <www.opbw.org>.

Ireland (1996), 'Working Paper Submitted by Ireland on Behalf of the European Union. European Community Collaboration with Developing Countries in the Field of Biotechnology', BTWC/AD HOC GROUP/WP.75, 18 July 1996, <www.opbw.org>.

Islamic Republic of Iran (1997), 'Working Paper submitted by the Islamic Republic of Iran: Article X. Economic and Technological Development', BTWC/AD HOC GROUP/WP.149, 20 March 1997, <www.opbw.org>.

Islamic Republic of Iran, Cuba and Pakistan (1998), 'Draft Resolution Submitted by Islamic Republic of Iran, Cuba and Pakistan: Fostering of International Cooperation for Peaceful Purposes in the Field of Chemical Activities', C-III/NAT.4, 19 November 1998.

Japan (1995), 'Working Paper Submitted by Japan: Japanese Cooperation in the Field of Biotechnology', BTWC/AD HOC GROUP/24, 13 July 1995, <www.opbw.org>.

Kelle, A. (1998), 'Strengthening the Biological Weapons Convention: A Role for Export Controls?', *The Monitor: Nonproliferation, Demilitarization and Arms Control*, Vol. 4, Nos. 2–3.

Kelle, A. (2003), 'Strengthening the Effectiveness of the BTW Control Regime – Feasibility and Options', *Contemporary Security Policy*, Vol. 24, No. 2.

—— (2004), 'Assessing the Effectiveness of Security Regimes: The Chemical Weapons Control Regime's First 6 Years of Operation', *International Politics*, Summer 2004.

Krasner, S. (1982), 'Structural Causes and Regime Consequences: Regimes as Intervening Variables', *International Organization*, Vol. 36, No. 2.

Littlewood, Jez (2005), *The Biological Weapons Convention: A Failed Revolution*, Ashgate, Aldershot.

Mathews, R.J. (1993), 'A Comparison of the Australia Group List of Chemical Weapon Precursors and the CWC Schedules of Chemicals', *Chemical Weapons Convention Bulletin*, No. 21.

—— (2004), 'The Development of the Australia Group Export Control List of Biological Pathogens, Toxins and Dual-Use Equipment', *Chemical and Biological Weapons Conventions Bulletin*, No. 66, pp. 1–4.

Morel, B. (1992), 'How Effective is the Australia Group?', in K. Bailey and R. Rudney (eds), *Proliferation and Export Controls*, University Press of America, Lanham, MD.

Müller, H. (1993), *Die Chance der Kooperation. Regime in den Internationalen Beziehungen*, Wiss. Buchgesellschaft, Darmstadt.

Müller, H. et al. (1993), 'From Black Sheep to White Angel? The New German Export Control Policy', *PRIF Reports*, No. 32, Peace Research Institute Frankfurt, Frankfurt/Main.

Netherlands (1995), 'Working Paper Submitted by the Netherlands: Implementation of Article X of the BTWC', BTWC/AD HOC GROUP/WP.45, 7 December 1995, <www.opbw.org>.

OPCW (2000), 'Decision, Implementation of Restrictions on Transfers of Schedule 2 and Schedule 3 Chemicals to and from States not Party to the Convention', C-V/Dec.16, 17 May 2000, <www.opcw.org/html/global/c_series/csp5/cv_dec16.html>.

—— (2003), 'Report of the First Special Session of the Conference of the State Parties to Review the Operation of the Chemical Weapons Convention 28 April – 9 May 2003', RC-I/5, 9 May 2003, <www.opcw.org/docs/rc105.pdf >.

Pearson, G.S., Dando, M.R. and Sims N.A. (2001), 'The Composite Protocol Text: An Effective Strengthening of the Biological and Toxin Weapons Convention', Evaluation Paper No. 21, University of Bradford, Bradford, July 2001, <http://www.brad.ac.uk/acad/sbtwc>.

Price, R.T. (1997), *The Chemical Weapons Taboo*, Cornell University Press, Ithaca, NY.

Roberts, B. (1995), 'Rethinking Export Controls on Dual-Use Materials and Technologies: From Trade Restraints to Trade Enablers', *The Arena*, No.2, CBACI, Alexandria, VA.

—— (1996), 'Technology Diffusion and International Security', in J. Brown (ed.), *Arms Control in a Multi-Polar World*, VU University Press, Amsterdam.

——(1998), 'Export Controls and Biological Weapons: New Roles, New Challenges', *Critical Reviews in Microbiology*, Vol. 24, No. 3.

Robinson, J.P.P. (1992), 'The Australia Group: A Description and Assessment', in H.G. Brauch, H.J. v. d. Graaf, J. Grin, and W. Smit (eds), *Controlling the Spread and Development of Military Technology*, VU University Press, Amsterdam.

Rosenberg, B. (1996), 'Incorporation of Dual-Use Export Controls in a Compliance Regime for the Biological Weapons Convention', *Chemical Weapons Convention Bulletin*, No. 33.

—— (2001), 'Allergic Reaction: Washington's Response to the BTWC Protocol', *Arms Control Today*, <www.armscontrol.org/act/2001_07-08/rosenbergjul_aug01.asp>.

Smithson, A. (1997), 'Separating Fact from Fiction: The Australia Group and the Chemical Weapons Convention', Occasional Paper No. 34, The Henry L. Stimson Centre, Washington, DC.

Special Conference (1994), 'Final Report: Special Conference of the State Parties to the Convention on the Prohibition of the Development, Production and Stockpiling of Bacteriological (Biological) and Toxin Weapons and on Their Destruction (BTWC)', BTWC/SPCONF/1, 19–30 September 1994.

Sweden (1999), ‘Swedish Review under the Chemical Weapons Convention Paragraph 2(e) of Article XI’, C-IV/NAT.1, 16 March 1999, <www.opcw.org/html/global/c_series/csp4/civ_nat1.html>.

Toth, T. (1999), ‘Time to Wrap Up’, *Chemical and Biological Weapons Conventions Bulletin*, No.46.

Tucker, J.B. (1998), ‘Strengthening the BTWC: Moving Towards a Compliance Protocol’, *Arms Control Today*, Vol. 28, No. 1.

United Kingdom (1995), ‘BTWC Article X: Areas of Biological Activity of Direct Relevance to the Convention’, BTWC/AD HOC GROUP/WP.7, 28 November 1995, <www.opbw.org>.

United States of America (1995), ‘Discussion of Potential Article X Issues. Working Paper Submitted by the United States of America’, BTWC/AD HOC GROUP/23, 13 July 1995, <www.opbw.org>.

—— (1999), ‘United States of America Export Controls and the Chemical Weapons Convention’, C-IV/NAT.2, The Hague, 29 April 1999, <http://www.opcw.org/html/global/c_series/csp4/civ_nat2.html>.

Notes

1. These were the EC 10 at that time – Belgium, Denmark, France, Germany, Greece, Ireland, Italy, Luxembourg, the Netherlands and the United Kingdom – plus Australia, Canada, Japan, New Zealand and the US.
2. This section is based on Kelle (2004).
3. Quoted in Feakes (2001, 47). Interestingly, while the Australian, Canadian, Swedish and US national statements on their review of national regulations to bring them into line with Article XI of the CWC are available online on the OPCW webpage, neither the draft decision put forward by Iran, Cuba and Pakistan (which is an official OPCW document), nor the opening statement of the Director General to the 5th Session of the CSP can be accessed online.
4. This section is based on Kelle (2003).
5. Parts of this section are based on Kelle (1998).
6. These Working Papers are Nos 126 (India), 142 (Austria and New Zealand), 147 (Friend of the Chair), 148 (Iran), 184 (Austria), 407 (NAM and other states), 424 (UK), 426 (Iran), 432 (China et al.), 443 (Australia et al.), 444 (UK), 452 (China et al.), and 453 (China), available at <www.opbw.org>.

Chapter 6

Nuclear Export Controls: Closing the Gaps

Adam M. Scheinman
Policy Director in the Office of Nonproliferation and International Security
National Nuclear Security Administration, US Department of Energy

Introduction

International crisis in the proliferation arena has opened multilateral export controls to intense scrutiny in recent years. Consider the following quote from International Atomic Energy Agency (IAEA) Director General Mohammed ElBaradei:

> [I]nternational efforts to limit the spread of technology through the use of export controls have left much to be desired ... The relative ease with which a multinational illicit network could be set up and operated demonstrates the inadequacy of the present export control system.[1]

Serious observers and non-governmental organizations have taken similar aim at export controls, recommending in some cases a total overhaul of the supplier regimes to remedy identified process, political or legal failures. This paper suggests a less ambitious – and more practicable – approach that sets a twin goal of tightening existing supplier restrictions and rules, and ensuring that states exercise their domestic responsibility to implement and enforce fully those restrictions and rules.

To set the context for these recommendations, this paper offers several observations about the current proliferation environment, followed by thoughts on the road ahead for controls on items and technologies needed for nuclear weapons. The focus is on nuclear proliferation, though the lessons are transferable to controls for missile technologies and those needed for chemical and biological weapons.

International Environment

The Challenge from Within the Non-Proliferation Treaty (NPT)

Over the last three years, the bedrock of the nuclear non-proliferation system – the NPT – has withstood a series of seismic jolts. These jolts have been the product of 'threshold' states that – unlike in prior years when the concern principally revolved around states outside of the NPT – are inside the treaty and have abused their position to access advanced nuclear capabilities. In capsule:

North Korea In 2002, North Korea conceded that it was pursuing a covert uranium enrichment programme, which was in direct violation of its legal non-proliferation commitments. North Korea then ejected IAEA nuclear inspectors, removed materials and facilities from IAEA safeguards, and in all likelihood resumed operations to recover and stockpile plutonium.

Iran In 2002, press reports from a dissident group revealed previously undeclared facilities in Iran, including a large uranium enrichment centrifuge, heavy water production plants and a heavy water research reactor which served no justifiable civilian purpose, but were certainly suited to a military nuclear programme. Iran's pursuit of a nuclear weapons capability has been a source of US concern for years. Many more governments share this concern, including those on the IAEA Board of Governors which has reported extensively and repeatedly on Iran's failures to comply with its safeguards commitments and on an 18-year, clandestine effort to acquire sensitive nuclear technologies and capabilities.[2]

Libya In late 2003, Libya announced that it would eliminate a nuclear weapons programme that it had developed in secret with the assistance of a vast network of brokers, front companies and agents led by Pakistan's A.Q. Khan. Information that has come to light as a result of the investigation of the Khan network revealed that Libya was well on its way to acquiring specialized technology, components and raw materials needed to produce weapons uranium. Libya was clearly closer to a nuclear capability than most realized or even suspected.

These cases point to cracks in the foundation of the nuclear non-proliferation regime; cracks that if left unchecked could place the entire global non-proliferation effort at risk.

The Risk of Nuclear Technology Leaking to Proliferant States or Terrorist Groups

Nuclear technology leakage from Pakistan highlights the growing concern of 'secondary' proliferation. Secondary proliferation has at least two meanings: (1) direct, illicit transfers of technology from states, including existing proliferant states, as well as emerging suppliers and trans-shipment countries, to other governments; and (2) illicit transfers arranged by intermediaries or other non-state actors that arrange transfers to governments or end-users seeking weapons-related technology. This is the model of the Khan network.

These two categories are similar in that the overriding aim of the seller and purchaser is to defeat export controls. However, they differ in terms of response. The first category places the onus on states, particularly but not exclusively those with non-existent or weak export controls, to take responsibility to regulate commerce and police activities conducted on their territory. The second category is clearly more troubling from an export control standpoint, in that rogue intermediaries drive the process, pushing technology on willing buyers. This requires a deeper commitment among all states and at all levels, including government agencies, law enforcement organizations, industry and even science and technology institutes, to be aware of nuclear technology transfer concerns and to prevent and if needed interdict illicit trade. Today, more than 90 per cent of all world trade volume moves in sea containers, exposing a wider number of countries to export control abuse. Encouraging broad adherence to the standards set by the international supplier regimes is therefore a clear and immediate priority.

The New Face of WMD Terrorism

In the latter phases of the Cold War, it became nearly an article of faith that nuclear war between the superpowers was unwinnable and must not be fought. Nuclear weapons were viewed more as instruments of politics and the province of arms control negotiators rather than tools of war and generals. This changed after the September 11 attacks. The international community had no choice but to assume that terrorists will seek out and use the most threatening, indiscriminate weapons to achieve their aims.

International regimes can help mitigate these dangers and steps are being taken in this direction. Examples include the Convention on Nuclear Terrorism adopted earlier this year by the United Nations General Assembly,[3] and import and export control guidance supplementing the Code of Conduct on the Safety and Security of Radioactive Sources endorsed by the IAEA in September 2004.[4] Perhaps more important for the prevention of nuclear terror are steps to protect nuclear or radiological materials and facilities from theft or sabotage. The US government and its partners, including those in the G8 and the IAEA, have well-established and extensive programmes to secure such dangerous materials from misuse through cooperative threat reduction activities.

The Implications of Nuclear Energy Growth

Nuclear power's promise as a global alternative to fossil fuel and other energy choices remains just that: a promise. Capital and infrastructure costs, public concerns about safety, waste and proliferation, and the slow pace of research and development have effectively held nuclear power growth in check. However, this is not necessarily an indicator of low proliferation risk. Drawing on the NPT's qualified promise of peaceful nuclear sharing, Iran has staked claim to a civil programme that lacks any reasonable economic or energy justification. The NPT's promise has also contributed historically to the spread of research reactors and nuclear technology projects, theoretically expanding the base of scientific experts available to support covert weapons programmes. These dangers may multiply over the next decades if nuclear power stages the comeback, particularly in energy starved regions or countries, for example, China and India, that some predict.

The greatest risk associated with nuclear energy growth concerns the further spread of enrichment and reprocessing capabilities. These capabilities can provide uranium and plutonium for nuclear fuel, but also for nuclear weapons. Over the last 15 years, the only NPT states that have sought to establish wholly new enrichment or reprocessing programmes are Iraq, Iran, North Korea and Libya. This line-up of countries speaks for itself. The economics of enrichment and reprocessing are such that it makes little sense for states with purely civil nuclear power programmes to enter that market. For this reason, activities that suggest an interest in enrichment technology deserve special scrutiny. To promote vigilance among suppliers, the US has distributed watch lists of items that fall beneath the NSG dual use control list specifications, but which nevertheless can contribute to enrichment or reprocessing programmes in Iran and North Korea.

Addressing the Challenge

What is being done, and what should be done, to meet these challenges? While there are many aspects of a response, what follows are several that have a more direct bearing on nuclear export controls and opportunities for their improvement.

Tightening Existing Restrictions

First, governments must address the NPT 'insider' threat by tightening restrictions on transfers of dangerous nuclear technology. A decision by North Korea or Iran to retain nuclear weapons or a nuclear weapons option could have a profound and potentially devastating effect on the regime. Fortunately, it is almost universally agreed that possession of nuclear weapons by those countries is unacceptable and must be challenged.

To address the immediate problem, the US government has launched a series of far-reaching initiatives designed to preserve and strengthen the nuclear non-proliferation regime, impose new supplier restrictions on nuclear enrichment and reprocessing technologies, and systematically shutdown clandestine proliferation networks.

In February 2004, in a speech before the National Defense University, President Bush outlined a set of initiatives that addresses each of these areas.[5] Key among them was a proposal to limit access to the most sensitive nuclear technologies – those related to enrichment and reprocessing – to states that already possess full-scale, functioning enrichment and reprocessing plants. The US government has interpreted this to mean the ten NPT states that had enrichment or reprocessing plants under IAEA safeguards as of 31 December 2003. The President also proposed that states foreswearing enrichment and reprocessing receive assured fuel supplies at reasonable cost.

Since 2004, these issues have been dealt with extensively in the G8 and the Nuclear Suppliers Group (NSG).[6] In 2004, the G8 agreed to refrain for one year from transferring enrichment and reprocessing technologies to additional states, and to work over the following year to amend the NSG Guidelines. NSG members have yet to agree on the precise terms for such restraint, and consensus continued to elude negotiators during the NSG's plenary session, held in Oslo, Norway in June 2005. Nevertheless, it is apparent that support among NSG members for such changes remains firm, and it is expected that agreement can be reached later this year.

Other points bearing on the NSG in relation to the NPT 'insider' problem deserve mention:

First, drawing from the President's February 2004 speech, the NSG is considering a proposal to make the Additional Protocol a new condition of peaceful nuclear trade. The NSG is nearing agreement on this point, although more diplomatic work remains to be done.

Second, at its Oslo meeting this year, the NSG endorsed the suspension of peaceful nuclear assistance to states that fail to comply with their international safeguards agreements. This was an overdue step and one that can help deter future violations. Currently, only Iran is both suspected of safeguards violations and receiving substantial nuclear support from an NSG member, for example, Russia.

Third, at its plenary meetings in 2004 and 2005, the NSG adopted a series of new recommendations that strengthen the normative core of regime, for example, by adopting the 'catch-all' principle for dual-use exports (that is, preventing exports of any item, whether it is on the NSG control list or not, which could make a contribution to a nuclear weapons programme), making effective implementation of enforcement measures in national laws and regulations an explicit requirement, and requiring that recipients have effective export controls as a new criterion of supply of nuclear and nuclear-related dual-use items.

Finally, in 2003, the NSG adopted changes to the Guidelines to make the prevention of acts of nuclear terrorism an explicit goal and a factor for export licensing decisions, and to encourage states to consider terrorist threats when designing and constructing new nuclear facilities.

Cooperative interdiction of proliferation trade is a new area of emphasis. In May 2003, President Bush introduced a new initiative – the Proliferation Security Initiative (PSI). PSI is billed as an 'activity' rather than a regime. It has no formal structure or rules, beyond a Statement of Principles endorsed by a group of PSI supporters in September 2003. The Statement of Principles, which has been endorsed publicly by more than 60 governments, aims to prevent trafficking of weapons of mass destruction (WMD) technology through active interdiction, such as ship boardings or seizures of suspicious cargoes travelling by air or land, and helps coordinate efforts to defeat proliferation networks. PSI has been supplemented by additional actions, including the recent US Executive Order to block proliferation transactions by freezing the assets of companies or individuals suspected of supporting WMD programmes.[7]

Increase the Formality of Obligations

Second, export controls should be made a legally-binding obligation. Unlike international safeguards, export controls are voluntary in nature (that is, they lack the standing of a treaty obligation), and have often been viewed as a requirement limited to supplier regime members. This mode of thinking is outdated and dangerous. Information that surfaced in connection with the Libyan procurements is a case in point. It is known now, for example, that Libya received exports of nuclear-related items produced in Malaysia, which is not a supplier regime member, and routed through various transit points before arriving in Libya.

This instance was not unique to Malaysia. Others, including members of the supplier regimes, likely knowingly or unwittingly supplied Libya with specialized equipment and technology. Closing this gap by making effective export controls and criminal penalties for WMD proliferation global requirements is a first order priority.

The United Nations Security Council (UNSC) has taken an important step in this direction by adopting Resolution 1540 in April 2004. Resolution 1540 creates an international, legally binding obligation to enact strict export controls and secure at-risk materials in line with international standards. A summary of the relevant operative paragraphs follows:

Operative paragraphs 1 and 2: calls on all states to refrain from providing any form of support, directly or indirectly, to non-state actors that attempt to develop, acquire or transfer weapons of mass destruction.

Operative paragraph 3: calls on all states to take and enforce domestic controls to prevent the proliferation of WMD and delivery systems, including laws and regulations to control the export, transit, or re-export of items needed for their production, as well as border controls and law enforcement efforts to detect, deter, and prevent illicit trafficking of such items.

Resolution 1540 represents a significant departure, in effect expanding to all states – rather than the five declared nuclear weapon states – the NPT's internationally binding prohibition on assisting others to acquire nuclear weapons. The Resolution has also had the ancillary and critically important effect of drawing three non-NPT states – India, Pakistan and Israel – under its umbrella. It is worth noting that in the last year, each of these governments has passed new or updated laws or regulations governing the control of exports of WMD-related items and technology.

Promote Implementation and Enforcement

Third, maximum effort should be made to promote implementation and enforcement of effective export controls. Accepting the UNSC Resolution 1540 obligation and implementing and enforcing it are separate matters. Implementation and enforcement of effective export controls and national laws against WMD proliferation is not trivial, and requires having in place an integrated set of requirements.

First, governments must exert political will. This involves not only legislating controls and educating exporters, but also an enduring commitment to implement export controls strictly and consistently, even in the face of other competing strategic or policy interests or changes in government.

Second, governments must have a dedicated bureaucracy of policy, technical, military, law enforcement, and intelligence groups capable of administering a national export control system, for example, by gathering the requisite expertise to assess proliferation risk in the review of licence applications or unlicenced trade. Non-governmental organizations can also facilitate export control capacity building, whether through training or development of proliferation information.

Third, law enforcement organizations must have the authority to inspect and detain suspicious cargoes and to deter violators through the threat of meaningful penalties. Enforcement organizations worldwide also need better tools and information to interdict illicit WMD-related trade. This requires access to technical experts, training, technology and commodity guides, intelligence information, and targeting strategies to ferret out violators.

Support for export control implementation has been a leading item on the US non-proliferation agenda. This includes international cooperation under the US government's Export Control and Related Border Security (EXBS) Assistance programme. From its original focus on a small number of 'source' countries in the former Soviet Union, the EXBS has since expanded to meet a broader, global threat. This programme, which involves the US Departments of State, Energy, Commerce, Homeland Security and Defense, provides training, expertise and equipment to help partners tighten up export controls worldwide.

Some argue that improvements to international export controls should be sought through reforms or an overhaul of the four multilateral supplier regimes (that is, the Nuclear Suppliers Group, the Missile Technology Control Regime, the Australia Group and the Wassenaar Arrangement), including, for example, the merging of the four into one or the establishment of a treaty-based international export control system. This approach may have appeal in terms of improved operation and enforcement of the regimes, but it is not without potential costs in terms of time, resources and attention diverted from efforts to deal with existing proliferation threats. The attitudes and preferences of roughly 40 governments speak to a multi-year negotiation for an outcome that is likely to provide only a marginal improvement over the current state of affairs.

Rather than address the specific arguments for or against overhauling the regimes, which are addressed elsewhere in this book, this chapter asserts that the immediate task is improving national capabilities to meet the export control standards set by the Nuclear Suppliers Group and by UNSC Resolution 1540. The greatest risks of proliferation today stem from countries like Iran or North Korea, and the agents, front companies and intermediaries which supply them, that together prey on states with weak or non-existent export controls. This gap is best addressed through a coordinated campaign of cooperation. This view is shared by many. In addition to the US EXBS programme, the European Union, Japan and Australia have each dedicated resources to promote export control development in their respective regions, and to make WMD export controls a leading item for discussion at regional security meetings. This is particularly crucial and useful in the regions of east and south-east Asia, which have not only developed a reputation as havens for terrorists, but are also hubs for trans-shipment trade.

A *sine qua non* for effective export control cooperation and performance is information sharing. This must take place at many levels. Within states, information sharing between and among government agencies and with exporters is critical. This is a particular necessity for 'catch-all' controls, which require access to entity lists, programmes of proliferation concern, supplier regime denials and so on, to deter or prevent the diversion of dual-use exports to proscribed users.

Between and among states, information sharing is a useful tool to address specific transactions that raise concerns and can be dealt with using diplomatic channels or through active interdiction. It is also an important requirement for states that provide and receive export control support. To be useful, these efforts must be coordinated to ensure that states needing help get it, that duplication of efforts are avoided, and that limited resources are put to the greatest effect.

Within regimes, the role of information sharing is also expanding. The United States has used NSG sessions to brief on programmes of proliferation concern, such as nuclear developments in Iran using commercial satellite imagery. The NSG has gone a step further and this year will refocus its information exchange meetings to emphasize procurement networks and consider creation of an *ad hoc* group to address specific intelligence issues and concerns.

Information sharing between the NSG and the IAEA is a more recent suggestion, and therefore less developed. Options might be to share NSG denial information with the IAEA so that it has a clearer picture of whether a state has declared all of its nuclear activities. Some states already do this on a limited and voluntary basis. Another option would be to integrate export control and IAEA safeguards information for the purpose of identifying and confronting suspicious activities, helping to target IAEA inspections, or answering questions that safeguards information alone cannot address. This would be a more standard version of the IAEA's *ad hoc* use of procurement data as a supplement to safeguards information in Iran and Libya. The IAEA may already be moving in this direction, through consultations that have started with the NSG Chairman and with establishment of a nuclear technology procurement unit that reports directly to the IAEA Deputy Director General for Safeguards.

Conclusion

One conclusion that can be drawn from this chapter is that the export control agenda is full and will remain that way for the foreseeable future.

Some argue that the failures that allowed Iran, Libya or North Korea to acquire sensitive nuclear equipment and materials point to the need for a new international export control system. The record tells a different story. We know now that these countries were pursuing capabilities for many years outside of public view. However, it was only the provision of key technology and equipment, supplied by a network that found a new way to proliferate – that is, using offshore companies to manufacture and ship prohibited items – that their nuclear programmes reached dangerous levels of sophistication.

Clearly, the international community needs better to understand export control gaps revealed by the network, but an overhaul of the supplier regimes is not what is needed to close them. The regimes have historically exhibited a capacity to evolve – adapting to change by enhancing strengths and eliminating weaknesses – to address proliferation supply threats. Regime evolution is what is taking place today, and it can be predicted that, with sustained high-level attention, the full range of proliferation concerns will be effectively addressed.

Notes

1. Mohammed ElBaradei, 'In Search of Security: Finding An Alternative to Nuclear Deterrence', Presentation to, Center for International Security and Cooperation, Stanford University, 4 November 2004.
2. See IAEA Resolutions at <www.iaea.org>.
3. International Convention for the Suppression of Acts of Nuclear Terrorism. See <www.un.org/News/Press/docs/2005/ga10340.doc.htm>.
4. See < www-ns.iaea.org/tech-areas/radiation-safety/code-of-conduct.htm>.
5. See <www.armscontrol.org/act/2004_03/Bush.asp>.
6. The Nuclear Suppliers Group is a voluntary regime of 44 countries that contributes to nuclear non-proliferation through the implementation of Guidelines for nuclear and nuclear-related dual use exports. The Guidelines are implemented by each participating government in accordance with its national laws and practices. For more information, see <www. nuclearsuppliersgroup.org>.
7. See <www.whitehouse.gov/news/releases/2005/06/20050629.html>.

PART III
National and Regional Case Studies

Chapter 7

Strategic Export Controls: A Case Study of Regulation of Executive Power and Parliamentary Accountability in the United Kingdom

John F. McEldowney[1]
Professor of Law
School of Law, University of Warwick

Overview

Export controls received concentrated media attention during the Arms to Iraq saga played out in all its detail before the Scott Inquiry[2] in 1996. The inquiry revealed a complex and detailed regulatory structure overseeing exports that lacked transparency, was of dubious legality and was subject to only weak parliamentary accountability. The focus of this chapter is on the command and control system of regulation over export control within the United Kingdom *post* the Scott Inquiry and the enactment of the Export Control Act 2002 which came into force on 1 May 2004. In the last annual *Report on Strategic Export Controls* (United Kingdom 2005; see also Taylor 2003), it was estimated for the year ended 2003, the value of exports of strategically controlled goods was £992.4 million. These exports make a significant contribution to the defence and security of the United Kingdom, as well as contributing to the multi-various international obligations to be met by the armed forces. In considering the regulation of strategic exports, an historical approach is adopted in drawing out the tensions between executive discretion and parliamentary controls. The main question addressed is how accountable is the new regulatory system? The main thesis advanced is that the system of export control is linked to the policy of the government of the day. In its early legal construct, it reflected the legal culture of the UK. Formally legalistic and highly structured in form, the *actualité* is of a pragmatic system that also reflects many of the strengths and weaknesses of a parliamentary system of *ad hoc* accountability. Thus the system of control is strongly driven by the government of the day, sustainable through political oversight and pragmatic decision-making subject to market forces. Party political decision-making is often interspersed with balancing different shades of multi-nationalism, especially in terms of the influences of the United States and Europe.

The growing significance of the European and international dimensions to regulation is reflected in the many changes to the UK system. Currently the legal regulation of export controls is a means of giving effect to international obligations. It provides a mechanism for the implementation of national and foreign policy objectives and the potential for parliamentary oversight and debate on the virtues or otherwise of a fundamental part of government policy (Ewing and Gearty 2000).

Export Controls: Regulation and Accountability

The chapter is focused on the historical and practical development of the system of export controls and restrictions (Scott Report 1996). It begins with the early history and traces the gradual development of a statutory regime of licences and restrictions that largely replaced the earliest use of prerogative powers. The Scott Inquiry and its findings are considered in the context of the Export Control Act 2002 and the system of reporting under the *Annual Report on Strategic Export Controls*. The system of strategic export control is assessed in terms of its efficacy and the question of whether there is sufficient accountability to Parliament. This is an important area for the consideration of legal controls and their scrutiny as part of the parliamentary process. It reveals the working of the less well-known Committees on Strategic Export Controls (the Quadripartite Committee) and assesses how this unique committee operates. While the main focus is on UK institutional systems of control, the chapter also addresses the European and international dimensions of export controls.

Legal and Historical Considerations: Prohibiting and Licensing Exports

It is necessary to begin with the history of the legal regime applicable to the import and export of goods (Smith 2004). The following account is drawn from the Scott Report and sets out the historical background. The legal regime for import and export controls reflects one of the strengths of the English common law when confronted with new or unforeseen problems. Existing doctrines were adapted and moulded to fit new circumstances. During the special circumstances of wartime, especially the two world wars, executive powers increased incrementally to meet the national emergency (see Ewing and Gearty 2000; Rubin 1994). In times of peace, little was done to redress the balance whereby the government of the day had acquired more powers and, through inertia, had failed to consider whether the newly acquired powers should be reduced. As a consequence, the powers to licence or prohibit the export of goods were deputed to the government with limited parliamentary oversight or accountability (Chester and Wilson 1968).

At the outset, it is necessary to distinguish between general controls for the *prohibition* of exports and controls that relate to their *licensing*. The general principle of prohibition of exports came from the use of the prerogative in time of war to embargo goods out of necessity. This use of prerogative powers had medieval origins. The common law crime of treason also applied to those found trading with the enemy under the Treason Act 1795. Combined together, the crime of treason and the power to prohibit exports, operated in the realm of discretionary power in the hands of the government of the day. An added element was state secrecy enhanced in the time of war or national emergency. This provided a useful cloak to guard against any unwarranted intrusion and accountability. It is doubtful today if many of the original prerogative powers remain, as a statutory regime for the prohibition of exports gradually developed during the nineteenth century, replacing the use of prerogative powers. It is certainly the case that in peace time there are no prerogative powers applicable to control trade between the UK and other countries.

The use of prerogative powers maintained executive controls administered through the War Office, reorganized after the Crimean War (Lindsay Keir 1948). The use of prerogative powers under the control of different government departments allowed the continued use of prerogative powers and their adaptation to changing circumstances. Section 8 of the Customs and Inland Revenue Act 1879 provided a general statutory power for Proclamation or Order in Council. Such powers only applied to a limited range of goods. It was unclear how far such an order might be varied and also whether there were limits on the number of countries where the export of goods could be prohibited. Some refinement to this general power was provided by section 1 of the Exportation of Arms Act 1900. This Act allowed specific countries to be identified that were perceived to pose a military threat to Britain or its allies. However, the limited range of goods that might be prohibited remained unaltered.

The First World War in 1914 provided a further opportunity to refine prohibition powers (Chester and Wilson 1968). Two Acts of Parliament, the Customs (Exportation Prohibition) Act 1914 and the Customs (Exportation Restrictions) Act 1914 extended the scope of legislative powers to include 'all articles of every description' during a period of war. After the First World War, a further legislative intervention under section 17 of the Finance Act 1921 provided an extension to cover all firearms, ammunition and 'weapons of any description'.

The prohibition of the export of goods covered a wide range of material including arms, ammunition and military stores, including food. In wartime, the prohibition was absolute to any destination and of goods of any description. In peacetime, the prohibition of goods had to be to a specific list of countries and the goods had to be likely used against the citizens of Britain or its allies.

Distinct from the question of the export of goods being prohibited to a specified country, there is the issue of how exports might be licenced. The legal authority for the licensing of exports, at time of war, was recognized as a prerogative of the Crown. However, there was no corresponding prerogative power to licence exports during peacetime. Paradoxically, the licensing of exports in the time of war also included goods that were prohibited and their export illegal. Licences for the export of prohibited goods could be issued by the Privy Council without any express statutory authority.[3] The power to grant a licence included powers to revoke or amend licences, exercised by the Privy Council through its Export Licence Department. From 1 March

1915, these functions were administratively transferred to the War Trade Department and later subsumed into the Imports and Exports Licensing Section of the Board of Trade. While the administration of the licensing scheme operated inside the Board of Trade, its legality acted under the Privy Council's jurisdiction and powers.

The split between the administration of the system of licensing and the legal powers of the Privy Council did not go unnoticed. At the end of the First World War, the legality of the operations of the War Trade Department in respect of licensing was raised in a report prepared for the Cabinet by Lord Emmott[4] who advocated some form of scrutiny to be undertaken by a suitably qualified committee to resolve disputes and maintain consistency in approach. Emmott, who was an experienced Head of the War Trade Department, also recognized the need for some form of inter-departmental co-operation. These specific proposals were not implemented at the time.

In 1921, the Commissioners of Customs raised doubts about the legality of the system of licensing operated by the Board of Trade. Following the opinion of the Law Officers, it was agreed that a specific power, authorizing the licensing of exports by the Board of Trade, should be inserted into the new Export and Import Order made in 1921. This power would be included in any subsequent orders, thereby recognizing the licensing authority of the Board of Trade.

Although the arrangements introduced since 1921 were of dubious legality, the government continued to make operational use of the powers available to them. A number of internal departmental reviews were carried out. In 1933, it was argued that there should be a specific Advisory Committee in the Foreign Office on Trading and Blockade in Time of War. This marked a major shift in the regulation of licensing powers. However the new arrangements did not last long. In 1937, it was recommended that the powers should revert to the Board of Trade. Further statutory regulation was needed to provide an efficient system of regulation.

The Import, Export and Customs Powers (Defence) Act 1939

In 1939, as a prelude to the outbreak of the Second World War, the government enacted the Import, Export and Customs Powers (Defence) Act 1939. The Act remained largely unnoticed and unknown amongst the plethora of legal powers necessitated by wartime emergency.[5] The 1939 Act had a number of distinct features:

- The Act could continue in force as determined by Order in Council.
- The Act was linked to the existence of an emergency such as wartime under section 9(3). However, the determination of whether or not there was such an emergency and when it might end rested on a subjective judgement made by the government of the day. The clear intention behind the 1939 Act was that the Act should be limited to wartime emergency.
- Many similar statutes such as section 1 of the Customs (Exportation Prohibition) Act 1914 rested on objective criteria as to whether or not an emergency was in existence.

- The main mechanism of control under the 1939 Act was the use of an order '… for prohibiting or regulating … the importation or exportation from the United Kingdom of … all goods …'. The Board of Trade was empowered to set out penalties that appear necessary for the due operation and enforcement of the order. This was an unusual power enabling the setting of criminal penalties without the direct authority of an Act of Parliament and for the scope and range of the criminal law to be altered without direct legal authority by Parliament.
- There were few controls over any new orders made under section 1 of the Act. They were subject to neither affirmative nor negative resolution, which was suitable for their wartime usage. The absence of parliamentary oversight was also a reflection of the intention to confine the use of such powers to wartime.

The 1939 Act remained in force and largely unaltered after the Second World War save for an amendment under the Import and Export Control Act 1990. Its main virtue was to place statutory controls on the licensing system for the export of goods, while at the same time not fully resolving doubts as to whether any vestiges of the prerogative may have survived (see Hale 1976, 297). More remarkable is that successive governments since the Second World War have depended on the 1939 Act, exploiting a loophole in the legislation which failed to stipulate clearly when an emergency was determined to end.

During wartime, the 1939 Act proved its worth in terms of providing a flexible regime for restrictions for supplies for wartime use. The limited availability of certain goods could be speedily addressed through regulatory controls to prevent their waste and to conserve existing supplies. At the end of the Second World War, the 1939 Act could be put to another use, namely freeing up export trade and removing whole sectors from licensing regulations. A plethora of wartime orders made under the Act achieved that result with the novel idea of adopting flexible foreign policies to regulate the export market in response to trade and international conditions taking root. The creation of foreign policy responses through the regulation of imports and exports became an accepted role for licensing regulations under the 1939 Act.

It is remarkable that a little known Act of Parliament and one intended for wartime emergency use became a major device for the government of the day in the regulation of trade. In peacetime, the policies implemented by the Act were diverse, including protecting 'animal welfare', the 'protection of the national heritage', and the use of orders to protect 'national security'. Why did the 1939 Act prove so useful? The answer appears to be that it provided widely drawn powers rarely subjected to parliamentary debate or accountability. The few debates that did occur were relatively minor affairs with little substantial review of the issues raised. This relieved the government of the day from the problems of any delay or difference of opinion over the implementation of any controversial policies. It also fitted an *ad hoc* purpose in allowing successive governments to respond to the challenges of a shifting international agenda and thus the flexibility needed to address issues for the future.

In 1944, the Law Officers gave their opinion on the question of extending emergency powers more generally beyond the currency of any wartime crisis. One view was that such powers remained valid for a 'transitional period' after the end of hostilities in Europe. This was extended when the war with Japan endured beyond the end of Nazism and the war in Europe. A further extension of time appeared necessary when it was conceded that the emergency legislation did not cease having effect once a final Peace Treaty was concluded. The ambiguity of when the 1939 legislation came to an end was fully exploited to the benefits of successive governments. However, as the Scott Inquiry was later to discover, there was cause for concern. The 1939 Act was similar to other wartime legislation, such as the National Registration Act 1939. A number of important court cases were heard relating to legal challenges as to the validity of extending wartime powers during peace time and by analogy the legality of the continuation of the 1939 Act. The earlier cases, such as *Wilcock v. Muckle* (1951) questioned the use of Acts of Parliament, passed during wartime, but used in peacetime. Objection was also taken to the misuse of legislation intended for a specific purpose to be made use of for a more general purpose. While substantial criticism was made of the practice of using wartime legislation, this fell short of challenging the legality of such practice. Despite judicial reservation, the case law of *Wilcock v. Muckle* only served to reinforce the idea that, strictly in terms of legality, the continued use of wartime legislation with an uncertain life expectancy could be countenanced by the courts (Scott Report 1996, vol. 1, paras C 137–41). While doubts remained over the legality of the continued use of the 1939 Act and there was a recognition that new legislation was needed, successive governments showed reluctance and timidity in taking any action. It must be remembered that the powers of the UK's courts fell short of holding that an Act of Parliament was unconstitutional or illegal.

In the 1950s, serious consideration was given by the Board of Trade to replacing the 1939 Act with permanent legislation. However, no action was taken until October 1958 when a White Paper was published recommending reform of emergency powers.[6] In particular, repeal of temporary emergency legislation, including the 1939 Act, was proposed. Following the White Paper, a Bill was introduced proposing reform of the main emergency legislation. But in the debate on the proposed reforms, the 1939 Act was singled out as an exception that was worth preserving. The importance of the Act was underlined, specifically in terms of the power to control the import and export of goods in the United Kingdom. The flexibility of the Act and the need to align legislation with the changing nature of government policy and the international order was cited as another reason for not changing the legislation. Strategic decision-making was also facilitated by the 1939 Act and the administrative difficulties of transferring into legislation the essence of government policy appeared to be a difficulty in providing major legislative reform.

This was a missed opportunity and no further reform was contemplated until the 1980s. In 1982, the then Attorney General expressed doubts on the continued use of the 1939 Act and argued that the powers under the 1939 Act were of dubious legality. In 1983, there was a direct legal challenge to the 1939 Act. The challenge took the form of a judicial review of a refusal to grant the applicant Chris International Foods Ltd a licence to import 220 tons of bananas from outside the sterling area. The main issue focused on whether the refusal was legal. The case was in the form of a judicial review of the refusal to grant such a licence and whether the powers were exercised in accordance with the requirements of the 1939 Act. There was considerable difficulty in fitting the refusal within the policy and objectives of the 1939 Act as the protection of banana imports fell outside the jurisdiction of wartime emergency legislation, the main rationale of the 1939 Act. The trial judge, Mr Justice Hodgson, ruled in the applicant's favour quashing the decision of the Secretary of State as this was an improper exercise of delegated powers. On the legality of the 1939 Act and its application to the banana case, the judge was reluctant to make any decision. Although the case went to a second hearing after the delegated powers judgment was answered by the Secretary of State taking the decision again, the trial judge at the second hearing upheld the legality of the 1939 Act as applicable to protecting Commonwealth supplies. While this reflected the state of administrative law in 1983, it is unlikely to stand up to the tougher standard of review prevalent in the last ten years (see *R. v. Blackledge* and others 1996; *The Cheng Poh v. Public Prosecutor* 1980). Doubts about the legality of the use of the 1939 Act outside clearly defined emergencies appear to have substantial support from recent legal analysis (Lindsay Keir 1948).

Much of the above information came to the notice of the public after the Scott Inquiry reported; the details of the report are considered below. Significantly, when the government gave evidence to the Scott Inquiry in 1994, it stressed the legality of the arrangements under the 1939 Act and argued that its use had been approved by Parliament. Various orders made under the Act[7] in 1980 regulating sanctions to Iran were debated in Parliament and this provided an opportunity for sufficient parliamentary scrutiny. The government also pointed to previous orders that received similar debates[8] and argued that this implied parliamentary authorization. The Scott Inquiry rejected this idea of implied authorization and argued that parliamentary debate fell short of authorization (Scott Report 1996, vol. 1, para. C1.33). This view had received support from the case law, noted above, where, *obiter dicta*, judicial comments on the 1939 Act expressed the hope that new legislation would be introduced, but stopped short of holding any illegality (McEldowney 2000).

The Import and Export Control Act 1990

Until the passage of the Import and Export Control Act 1990, the legal powers to licence and control exports rested on the 1939 Act. The continued use of the legislation was later described by the Scott Inquiry as 'a reprehensible abuse of executive power' (Scott Report 1996, vol. 1, para. C1.34). In the government's view, the 1939 Act facilitated a difficult task of regulation, which was best done discretely and far removed from publicity or detailed inquiry. The 1990 Act had, as its main purpose, the removal of section 9(3) of the 1939 Act, thereby effectively making the 1939 Act permanent. Effectively, this allowed wartime powers to be freely available during peacetime and, as most of the powers were exercised through subordinate legislation, the 1990 Act entrenched the absence of parliamentary control and supervision. The justification for doing so came from a series of postulations used to justify the 1990 Act and later available to the Scott Inquiry.[9] These included the desirability of placing on a firm legal foundation the entire scheme for the regulation of export control. The arguments against appear to stem from the absence of available parliamentary time and a reluctance to open up the system of export controls to public scrutiny. The Scott Inquiry examined many official documents detailing the discussions on the possible way forward[10] on drafting the 1990 Bill. Party political considerations also appeared to be relevant in the final arrangements agreed for the 1990 Bill. Paradoxically, one of the arguments that held influence was the idea that the flexibility inherent in the 1939 Act allowed the government sufficient flexibility to incorporate international obligations into domestic law through executive action, thus avoiding parliamentary control. The 1990 Act thus facilitated this approach and further relied on the continued use of subordinate legislation without parliamentary scrutiny or control (Export of Goods [Control] Order 1991). The 1990 Act did not enhance parliamentary scrutiny and failed to address this systemic weakness in the export control system. The government's concern about parliamentary scrutiny and fears about publicity in the media contributed to its general reluctance to undertake a comprehensive review of the export control regime. There were also concerns about finding parliamentary time to debate and discuss the issues involved. At the same time, there were doubts about how market-sensitive information should be handled by the executive.

The Findings of the Scott Inquiry and its Aftermath

The Scott Inquiry and its report in February 1996 drew a number of conclusions from an extensive analysis of the system for the regulation of exports. The inquiry was set up following the collapse of the prosecution of a number of directors of Matrix Churchill, a now defunct machine tool company based in Coventry. Specific attention was given to the unreliability of the controls in place on dual-use goods. Scott's report highlighted a number of key deficiencies in the 1939 Act and the absence of a transparent and accountable system of parliamentary control. The findings proved conclusive in leading to the replacement of the 1939 Act and a much needed comprehensive review of the subject. The main findings of the Scott Inquiry may be summarized as follows:

- the 1939 legislation was based on wartime emergency legislation and lacked the necessary parliamentary supervision and control appropriate for a modern democracy;

- the system of regulation left too much discretion in the hands of the executive and should be replaced;
- government policy on export controls is too tied up with the system of enforcement, any such linkages requires reform;
- there should be a thorough review of the legislation at the earliest possible time;
- there is a general lack of accountability and transparency in this area of policy and in prosecution discretion (Scott Report 1996, vol. 1, ch. 2, paras K 2.1–6).[11]

Following Scott's recommendation, there were a number of reviews within government of the existing law and the statutory arrangements set up under the 1939 legislation. The Labour Party, in opposition, made use of the Scott findings to criticize the government of the day. Such criticism gained credibility with the electorate and although there was a parliamentary debate on the Scott Report, no minister resigned or was rebuked. The then Conservative government won the day by the narrowest of margins, but this added to the growing lack of public support in the government's conduct. The Labour Party made reform of the export control system an election pledge. In May 1997, after the election of a new Labour government, the government decided to provide an annual publication of the strategic export data alongside a promise to adopt and implement the European Union (EU) Code of Conduct for Arms Sales. In July 1997, the government set up a review of the criteria used for determining export licensing involving coordination between four government departments, namely the Department of Trade and Industry (DTI), the Ministry of Defence (MOD), the Foreign and Commonwealth Office (FCO) and the Department for International Development (DFID). The new criteria that emerged included assessing whether or not there was an identifiable risk that 'the proposed export might be used for internal repression' (Foreign and Commonwealth Office Press Release, 28 July 1997). At the same time, mounting pressure for an EU Code of Conduct for Export Controls from the French government began to gain results. Eventually, the UK's criteria became incorporated into an EU Code of Conduct for Exports on 26 October 2000.

In July 1998, the government published a White Paper detailing proposals for new legislation and setting in place new criteria for arms sales (United Kingdom 1998). The White Paper soon led to the Draft Export Control and Non-Proliferation Bill as a consultation document in March 2001 (United Kingdom 2001a). The Labour government also favoured a general tightening of controls on strategic exports and a more human-rights focus on the countries that might be considered as the final destination for the licensing exports. In fact, the United Kingdom and French governments jointly proposed in June 1998 that there should be an EU Code of Conduct.[12] This was supported by the German government for tactical reasons to influence the final content of the Code. The EU Code of Conduct upheld eight important principles of international law including the desire to preserve regional peace, security and stability. Respect for human rights in the country of final destination was regarded as a fundamental part of the new arrangements. Greater intra-government cooperation was urged and consultation over policy was recommended to take place on a regular basis. In support of greater transparency, the government agreed the publication of annual reports.[13]

While the new EU Code has much to recommend it, critics have suggested that the motivation of the French and German governments was to adopt a code that would be weaker in content than if they had waited for the momentum to build from other member states. Thus, the Code has little in terms of legally binding restrictions and is aspirational in tone rather than prescriptive in content. However, the existence of the Code is a step towards greater transparency and it does alert exporting countries to consider the regime of the countries where the end use of the relevant material is likely. This aspect of export control is the most difficult to anticipate (Smith 2004).

The Export Control Act 2002: Background and Strategic Analysis

It must be remembered that the United Kingdom spends on average £9.1 billion on defence procurement each year (Taylor 2003). At the same time, it is estimated that from 1998 to 2002, exports for defence equipment and services provides jobs for over 86,000 in the United Kingdom defence industry. The estimate of the value of strategically controlled goods is £992.4 million. This is in the context of an annual average of £5 billion for the arms industry as a whole. In that context, the export of material and the supply of arms and military goods constitutes an important part of the United Kingdom export industry.

The opportunity to reform the law on the regulation of exports was taken to consider the role of parliamentary scrutiny and the importance of greater transparency. One reason was the high profile accorded to the findings of the Scott Inquiry, with the inevitable damage to the reputation of many politicians, when no minister resigned or was held publicly accountable for any shortcomings revealed in the Scott Report itself. A further reason is that media speculation had been heightened to find abuses within the existing system. This proved embarrassing and counter-productive in securing for UK companies lucrative contracts. The considerable legal uncertainty left by the failure to reform the 1939 Act remained to be addressed, leaving the newly elected Labour government no option but to reform the law. Finally, the responsibility to be seen to take a lead in limiting arms supply and ensuring an adequate licensing system became a matter for the European Union at the instigation of the UK, France and Germany. This required a new regulatory system that was compatible with European and international treaty obligations.[14] The importance of Europe's growing foreign and security policy should not be overlooked in terms of the United Kingdom's desire to participate and take a lead role. This has reinforced the need for an institutional basis for regulatory controls and given a momentum to cooperation and collective agreements (Smith 2004, 239–63).

Regulating export controls also fits within the overall system of international agreements. The UK, as one of the five countries maintaining a nuclear weapon capability, had signed up to an international agreement on limiting nuclear proliferation.[15] Since 1992, the Zangger Committee, charged with interpreting and coordinating nuclear supply policies, issued new guidelines on dual-use goods, such as machine tools which may form part of a nuclear capability. The setting of criteria to form a control list of items and their application in terms of end-use proved an important way to set parameters of control. Consequently the United Kingdom decided to improve the substantive law and the system of controls through the introduction of the Export Control Act 2002.

The new legislation which came into force on 1 May 2004 provides a comprehensive modernization of the existing law applicable to the export control regime. As explained above, this is a long overdue reform. The new Labour government, less than a year after being elected to office in 1997, embarked on reform. In 1998 the government's White Paper (United Kingdom 1998) outlined the case for a radical overhaul of the entire system of export controls. In the government's view, the export control regime was inextricably linked to the question of aid policy and the role of arms trade. The government announced on 25 March 1999 that it would publish an *Annual Report on Strategic Export Controls*. The first report covered the period from 2 May to 31 December 1997, and since then there have been annual reports, the latest, published on 24 March 2005, covers 2003 (United Kingdom 2005). The reports are the result of collaboration between the different participating departments[16] and are intended to introduce a new level of annual review and monitoring. Policy matters are outlined, including licensing decisions and information on specific issues that emerged over the past year. The annual reports are reviewed by the newly created Quadripartite Committee discussed below (Rubin 1994).

The Export Control Regime under the Export Control Act 2002

The Export Control Act 2002 replaces entirely the Import, Export Customs (Defence) Act 1939 and its remit includes new powers to cover the transfer of technology by intangible means, overseas trade including the regulation of trafficking and broking between third countries, and powers to regulate technical assistance to counter weapons of mass destruction programmes. The 2002 Act also takes account of the 11 September 2001 events and provides measures in response to the United Nations (UN) Security Council Resolution 1373 (2001). Thus, the new legislation is much more comprehensive than its predecessor Act and incorporates the anti-terrorism elements as part of the export control regime. It is therefore essential that the 2002 Act should also be read alongside the Anti-Terrorism, Crime and Security Act 2001.

The 2002 Act addresses the main deficiencies in the law identified in the Scott Report. The main structure of the legislation is as follows. Section 1 gives the Secretary of State order-making powers to set controls over the export of goods. This is an all embracing power allowing for the classification and organization of goods. Similar powers are provided under section 2 for the control of the transfer of technology.[17] These are widely drafted and provide an important mechanism for control. Section 3 applies to the provision of technical assistance, section 4 is applicable to the operation of trade controls giving the Secretary of State wide powers in relation to any goods.

There are a miscellaneous number of powers found in sections 5–11 of the Act, covering the adoption of European Community law, and supplementary powers covering the adoption of international agreements and their application. Section 13 provides for the express use of parliamentary scrutiny of secondary legislation made under the Act and section 5 provides clear and explicit powers to control goods and technology assistance. In the past, such controls were left to executive discretion under the 1939 Act. Now the 2002 Act provides explicit legislative powers. In addition, there are clear and explicit powers to impose controls on exports from the United Kingdom, on the provision of technical assistance overseas, on the acquisition, disposal or movement of goods or other 'trafficking activities', that apply EU legislation for the control of dual-use goods. The legislation is also clear about the responsibilities on the Secretary of State which proscribe licensing procedures, an annual report to Parliament, guidance on the general principles to be followed when licensing powers are being used, and to vary the range of penalties and controls over the various offences committed under the legislation. There is also an important principle of integrated controls that provide inter-departmental regulations to enable each relevant government department to coordinate their respective roles.

The 2002 Act may be seen as a work of consolidation as well as reform. The Act sets powers that sweep away a rag-bag of secondary powers,[18] and provides a coherent framework of controls, replacing past executive discretion with an appropriate level of parliamentary scrutiny. The practical operation of the system of export controls in the United Kingdom is based on detailed forms downloadable from the Export Control Organization of the DTI with detailed criteria and instructions for obtaining a licence. The use of secondary legislation under the 2002 Act has continued[19] and the details of executive powers have been preserved in the statutory arrangements.

The continued use of wide discretionary powers, albeit under a statutory regime, rather than the prerogative, highlights the difficulty of achieving the appropriate regulation of this area. It also shows the requirements of flexibility and the importance of vigilance in the area of weapons of mass destruction proliferation. As already mentioned, the existing controls on chemical, nuclear and biological weapons were strengthened by the Anti Terrorism, Crime and Security Act 2001. This makes it an offence to knowingly cause a nuclear explosion, to engage or participate in the production of a nuclear weapon or to transfer a biological, chemical or nuclear weapon. Events since 11 September 2001 have led to the adoption of UN Security Council Resolution 1373 (2001) and a review of the existing controls under the 2002 Act in respect of the main areas of concern relating to export controls.

This underlines the need for co-operation at European and international levels. At the international level, the 2002 Act is supportive of the international agreements entered into by the United Kingdom including the Wassenaar Arrangement agreed in Vienna on 10–12 December 2003 (see <www.wassenaar.org>), aimed to permit participating states with a forum to discuss and collaborate on the control and regulation of dual-use technologies. The idea is to provide a system of control that effectively guards against the proliferation of terrorist networks and to limit arms sales and the use of dual-use goods. In addition to the Wassenaar Agreement, there is also the need to continue to prevent the proliferation of nuclear weapons. This is monitored by the Nuclear Suppliers Group and the Zangger Committee, setting guidelines and monitoring their implementation. The Group has 44 participating governments and the European Commission acts as a permanent observer. There are various groups within the system, each charged with responsibility to control the use of missile technology, emphasizing the need for international cooperation in order to prove effective.[19]

At a European Level, there has been much agreement. Since 1997 and the election of the new Labour government, the development of criteria for judging export licences for military and dual-use equipment has developed. The national criteria drawn up then have been supplemented and agreed in an EU-wide Code of Conduct on Arms Exports. This was consolidated on 26 October 2000 and has been refined. There are eight criteria, currently under review,[20] as follows:

- respect for the UK's commitment to sanctions agreed by the UN Security Council and European Community and other international agreements;
- respect for human rights and fundamental freedoms in the country of final destination;
- consideration of the internal situation in the country of final destination in terms of tensions and armed conflict;
- preservation of regional peace, security and stability;
- consideration of the national security of the United Kingdom, external relations and the interests of allies, EU member states and friendly countries;
- the behaviour of the buyer country with regard to the international community and attitudes to terrorism, respect for international law and alliances between countries;
- consideration of a risk that the equipment will be diverted within the buyer country or re-exported under undesirable conditions;
- consideration of the compatibility of the arms exports with the technical and economic capacity of the recipient country, taking into consideration that it is desirable that states should achieve their legitimate needs for security and defence with the least diversion for armaments of human and economic resources.

The government is expected to give attention to other factors, such as the national interest of the United Kingdom. This includes the potential effects on the economic interests and long standing stability of democratic trading countries, the potential effect on future diplomatic relations between the United Kingdom and the recipient country. Other matters for consideration include the potential effect on any collaborative defence production or procurement project with allies or EU partners and finally, the protection of the United Kingdom's essential strategic base.

It is questionable whether the above criteria are sufficiently robust to prevent material ultimately going to countries that will use weapons against western interests. This raises questions about accountability and how this is assessed in terms of the adequacy of parliamentary controls.

Transparency and the Quadripartite Committee: The House of Commons Defence, Foreign Affairs, International Development and Trade and Industry Committees

A significant development in the system of parliamentary scrutiny of export controls in the United Kingdom is the creation of the Quadripartite Committee (Natzler and Hutton 2005). Since 1979, the establishment of departmental select committees has provided a more coherent approach to government accountability. This has allowed a systematic approach to scrutiny as well as an evolutionary approach in the development of the functioning of select committees in general (Natzler and Hutton 2005, 88–106). The Quadripartite Committee was started in 1999, notably before the Export Control Act 2002 was enacted. The Quadripartite Committee was achieved through the four departmental select committees – Defence, Foreign Affairs, International Development, and Trade and Industry – collaborating together and deciding to act as an effective intra-departmental select committee to monitor the work of four different departments. The Quadripartite Committee permits the select committees from the relevant four departments to combine and work together to examine the government's policy on strategic export controls. This is a unique arrangement. It allows the combined strengths of the four select committees to come together, raising the level of expertise and permitting joined-up scrutiny of government policy across a range of specialist subject areas. This is intended to allow greater transparency than hitherto and restore the balance between the executive and Parliament in favour of the latter.

How has the new system worked? Early indications are that the Quadripartite Committee has shown its potential to be effective. This may be measured in terms of information and greater transparency. There have been a number of annual reports[22] supplemented by special reports covering specific issues. In the early stages, the work of the Committee was to continue sustained pressure on the government to introduce the Export Control Bill and having adopted the EU Code of Conduct for Export Control to give the subject sufficient transparency. The first report published in July 1999 was followed by a second annual report on 3 November 1999 and the government's response.[23] Later in February 2000 and July 2000, two further reports were published with the government's response.[24] These early reports laid the basis of developing different themes as a basis of effective accountability. First, the desirability of achieving improved scrutiny in the United Kingdom through transparent systems of scrutiny linked to other Member States in the European Union. Second, encouraging the adoption of multinational agreements and bringing the US into agreement with the EU Code. There were concerns about allowing the

Committee prior scrutiny of licence applications. Third, the Committee was able to scrutinize nearly 10,000 applications, a sign of the seriousness of purpose and the dedication of the Committee to make its mark.

The annual reports for 2001, 2002, 2003 and 2004 follow a similar pattern, developing some of the principles of review[25] identified earlier. The findings of the latest report covering the year to 2003 may be summarized as follows:

- the Committee has found a sustained focus in its work and this has allowed 'real progress' in the development of high level and constructive analysis of government policy;
- the Committee has only been able to look in detail at a small number of licensing decisions;
- the profile of the Committee and its role and remit could receive better publicity and be better resourced;
- the Committee has experienced delays in receiving information from the government and these delays have diminished the effectiveness of the committee.

An important resource in monitoring the working of the Quadripartite Committee comes from the pressure group Saferworld who undertake regular audits of the system (Isbiter and Kirkham 2004). This increases the pressure on the government to adopt a pre-scrutiny of the system of export licences. It appears that the Quadripartite Committee has worked well and shown the strength of select committees combining together when attempting to tackle complex and detailed problems. These are early days but there are a number of improvements proposed to enhance the visibility of the work of the Committee. The setting-up of a dedicated website and including the addition of the Committee to the alphabetical list of committees on the parliamentary website are steps in the right direction. The government has consistently rejected the idea of prior scrutiny of sensitive export licence applications. The Committee, however, has highlighted the continuous need for better information and improved scrutiny. One of the main recommendations made by the Committee's first report in July 2000 was that there should be a principle of prior parliamentary scrutiny conferred upon the Committee (United Kingdom 2000). Such prior scrutiny would involve the Committee in a two stage process. Stage 1 notification includes all licence applications including those for dual-use goods licences. The second stage would involve notification where the Committee would advise the government of those applications where the Committee would receive more information.

The government has rejected this proposal and argued that such scrutiny would be inappropriate given the average of 12,000 or so export licence applications each year. The recommendation for prior scrutiny has been reiterated by the committee, but to no avail.

One of the advances undertaken since the 2002 Act came into operation is the development of improvements in cooperation between government departments. This was achieved through a number of initiatives. In 2003 the work of the Joined-up and More Efficient Working in Export Licensing (JEWEL) project was completed. This project introduced many changes in the export control regime, putting in place important organizational benefits to enhance the system of licensing. This included establishment of decision-making systems intended to speed up decisions on less complex cases. Also included were systems intended to promote staff induction and training programmes and measures to improve the relationship with exporters and the transparency of criteria used to assess export controls. A major feature of the regulatory system is new information technology developments that enhance the profile of export controls. The effectiveness of the JEWEL project is not in doubt, but there are concerns about its longer term viability. In the 2004 budget statement, the Chancellor of the Exchequer made references to efficiency savings. This will effectively reduce the number of staff and the operational capability of the export control team.[26] This has resulted in the expression of major concerns by the Quadripartite Committee and the need to continue to place the export control system at the top of government priorities.[27] Recently, however, the government has abandoned its plans to privatize the Export Control Organization (*The Guardian* 2005). There remains active consideration to the question of whether the introduction of a charging scheme for export licences might alleviate the costs concerns and secure financial saving on public expenditure.

The Quadripartite Committee has also expressed disappointment over the fact that on three occasions, the government missed deadlines with supplying information. This has impeded the effectiveness of the Committee. However, there are advances such as the publication of quarterly data by government. There are concerns about the remit of the new legislation, especially in its territorial scope. There are ongoing controversies such as whether the arms embargo to China should remain. The United Kingdom also provided Iraq, Saudi Arabia and Kenya with various small arms weapons during 2004–5 (ibid.).

The cornerstone of the current system of export control is the adoption of the European Code of Conduct on Arms Export, currently under review. Among the considerations being given in the review are questions of licensing production overseas, the use of arms brokering agreements, intangible technology transfers and an increase in transparency standards. In the future, it is hoped that an updated version of the Code of Conduct will be published following the conclusions and recommendations from the review.

The Quadripartite Committee offers the potential for a different form of parliamentary review than that offered by a solitary committee. While it lacks the status of the Public Accounts Committee with the latter Committee's link to the National Audit Office, the Quadripartite Committee offers the potential to expand the range of scrutiny available to select committees. The Quadripartite Committee adopts the technique of inquiry, common to other select committees, but through the expertise and experience of four key committees it offers more. A wide-ranging scrutiny targets specific issues and, in doing so, provides a unique opportunity to develop and strengthen parliamentary scrutiny. The fact that the government has been reluctant to allow pre-scrutiny of licences underlines the fact that the Quadripartite Committee must continue to seek to improve its status and enhance its role. Such criticisms aside, the Committee has established its credentials and sought to improve its position. This takes time and there will be sufficient opportunities in the future, such as the Review of the EU Code and its implications. There are also ongoing debates about the incorporation of goods for re-export and the pressure from France and Germany to lift the EU arms embargo to China. Saferworld, in its annual audit of the UK export control regime, has identified areas of concern, many areas relate to the case studies that are country specific but also include general principles.[28] This complements the scrutiny of the Quadripartite Committee and ultimately strengthens the ability of Parliament to hold government to account.

Conclusions: Lessons for the Future

The modern system of export control in the United Kingdom owes much to the lessons learned from its historical origins and the development of prerogative powers (Oakes and Youngs 2001). The 1939 Act had become discredited and the absence of appropriate parliamentary scrutiny owed much to the failures of successive governments, the inertia of Parliament and the inadequacy of select committee scrutiny. The turning point came with the Scott Report and the recommendation to undertake a comprehensive review of the export control system. This was followed by a protracted debate on the future of export controls and the absence of adequate parliamentary supervision. The Export Control Act 2002 is an improvement on the previous legislative regime. Past doubts about the legality of controls have been resolved through a comprehensive statutory system for the licensing and control of exports. Much-needed inter-departmental cooperation appears to have been put in place. There is greater transparency than in the past with the system of annual reports and reviews (Isbister and Kirkham 2004). The Quadripartite Committee system offers a unique system of control that is innovative and reflective of the need to address the details of a multi-faceted area that is growing in importance as well as complexity. The increase in parliamentary scrutiny is showing signs of making its mark already. The recent announcement that the government is not going to privatize the Export Control Organization is a signal of the role of the Committee in questioning government policy (*The Guardian* 2005). The government has provided support for a strong defence industry while maintaining a strategic approach to limiting exports that may fall into the wrong hands. Setting the appropriate balance is difficult, but not impossible, once the United Kingdom's national export control system has become integrated into a European and international system of control. One of the achievements of the 2002 Act is to bring greater coherence to the United Kingdom system that has allowed convergence with the European system. Recently, the Quadripartite Committee concluded:

> We believe that the UK's export control system has improved substantially in this Parliament. As … a result of the legislation passed in 2002, subsequent delegated legislation, changes in reporting practice and the JEWEL review, we now have generally efficient and reliable export controls (United Kingdom 2005, paras 172–3).

There is little room for complacency as events over the past few years have proved in terms of terrorism. The provision of data and the enhanced system of parliamentary scrutiny through the Quadripartite Committee has not inhibited exports or limited the efficiency of government policy. Instead it has given rise to an increased confidence that the system in place is no longer based on the residual discretion of the government of the day but is drawn on more entrenched systems of parliamentary accountability. However, there are signs of the limitations in the system of control, and the failure of the government to abide by timetables to give evidence is a worrying signal. If viewed from the perspective of its long history, the United Kingdom's export control system has improved considerably, notably in its linkage into European and international obligations. It must not be allowed to drift back to the past practice of largely unfettered executive discretion. This calls for continued vigilance and the development of working patterns and time-tables with the Quadripartite system of Committees. The Quadripartite Committee offers Parliament an innovative and useful case study of how its scrutiny of government might be improved. Changes in the scrutiny of export controls, comes at a time when there is a re-organization of Customs and Inland Revenue services. The United Kingdom's assumption of the presidency of the Group of Eight also offers opportunities to provide a global system of regulatory control coupled to the growing likelihood of a new International Arms Trade Treaty. The Export Control Act 2002 provides a fresh start to the system of export controls and has generated the expectation of the future strengthening of parliamentary accountability.

References

Blakeney, M. (2003) 'Export Controls in the United Kingdom', *International Trade Law and Regulation*, Vol. 9, No. 6.

Chester, D.N. and Wilson, F.M.G. (eds) (1968), *The Organization of British Central Government 1914–1964*, George Allen and Unwin, London.

Ewing, K.D. and Gearty, C.A. (2000), *The Struggle for Civil Liberties: Political Freedom and the Rule of Law in Britain 1914–1945*, Oxford University Press, Oxford.

Foreign and Commonwealth Office Press Release, 28 July 1997.

Hale, M. (1976), *Prerogatives of the King*, ed. D.E.C. Yale, Selden Society, London.

Isbister, R. and Kirkham, E. (2004), *An Independent Audit of the UK Government Reports on Strategic Export Controls for 2003 and the First Half of 2004*, Saferworld, London.

Lindsay Keir, D. (1948), *The Constitutional History of Modern Britain 1485–1937*, 3rd edn, Adam and Charles Black, London.

McEldowney, J.F. (1997), 'The Scott Report: Inquiries, Parliamentary and Government Control in Britain', *Democratization*, Vol. 4.

—— (2002), *Public* Law, 3rd edn, Sweet and Maxwell, London.

Natzler, D. and Hutton, M. (2005), 'Select Committee: Scrutiny a la Carte?', in P. Giddings (ed.), *The Future of Parliament?*, Macmillan, London.

Oakes, M. and Youngs, T. (2001), *The Export Control Bill*, House of Commons Research Paper 01/64.

R v. Blackledge and others [1996] 1 Cr. App. R. 326.

Rubin, G.R. (1994), *Private Property, Government Requisition and the Constitution 1914–1927*, The Hambledon Press, London.

Scott Report (1996), *Report of the Inquiry into the Export of Defence Equipment and Dual-Use Goods to Iraq and Related Prosecutions*, HC 115.

Smith, Michael, E. (2004), *Europe's Foreign and Security Policy*, Cambridge University Press, Cambridge.

Taylor, Claire (2003), 'UK Defence Procurement Policy', House of Commons Research Paper 03/78.

The Cheng Poh v. Public Prosecutor [1980] AC 458.

The Guardian, 21 July 2005.

United Kingdom (1998), *Strategic Export Controls White Paper*, Cmd 3989, July 1998.

—— (2000), *Strategic Export Controls: Further Report and Parliamentary Prior Scrutiny*, Quadripartite Committee, Session 1999–2000, HC 467.

—— (2001a), *Consultation on Draft Legislation: The Export Control and Non-Proliferation Bill*, Cmd 5091, March 2001.

—— (2001b), *Strategic Export Controls: Further Report and Parliamentary Prior Scrutiny*, Quadripartite Committee, Session 1999–2000, HC 225.

—— (2005), *Strategic Export Controls: HMG's Annual Report for 2003, Licensing Policy and Parliamentary Prior Scrutiny*, Quadripartite Committee, Session 2004–05, HC 145.

Wilcock v. Munckle [1951] 2 KB 844.

Notes

1. I am grateful to Sarah Davies, Clerk to the Quadripartite Committee for advice. Opinions expressed are my own and I am responsible for any errors.
2. Inquiry into the Export of Defence Equipment and Dual-Use Goods to Iraq and Related Prosecutions, chaired by Sir Richard Scott, 15 February 1996, hereinafter the Scott Inquiry. See McEldowney (1997, pp.135–56).
3. This is implied as a prerogative power of the Crown in the Customs (War Powers) Act 1915 and the Trading with the Enemy and Export of Prohibited Goods Act 1916.
4. Alfred Emmott (1858–1926), first Baron Emmott, Head of the War Trade Department from 1915 until 1919.
5. The National Registration Act 1939, the Prevention of Violence (Temporary Provisions) Act 1939, the Emergency Powers (Defence) Act 1939.
6. Emergency Powers (Defence) Act 1939, the Supplies and Services (Transitional Powers) Act 1945, Emergency Laws Transitional Provision Act 1946.
7. See: The Iran (Trading Sanctions) Order SI 1980 No. 737 and the Export of Goods (Control) (Iran Sanctions) Order SI 1980 No. 735.

8. Examples include the Defence Powers (Continuance) Order 1969.
9. Details may be found in the Scott Report (1996, vol. 1, paras. C.1.66–1.150).
10. DTI/256. 19746, 19748, 19754 (Scott Report 1996, vol. 1, paras. C1.66–1.150).
11. There is a general discussion in Oakes and Young (2001).
12. The debates covering the Code of Conduct may be found at H.C. Deb. 28 July 1997 c27w, and H.C. Deb. 16 June 1998, c193w.
13. *Strategic Export Controls Annual Reports*, 1997–current available from the DTI, MOD or FCO.
14. European Community (EC) Regulation 1334/200, in force from 2004. See Blakeney (2003).
15. 1968 Nuclear Non-Proliferation Treaty in force from 1970.
16. The departments are the Ministry of Defence, the Foreign and Commonwealth Office, the Department of Trade and Industry, the Department of International Development. See <www.fco.gov.uk/reports/strategicexportcontrols>.
17. Schedules 1 and 2 of the Export of Goods, Transfer of Technology and Provision of Technical Assistance (Control) Order 2003 and the EC Regulation 1334/2000 (20 June 2000).
18. Specifically delegated powers under the Export of Goods (Control) Order 1994, as amended, the Dual-Use Items (Export Control) (Regulations) 2000 under the European Communities Act 1972.
19. See the Export of Goods, Transfer of Technology and Provision of Technical Assistance (Control) (Amendment) Order 2005, SI 2005, No. 468. The Trade in Goods (Control) (Amendment) Order 2005, SI 2005, No. 443, the Trade in Controlled Goods (Embargoes Destinations) (Amendment) Order 2005, SI 2005, No. 445.
20. Missile Technology Control Regime (MTCR) held its 19th plenary meeting in Seoul, 6–8 October 2004. There is also the International Code of Conduct Against Ballistic Missile Proliferation (ICOC) since 2002, set up at The Hague on 25 November 2002. The Australia Group is an informal network of countries intended to harmonize export licensing controls.
21. It was expected the review would be completed later in 2005.
22. The first report was published in July 1999 as the *First Joint Report: Strategic Export Controls 2000. Fifth, Third, Second and Ninth Special Reports of the Defence, Foreign Affairs International Development and Trade and Industry Committees* HC 540 Session 1998–1999.
23. *Third, Second, Third and Fourth Reports of the Defence, Foreign Affairs, International Development and Trade and Industry Committees*, HC 225 Session 1999–2000. The government's response may be found at Cmd 4799.
24. *Eleventh, Seventh, Seventh and Eleventh Reports of the Defence, Foreign Affairs, International Development and Trade and Industry Committees*, HC 467 Session 1999–2000. The government's response is at Cmd 4872.
25. *House of Commons Defence, Foreign Affairs, International Development and Trade and Industry Committees Strategic Export Controls Second Joint Report for 2002–3*, HC 474 Session 2002–3.
26. During 2003–4, the export control team had 166 staff, the number of which is expected to fall to 136 by 31 March 2005 and 109 by 31 March 2006. See United Kingdom (2005, para. 70).
27. Similar concerns are set out in the Saferworld audit report: (Isbister and Kirkham 2004).
28. Examples include Brazil, Colombia, Egypt, Iraq, Jamaica, Jordan, Kenya and many more.

Chapter 8

The 11th Commandment?

Bent L. Andersen

Assistant Director, Danish Agency for the Development of Trade and Industry, Ministry of Economic and Business Affairs, Denmark

Maja S. Thagaard

Danish Agency for the Development of Trade and Industry, Ministry of Economic and Business Affairs, Denmark[1]

Introduction

'*Thou shalt not contribute to the proliferation of weapons of mass destruction.*'

The purpose of export control is simple and clear. Being self-evident and universal the message almost has the characteristics of a potential new 11th commandment.

However, the international system of export controls consists of a complex nexus of interrelated international treaties, organizations and multilateral export control regimes, and the scope is increasing. In fact, only a few people outside the narrow circles of government officials, who actively participate in international meetings and negotiations with regard to export control, fully understand the system. Furthermore it is often unclear to companies when there is a risk of proliferation and how the export control systems work.

The complexity of the system thus represents a fundamental challenge to the future effectiveness of export controls. Creating a simpler, more harmonized, transparent and credible export control system should therefore be put high on the international agenda to ensure efficient export controls, which all countries agree are crucial for future security.

The need for a thorough discussion on the complexity of the system is also underlined by another dilemma. On the one hand, politicians ask for more control in responding to the threat from terror attacks, while on the other hand, they also ask for removal of administrative burdens and trade barriers in responding to the pressure from globalization.

Since the September 11 terrorist attacks in New York and Washington in 2001, international focus on export controls as a means to combat the proliferation of weapons of mass destruction (WMD) has increased dramatically. The terror attacks in Madrid in 2004 and London in 2005 clearly underlined the threat from terror attacks in western countries and reminded us that the use of WMD in terror actions could have unprecedented consequences.

At the same time, the globalization of trade and rapidly growing technological developments pose significant challenges to all western countries where the development of high tech products, research and technology, innovation and open global markets are seen as decisive means to ensure future growth and wealth in the competition against upcoming competitors from China and other developing economies.

The international export control system thus exists in a difficult balance between security policy considerations and commercial interests. It must develop efficient controls without hampering legitimate trade and without drowning international high technology trade, research and development in a huge and inefficient bureaucracy.

To ensure efficient control before an export takes place, close cooperation with the companies involved is vital. With the emergence of the internet, it is possible to transfer sensitive technology anywhere with a click of the mouse. Traditional border control is no longer sufficient and has to be supplemented by a close cooperation with the companies who must apply internal compliance systems.

This is also an immense challenge because such cooperation will only be efficient if the system is credible to companies, offering clear rules, easy procedures and reasonable lists of products and technologies under control. The development of Corporate Social Responsibility policies in multinational companies will, together with the risk of being exposed in the world media overnight if something goes wrong, be helpful in fostering cooperation with industry. However, tough penalty measures, spot checks, audits and control visits are needed to emphasize the seriousness of export controls.

This chapter offers an insight into the challenges for the international export control system, seen in a practical perspective from a small administration in a small state, building on experiences from international cooperation and national implementation. The focus will be on the national implementation of international rules and regulations, the handling of applications for export licences, and enforcement and compliance.

It is shown here that the overall effectiveness of export controls is compromised by the complexity of the system and huge divergences in national implementation and administration of regime guidelines. This chapter also points at the lengthy decision-making processes, lack of coordination and a built-in reluctance towards fundamental reforms of the existing system as major challenges.

The chapter concludes that the effectiveness of the existing system of export controls could be enhanced significantly, but this calls for the ability and willingness of member states to think outside of the box with respect to the future organization of international cooperation in export controls.

The Complex Global System of Export Controls

The global system of export controls is very complex. It is built on three non-proliferation treaties: the Nuclear Non-proliferation Treaty (NPT), the Biological and Toxin Weapons Convention (BTWC) and the Chemical Weapons Convention (CWC), which have been negotiated and adopted within the framework of the United Nations (UN).

The multilateral export control regimes, the Nuclear Suppliers Group (NSG), the Missile Technology Control Regime (MTCR), the Australia Group (AG) and the Wassenaar Arrangement (WA), supplement the non-proliferation treaties by controlling and monitoring the transfers of sensitive items, which can be used in relation to WMD.

In addition, UN Security Council Resolution 1540 in 2004 imposed a legal obligation on all states to control the export of weapons of mass destruction, their delivery systems and related items.

All together, the three treaties, UN Security Council Resolution 1540, a number of implementing organizations, the four export control regimes and new initiatives such as the Proliferation Security Initiative and the expected changes in the Convention for the Suppression of Unlawful Acts against the Safety of Maritime Navigation, the international system of non-proliferation becomes a very complex nexus of legally binding rules, politically binding regulations, guidelines, norms and principles (see Figure 8.1).

On the basis of this, each nation must implement national legislation and set up national administration to meet all the international requirements. As each country has its own special traditions and administrative systems, this is done in numerous different ways, making it a jungle for multinational companies to manage export control. The risk of creating loopholes and trade distortions is clear.

In the European Union (EU), the formal export control measures decided in the export control regimes are implemented in EU Regulation 1334/2000, setting up a Community regime for the control of exports of dual-use items and technology. But even between the 25 member states, a peer review in 2004 showed that the practical implementation differs considerably despite close cooperation over many years.

The export control regimes are politically binding multilateral arrangements, which, for example:

- establish lists of critical products and technologies, which requires an export licence;
- adopts guidelines with regard to administrative procedures, for example procedures for handling licence applications;
- shares information on critical end-users, WMD-programmes, routes of proliferation and procurement trends.

As in most international organizations with regard to multilateral treaties, all decisions in the export control regimes have to be adopted by consensus. This implies a long decision-making process which impedes adjustments necessary for security policy reasons. Also, the fact that changes in the control list may cause changes in national legislation slows down the process.

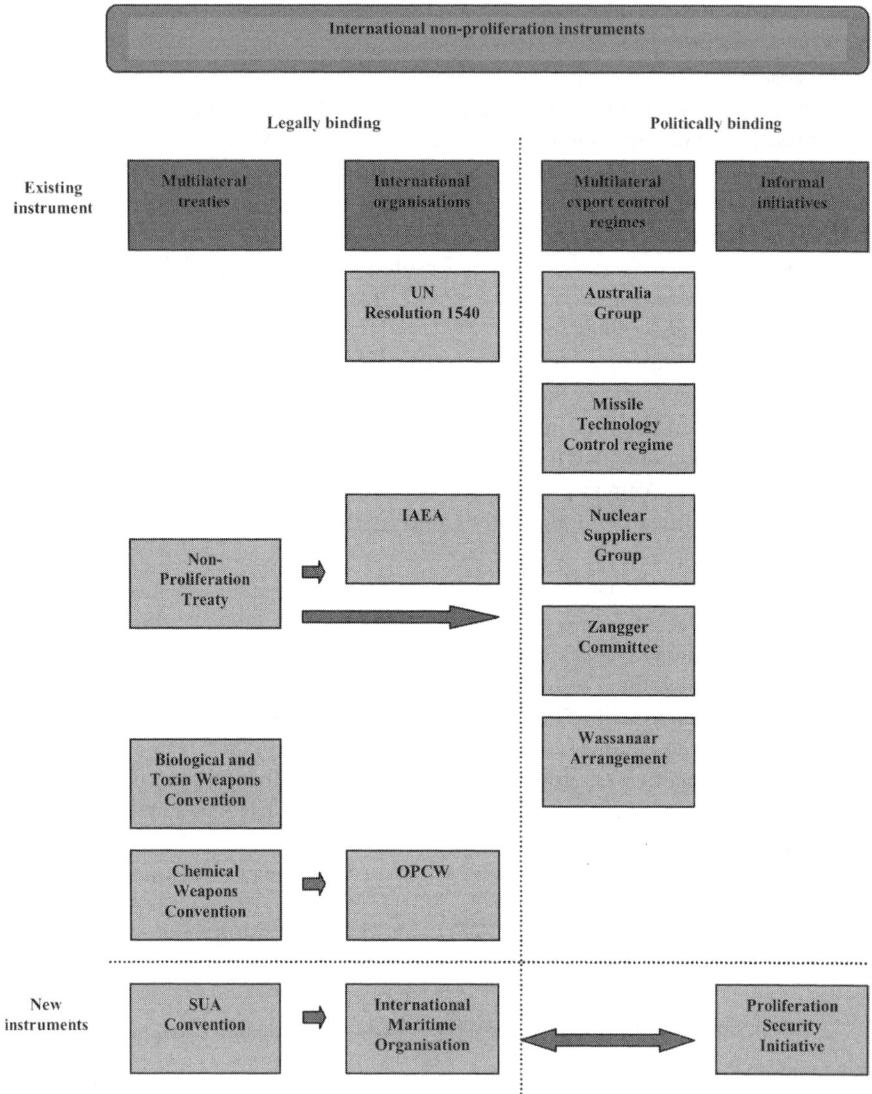

Figure 8.1 International Instruments Dealing with Export Control

This is one of the reasons why there is an increasing use of the less binding 'guidelines' and 'statements of understanding', which are more likely to be accepted by participating states because they are not obliged to implement them nationally, and accession to the agreements themselves often can take place on a purely administrative basis without the need to involve national legislatures. On the other hand, the request for annual reports on implementation puts pressure on participating states and has proven to be an efficient tool to pave the way for gradual harmonization and strengthening of controls.

As a safeguard against proliferation of WMD, the export control system is only as strong as its weakest link. In the current system, there is a risk that small states with small administrations will become the weaker links because it is a difficult and tremendous task to follow all discussions in the various organizations and regimes and keep track of all new obligations which must be implemented nationally. The number of international meetings, the amount of necessary intelligence information, the national implementation of rules and the necessary national administrative set-up to handle applications, enforcement, information and the dialogue with industry is the same, no matter the size of the country and no matter the number of applications. Therefore, in small countries, this places a heavy burden on the few officials dealing with export control. Just covering relevant meetings in the four export control regimes is overwhelming for these countries.

Seen from the perspective of the many small states, the call for simplicity, harmonization and coordination in the field of export controls is a logical next step in ensuring the effectiveness of the system.

The Danish Approach to Export Controls

Denmark is a small country with fewer than six million inhabitants, and although Denmark has always had a considerably large proportion of international trade, the annual number of licences related to dual-use exports does not exceed 200.

The Danish political basis for export control reflects the dilemmas mentioned in the introduction. A clear positive position towards open international trade, close international cooperation and the removal of trade barriers as a means to cope with globalization. At the same time, Denmark has a strong commitment in working towards international security and stability – with military presence in the Balkans, Afghanistan and Iraq, and now also as a member of the UN Security Council.

Although Denmark is a small country, the administration of export controls involves a great number of government agencies; including the Ministry of Foreign Affairs (political issues), the Ministry of Justice (export of weapons), the Ministry of Defence (expertise), the Ministry of Tax and Customs (enforcement), the Ministry of Science and Technology (expertise), the National Agency for Enterprise and Construction (NAEC) under the Ministry for Economic and Business Affairs (export of dual-use products), the Intelligence Services (intelligence information), the government institutions which are part of the national preparedness (expertise) and the Federation of Danish Industries.

However, only a very limited number of people in each agency (often one or two) are devoted to the task of export controls, and export control has a marginal placing in all institutions. As a consequence, efficient national cooperation within the Export Control Advisory Group chaired by the National Agency for Enterprise and Construction plays an important role for the daily personal coordination between all involved Danish officials. In international export control, this close personal cooperation is often an advantage compared to big countries, where coordination takes a lot of resources.

The legislative basis of Danish export control with dual-use items is the EU Regulation 1334/2000.[2] The regulation determines rules for export of dual-use items which require a licence to be exported from the territory of the European Community. These controlled items are listed in an annex to Regulation 1334/2000. The annex is a consolidated list of the four regime control lists. It is updated on a yearly basis in order to implement decisions adopted with regard to controlled items in the export control regimes. In accordance with the so-called 'catch-all' clause of Regulation 1334/2000, a licence is also required for export of non-listed items if there is a concrete risk that the items in question are determined for use in relation to WMD. Regulation 1334/2000 is supplemented by national legislation, which determines administrative procedures and sets up penalties for violation of the export control rules. The maximum penalty is imprisonment for no more than six years.

Besides representing national interests in international negotiations within the export control regimes and other international organs which deal with the issue, the tasks related to maintaining a national system of export controls are mainly:

- national implementation of international rules and regulations;
- handling of applications for export licences;
- enforcement and compliance.

National Implementation of International Rules and Guidelines

When a decision with regard to export control has been adopted in one of the four international regimes, each member state has to ensure national implementation. The decentralized nature of international export controls means that national implementation is complex. In Denmark, the legally binding international non-proliferation treaties are implemented in national legislation under the Ministry of Foreign Affairs. The lists of controlled dual-use items established in the export controls regimes are implemented through EU legislation and legislation under the Ministry of Economic and Business Affairs. Export of weapons is legislated by the Ministry of Justice. Best practice guidelines and statements of understanding that intend to guide member states' behaviour are usually implemented in the administrative procedures and practices.

In recent years, the number of best practice guidelines and statements of understanding adopted in the international regimes has been increasing. Within the AG, the guidelines for the transfer of sensitive chemical and biological items have been revised to include transit and trans-shipment controls in the recipient state as a criterion for supply. Similar considerations have taken place within the MTCR. In the WA examples of recently adopted statements of understanding are the statement of understanding with regard to arms brokerage, and statement of understanding on control of non-listed items.

Guidelines and statements seem to be an effective way to affect member states' behaviour in relation to export controls. As they are not obligatory for participating states and they can often be implemented on an administrative basis, it is much easier to agree on these. Nonetheless, the requirements to report on the progress of national implementation will encourage implementation in each member state. It seems to be a useful alternative way of ensuring a more harmonized and efficient export control by finding practical solutions instead of having endless theoretical discussions on formal rules.

Even if there is some useful progress, it is still a fact that the implementation of best practice guidelines and statements of understanding varies significantly in individual member states, just like the general implementation of export control. Presumably the biggest differences occur in relation to 'catch all'.

Consequently, export control cases which in principle are similar, will be handled differently in individual participating states. On the one hand, there is a risk that different national practices will create loopholes in the system of export controls. This could give potential proliferators the opportunity of licence shopping. That is, seeking to procure the same item in several countries, hoping that at least one will issue a licence. On the other hand, differences in national implementation can create trade distortions for industry when systems differ and countries have differing evaluations of commercial and security policy aspects. The Danish experience is that 'catch all' cases especially are evaluated very differently and that cases, which would result in denials in Denmark, might not even require a licence in other countries.

The implementation of export control regulation deriving from the four export control regimes is complicated by the fact that the same issues are discussed in all four regimes but result in different decisions.

Although the regimes share a common goal of non-proliferation of WMD and are often therefore faced with the same external challenges, there is little formal coordination of the work agenda between the regimes. Similar issues are often discussed more or less simultaneously in several regimes. This is both unnecessarily resource demanding and inconsistent, often leading to different decisions which means that national administrations have to handle several sets of procedural guidelines dealing with the same issue. One example is the discussions on transit and trans-shipment controls which have taken place in the framework of the AG, the MTCR and the WA.

Another example of different solutions reached among the four regimes is the discussion of 'catch-all'. Due to continued technological developments, the regime control lists are not exhaustive lists of all civilian items which could be used for military purposes. The overall principle of 'catch-all' is to ensure that member states have the capacity to restrict trade in *non-listed* dual-use items if the items are intended for military use in one respect or another. This is done by authorizing governments to require a licence for the export of non-listed items under certain circumstances. Typically, the implementation of the 'catch-all' principle will require adoption of new legislation.

Table 8.1 'Catch-all' Clauses in the Four Regimes

Regime	Adoption	Scope	End-use	A licence is required
AG	2002	All states	Use in connection with chemical or biological weapons activities	(a) If the exporter is informed by the authorities that a licence is required; or (b) if the exporter is aware that the non-listed items are intended to contribute to chemical or biological weapons activities
NSG	2004	Not specified	Use in connection with a 'nuclear explosive activity'	Not specified
MTCR[3]	–	–	–	–
WA	2003	Destinations subject to arms embargos	Military end-use	(a) If the destination is subject to arms embargos; or (b) if the exporter is aware that the products are intended for military end-use

As indicated in Table 8.1, the discussion of 'catch-all' has led to different results in the four regimes, both with regard to the scope of the 'catch-all' clause, the intended end-use and the conditions under which a licence is required. Furthermore, during implementation of the different 'catch-all' clauses, it has become apparent that participating states administer the 'catch-all' clauses very differently. In some states, 'catch-all' only applies if the government has enjoined the exporter to apply for an export licence. In other states, as in Denmark, the exporter has to be personally aware of 'catch-all'. If the exporter has grounds for suspecting that an export of a non-listed item is intended for uses other than civilian uses, the exporter should contact the authorities, who will decide whether a licence is required. This means the exporter can be prosecuted if the authorities can prove that the exporter prior to the export had ground for suspecting that the item was intended for illegal use.

While acknowledging that the existing regimes function on the basis of their respective traditions and institutional dynamics, merit could be gained from a more formalized coordination between the regimes. The system of export controls as such would benefit from a more focused and coordinated effort while, at the same time, national administration would be more effective.

Handling Applications for Export Licences

On average, Denmark reviews approximately 200 applications for export licences every year. The relatively small number of applications reflects the fact that Denmark is a small state, but also that many licences are open individual licences which are valid for exports of specified products for specified markets for two years. In comparison, the United States Bureau of Industry and Security (BIS) reviewed more than 12,000 licence applications in 2003.[4] The number of annual licences also exceeds well over 10,000 for countries such as the United Kingdom and Germany.

When a Danish exporter wishes to export an item which is subject to export control, either because it appears on the list of controlled items contained in Annex I of the EU Regulation 1334/2000 or because 'catch-all' applies, an application for a licence is send to the NAEC. The decision on whether to issue a licence or deny the export is based on national discretion, but considered with reference to:

- the lists of controlled items;
- technical specifications of the items;
- intelligence information.

The Lists of Controlled Items

Export control is based on international lists of items which can only be exported from the territory of the member state if a licence has been issued by the national authorities. The listed items are items which are developed and produced for civil purposes and which, if they fall into the 'wrong hands', can be used in relation to one of the three categories of WMD, missiles or conventional weapons. Each of the four international export control regimes maintains its own list (see Table 8.2).

The AG list consists of biological agents, chemical substances and production equipment which can be used in relation to chemical or biological weapons. The NSG list consists of nuclear related materials and equipment which can be used in relation to nuclear weapons. The MTCR list consists of items which can be used in relation to missiles. The WA dual-use list is related to the WA munitions lists. The munitions lists control trade in conventional weapons. The WA dual-use list consists of dual-use items which can be used in the development or production of an item from the WA munitions list.

As with all other decisions adopted in the regimes, decisions to change the control lists have to be adopted by consensus. But in contrast to statements of understanding and best practice guidelines, which are only subject to implementation in administrative procedures, decisions to change the control lists will often have to be included in the national legislation of member states. This means that the process of agreeing to changes in the control lists can be lengthy.

Table 8.2 The Regime Control Lists

Regime	Controlled items	Proliferation risk
AG	• Biological agents (e.g. yellow fever virus) • Chemical substances (e.g. ricin) • Production equipment (e.g. specially designed pumps)	Chemical and biological weapons
MTCR	• Products and technologies that can be used in relation to missiles (e.g. specially designed navigation equipment)	Missiles
NSG	• Materials, products and technologies that can be used in relation to nuclear weapons (e.g. uranium isotope separation equipment)	Nuclear weapons
WA (Dual-use list)	• Products and technologies that can be used in the development or production of an item on the WA munitions list (e.g. specially designed optical fibres)	Conventional weapons

According to individually adopted procedures and criteria, each of the four control lists is updated yearly. This is done on the basis of national proposals to either add new items to the lists or – even though more seldom – to remove existing items from the lists. In a world where rapid technological development and globalization of trade is a fact of life, it is vital that the control regimes can respond without delay to the development of new products and technologies that pose a risk in relation to the spread of WMD. At the same time, it is important that items which, due to technological development, have become irrelevant in the context of export control because they have been replaced by new technologies, are removed from the lists. If not, the continued existence of such 'dead-wood' on the control lists will place unnecessary economic and administrative burdens on both national administrations and industry.

The principle of continuous updating of the lists is crucial for the overall effectiveness and credibility of the international system of export controls. However, the current practice leaves room for improvement, especially because the process is very slow and the attitude of participating states is extremely conservative. One possible way forward could be to undertake an extraordinary list review in each of the four regimes with a view to removing the 'dead-wood' of the list once and for all, and to focus controls on the most sensitive items. In addition, action could be directed towards ensuring that sensitive items added to the control lists in the future are made subject to an automatic review, for example five years after they have been included on the lists. By doing this, all items on the control lists would be reviewed automatically, independent of the capability of national authorities to put forward proposals.

Technical Specifications of the Items

The decision on whether an item is covered by export control because it is either listed on one of the four control lists or because it is covered by the 'catch-all' provisions is not an easy task. Technical evaluation of dual-use items in relation to export controls requires state-of-the-art technical knowledge as well as a thorough understanding of export controls in general and the control lists in particular.

The task of evaluating technical specifications of dual-use items requires technical expertise in a wide range of technical issues, including chemical substances, human pathogens, laser equipment, telecommunications equipment and encryption software. The small number of Danish licence applications each year render it impossible to establish a team of technical experts dedicated solely to this task. Instead the task is accomplished by technical experts from, for example, the Ministry of Defence, who are primarily assigned to other responsibilities. Accelerating technological development, combined with an increased level of research and development taking place in the private sphere outside the circles of military research institutions, exacerbates the challenges met by the technical experts, who have to establish whether an item is covered by export control. The fact that different member states often come to different conclusions when evaluating the same item only underscores this point. The difference in technical evaluations creates unwanted trade distortions. In small states, the limited number of applications means that the technical experts seldom get into a routine in dealing with export controls. This can cause delays in the application process and there is a risk of ambiguous evaluations with possible disadvantages for the exporter, especially in countries like Denmark where security concerns will be given priority in doubtful cases.

The difficulty in maintaining state-of-the-art expertise in all the areas of the control lists and the problem of national discrepancies in technical evaluations challenge the effectiveness of the export control system. This could be remedied by setting up an international group of experts who could assist member states in their technical evaluations. The appointed persons could serve as impartial technical experts, lending their support at the request of member states. In cases of different national evaluations, member states could request a third opinion from the group of technical experts. Furthermore, the group of international experts could be involved in the process of reviewing and updating the control lists. The group could act informally through more or less formalized networks of national experts, or as a formal group established as a secretariat. The EU has, in 2005, established a voluntary 'pool of experts' from different member states to help, in particular, the many small countries within the EU to make technical evaluations.

Intelligence Information

Information on proliferation trends, front companies, critical end-users and developments of illegal WMD-programmes is crucial to ensuring that dual-use items are only exported for peaceful purposes.

The decision on whether to issue a licence or to deny an export is made after careful consideration of intelligence information on these issues. In this respect, the regimes serve as very important fora for information exchange between participating states. Besides informal information exchange on trends of proliferation and so on, the regimes have also set up formal procedures for exchanging information on licence decisions, primarily with respect to denials.

The exchange of information on licence decisions serves several purposes. One is to exclude the possibility of licence shopping by potential proliferators, who might procure the same item in several countries, hoping that at least one will issue a licence. Another is to avoid one member state unintentionally 'undercutting' a licence decision taken in another member state, by allowing the export of an item to an end-user which has been denied in another member state. Besides closing a potential loophole in the system of export control, the purpose of the 'no undercut' policy is to ensure a level playing field for industry.

Table 8.3 Procedures for Exchanging Information on Licence Decisions

Regime	AG	MTCR	NSG	WA
Notification of denials	Yes	Yes	Yes	Yes
Notification on licences	No	No	No	Yes (only with regard to items on the very sensitive list)
Deadline for reporting	No	No	No	Yes (no later than 60 days, but only for items on the very sensitive list)
Electronic submission	No	No	Yes	Yes

Even though all four regimes have adopted procedures for exchange of information with regard to exports (see Table 8.3), great discrepancies in these procedures hamper the overall effectiveness of the information exchange. Only one regime, the WA, has adopted procedures for exchanging information on approved exports and in this regime, the information on approved exports is restricted to licences for items on the 'very sensitive' list. The absence of information sharing on approved exports in the other regimes means that is it difficult for member states to get the full picture when reviewing an application for a licence. Small countries with only few licence applications are particularly dependent on knowledge about the licence decisions of other countries.

In principle, member states are expected to report denials on export licences without delay within all the regimes. But with the exception of the WA, no regime has actually set deadlines for reporting of denials, and the deadlines within the WA only apply to the very sensitive dual-use items. Two of the regimes, the NSG and the WA, have established information systems which make it possible for member states to submit their denial notifications electronically. Within the AG and the MTCR, denial notifications are distributed to member states in hard copy through the chairs of the regimes. The absence of deadlines for reporting information on denials and the practice of submitting the data in hard copy mean that, often, the exchange of information is slow and incomplete. This affects the full and effective implementation of the 'no undercut' policy, because, in practice, it is difficult to establish whether a potential export actually involves a transaction which has been denied by another member state. Also the long lag between the time when a denial is issued in one member state and the time this information is received in the other member states weakens the system. In combination with increased globalization of trade, this makes the current system of information exchange unsuited to guaranteeing the absence of licence shopping and the establishment of an effective 'no undercut' policy.

The adoption of one set of guidelines for all the regimes for exchanging information on licence decisions would make the task of implementing these more comprehensible for each member state. With the WA procedures as a model, this new set of guidelines should include deadlines for the submission of reports on licence decisions. Furthermore, consideration should be given to extending the information to include information on approved licences. Finally, the establishment of one central electronic information system with a central database of licence information and some intelligence information could replace national databases. This would be much more cost-effective for member states, while at the same time, reducing the risk of error in the data in different national databases which have been built on the basis of information from the regimes.

Enforcement and Compliance

Border control is a central part of export control. However, in recent years, it has become apparent that traditional border control is no longer sufficient to ensure the enforcement of export controls. The growing number of intangible transfers (ITT), that is, electronic transfer of controlled knowledge and software, which are virtually impossible for authorities to control, only underscores this point. This means that cooperation with industry is a precondition for effective enforcement of and compliance with export control regulations.

The universal adherence to the three non-proliferation treaties indicates that the norm against WMD is widespread. The purpose of export control is evident to most companies. No company wishes to be connected with the proliferation of any of these categories of deadly weapons or their means of delivery. In particular, no company wants to be exposed in the media worldwide overnight if there is any doubt whether or not export control regulations are broken and a company has contributed to the proliferation of WMD. The media does not wait for evidence and a fair trial. So if a company does not have a proper answer at hand, the image of the company will be damaged for many years, even if there has been no violation of export control regulations.

However, in order to comply with export control, industry has to be aware of the rules. The Danish experience from implementing export controls is that companies producing dual-use items are not sufficiently aware of export controls. The hard core of 100–200 companies regularly applying for licences and receiving information and control visits from the NAEC know the system, although the knowledge is often held by a few people, making compliance vulnerable to personnel changes in the company. But outside this hard core, another approximately 2,000 Danish companies, which may apply for licences from time to time, are considered not to have sufficient knowledge of export control. Targeted information from the NAEC, the intelligence services, the ministry of Foreign Affairs and the Federation of Danish Industries generally resolves the problem in actual cases, but knowledge of 10 per cent of the companies potentially involved could be improved.

One reason for lack of knowledge is simply that companies are not familiar with the potential WMD-use of their products which, as far as the companies are concerned, have been produced for customers they trust and for civilian purposes only. This means that national administrations are faced with an important challenge of informing their industry about rules and risks in order to ensure compliance.

It is often said that the complex nature of export controls means that few people outside the narrow circles of government officials, who participate actively in regime meetings and negotiations, fully understand the system. The need to inform industry about the rules as a means of enforcement is widely recognized within the regimes. But so far, this task has primarily been left to each member state to undertake nationally.

However, the companies which have to comply with the rules often have activities beyond the borders of each member states and operate worldwide. It could be argued that coordinated information would be beneficial, perhaps within the regimes. More attention could be given to developing the regime websites and holding information meetings and seminars with the participation of industry representatives and organizations representing industry. This would raise awareness of the non-proliferation purpose of export controls and give valid input to future non-proliferation initiatives in the regimes.

Much more important though is the extension of internal compliance programmes in companies which will enable them to comply with day-to-day export control regulations. Numerous applications and time spent waiting for answers from the authorities could be avoided if compliance programmes combined with control visits (audits) from the authorities can result in general licences covering specific products to specific customers, for example, for two years. Companies will of course always have to contact the authorities in very sensitive cases.

Compliance programmes are very similar to, for example, quality control management or environment control systems, and consist of a number of elements which should be developed and implemented in the company, for example:

- issuing an export control policy by the management (the CEO);
- setting up an export control organization and appointing employees responsible for enforcement of export control (for example, educating employees, updating information from authorities, advising on applications);
- procedures for products and customers of proliferation concern;
- internal and external audits (control visits by authorities).

There are at present no international standards for international compliance programmes, but the idea is worth pursuing for several reasons. First, the number of intangible transfers, where internal control is decisive, is growing. Secondly, the establishment of international standards for internal compliance would harmonize the implementation of the regime guidelines and agreements. Thirdly, if multinational companies could comply with export controls in several countries by implementing one international internal compliance programme instead of having to familiarize themselves with a number of different sets of national rules and procedures, 'in house' enforcement export controls would be easier and more efficient. Finally, widespread implementation of international compliance programmes would surely raise awareness of export controls in general.

Conclusion

The clear and simple message of export controls – 'thou shalt not contribute to the proliferation of WMD' – has materialized in a very complex system of international treaties, organizations, rules and regulations. This hampers the effectiveness of the system, not least because it is difficult for industry to understand the rules to which they have to comply. Also, the complex system and the huge differences in national implementation create trade distortions and loopholes.

In this chapter, we have identified a number of problem areas in the present export control system where reforms or improvements should be considered for carrying out more efficient control. To be successful, this control should, at the same time, be credible to industry, with which close cooperation is needed, and create a level playing field across increasingly integrated markets.

Individually, the regimes are striving to adapt to changes in the international context. Progress is achieved, but so far only slowly by a step-by-step approach which complicates the system of export control even more.

The need to reconsider reforming the system of export control is obvious. But in practical terms, reform is very difficult to carry out, because it involves many countries and touches upon sensitive questions, such as national competence in security policy areas, confidential intelligence information and commercial interests in high technology products. In this respect, the implementation of UN Security Council Resolution 1540 offers an opportunity to rethink the entire organization of international cooperation in export controls.

The future effectiveness of export controls could be enhanced significantly. But this requires capacity and willingness among participating states to think outside the box with respect to the future organization of international export controls.

Irrespective of what kind of scenario is considered, cooperation between industry and the authorities is crucial for effective export controls. In the global industry with extensive use of technology transfers on the internet, the understanding and active support of industry and implementation of internal compliance systems is absolutely necessary for an efficient export control system. At the same time, the relationship is delicate, because it requires that the enterprises balance immediate commercial interests and security policy considerations which might not be clear and which traditionally have been the responsibility of the authorities. It is not impossible, though, because companies fear being exposed in the international media and having their image ruined for years because of dubious exports. But it has to be constantly supported by, on the one hand, severe penalty clauses, control visits, spot checks and awareness campaigns to underscore the importance of export controls, and, on the other hand, transparency and simple, harmonized rules in order to ensure credibility and support from industry.

Notes

1. The views expressed are solely those of the authors. They do not necessarily represent the policy of the Government of Denmark.
2. Council Regulation (EC) no 1334/2000 setting up a Community regime for the control of exports of dual-use items and technology.
3. Within MTCR no common 'catch-all' clause has been adopted. In 1999 member states agreed to encourage when appropriate the implementation of national measures to prevent exports of sensitive non-listed items if they are destined for missiles capable of carrying WMD.
4. Bureau of Industry and Security, *Annual Report Fiscal Year 2003* < www.bxa.doc.gov/News/2004/03AnnualRept/index.htm#Chap2>.

Chapter 9

A Regional Export Control Regime in East Asia: From No Regime to a Soft Regime

Takehiko Yamamoto
Professor, School of Political Science and Economics, University of Waseda

Introduction

It is no exaggeration to say that East Asia is nowadays the most vibrant region in the world. This does not mean, however, that it is an established market in safe hands. Its diverse conditions ironically make it more vivacious and unstable simultaneously. It is also the case that strategic circumstances in East Asia are significantly influenced by changes in United States foreign policy, mainly due to the residual effects of the Cold War in the region. US foreign policy has perhaps been rather more impulsive since President George W. Bush took office for his first term in 2001. The George W. Bush administration recognizes, for example, China as a 'strategic competitor', changing from the 'constructive engagement' stance that the Clinton administration took from its inauguration in 1993. Moreover, the Bush administration's attitudes towards North Korea are even more hawkish and uncompromising than the Clinton administration. Most state actors, if not all, in the region are in agreement that the multilateral non-proliferation export control regimes related to weapons of mass destruction (WMD), such as the Nuclear Suppliers Group (NSG), Missile Technology Control Regime (MTCR), Australia Group (AG) and the Wassenaar Arrangement (WA), ban the transfer of sensitive dual-use goods and technologies to North Korea. Particularly after September 11 2001, the United States decided to strengthen the postures of export controls, and other countries, more or less, also agreed to do so in some way. The Proliferation Security Initiative (PSI) and the Container Security Initiative (CSI) are cases in point. It will be herein examined whether these initiatives contribute to the bringing about of a *de facto* regional regime of export controls in East Asia. Japan, one of the major actors in the region, has actively taken part in creating a market-led trading system in this region in the past several decades. Now, questions of whether and how Japan would manage a regional institution-oriented export control regime should also be scrutinized.

This chapter consists of four sections. First, the theoretical basis for analyses of regional dynamics of multilateral export controls in East Asia will be discussed from three levels of analyses in international relations (IR) theories. Second, geo-strategic interactions among major actors in East Asia will be analysed. In particular, changes in patterns of interactions after the end of the Cold War will be focused upon. Third, functional and structural characteristics of an emerging export control system, as well as a possible 'soft regime' of export control in East Asia will be discussed from various perspectives. Fourth, the export control policies adopted and practised by both the Japanese government and business community will be described briefly under the assumption that Japan has played a significant role in strengthening the multilateral regimes of export controls since its joining the Coordinating Committee of Export Control against the Communist countries (COCOM) in 1952, and also has a pivotal position in making a regional export control regime in East Asia.

Theoretical Framework for Analysis

It seems that the dynamics of constructing a regional export control regime has theoretical connotations based on political realism, neoliberal institutionalism and social constructivism. The concept of export controls firstly implies the momentum of power politics, as well shown in the 44-year-long COCOM embargo against the Communist bloc, in the context of the Cold War. The existing WMD-related export control regimes and the WA today function similarly and therefore could be understood in the same vein. These regimes, at the same time, are interlinked as multi-dimensional institutions on the basis of a gentlemen's agreement. The common norms of non-proliferation have been formulated among the members during the process of intertwining these multi-dimensional institutions. Moreover, a sense of security identities has been constructed among them. It is safe to say, in this way, that these three schools of thought have theoretical relevance in examining and analysing the concerns and problems of export controls at both global and regional levels.

COCOM was the institutional bedrock for economic warfare that the United States designed to maintain the technological advantages of the West against the Soviet-led Communist bloc, under the so-called 'containment' strategy during the Cold War (Mastanduno 1992; Cupitt 2000). Controlled items in the COCOM regime, therefore, covered a wide range of dual-use high-tech goods and technologies for its original purposes. However, the purpose of the 'containment' strategy of the West changed in the wake of the split in the Communist bloc, especially since the early 1980s. At this time, the Reagan administration eased drastically the ban on dual-use goods and technologies to China for the reason of militarily competitive strategy against the former Soviet Union. When we look back on the stringent export control strategy pursued against China during and after the Korean War, such changes in targeted embargo policy illustrate well the awful aspect of power politics in export controls. This is the reason why the realist paradigm of international relations has, to a considerable degree, relevance in the analysis of export control issues.

Meanwhile, under the COCOM regime, there had often been, legally or illegally, flows of sensitive goods and technologies to the Communist bloc. As shown in the 'pipeline sanction' against western European countries in 1982 as well as the 'Toshiba sanction' in 1987 by the Reagan administration, sanctions diplomacy within the COCOM regime had been practised by interested state actors in the model of a 'prisoner's dilemma'. As a result of regime members' exchange of economic sanctions and retaliations against each other, the states concerned had learned the effect and significance of long-standing interests in abiding by norms and rules of economic containment. In other words, as neoliberal institutionalists argue, a number of lessons were learned from the synergistic effects of the 'shadow of the future'; that is, the long-term interests of cooperation in terms of embargos against common security threats, rather than short-term interests gained by defection from a regime's norms and rules (Martin 1992). It should be noted, therefore, that the neoliberal paradigm of international relations also has theoretical relevance for the analysis of export control issues.

With the ending of the Cold War, former COCOM members, along with some former targeted states (Russia, East European countries) agreed on the establishment of a new international export control regime, the WA. 'The WA was designed to promote transparency, exchange of views and information and greater responsibility in transfers of conventional arms and dual-use goods and technologies, thus preventing destabilizing accumulations'.[1] Although there has been much controversy over the controlled items among the members, the agreement was made so as 'to continue the use of the COCOM control lists as a basis for global export controls on a national level', adapting the concept of 'non-proliferation'.[2] The concept of non-proliferation originated from the Treaty on the Non-Proliferation of Nuclear Weapons (NPT). This treaty does not aim to abolish nuclear weapons. It endeavours rather to maintain a *fait accompli*, that is, the perpetual distinction between the haves and the have-nots of nuclear weapons. Since the WA adapts the concept of non-proliferation, its stance naturally intends to uphold the firm division between technologically advanced industrialized states and the others.[3] With regard to such WMD-related regimes, such as the NSG, the AG and the MTCR, their basic norms and rules are very similar to the WA, even if their individual control lists differ.

As is well known, the common norms of multilateral export control regimes have changed from Cold War containment theory to non-proliferation logic. At the same time, the target of security trade controls has expanded under this logic to non-state actors, such as terrorist groups, especially after September 11, so that the economic statecraft of every state concerned in terms of export controls becomes far more complicated and multifaceted than during the Cold War era. More to the point, in East Asia where many Cold War features still remain, export control policies tend to be based on security-oriented rationales, as political realists straightforwardly indicate. Meanwhile, confrontations between the communist states and others in the post Cold War era today are much more often economic than military in character, even in East

Asia. Economic interdependence among states in East Asia has grown rapidly, year after year, owing to the spread of neoliberal economic reforms and marketization dynamics in the East Asian countries. In fact, Japan's largest trading partner in the 2004 fiscal year was China, exceeding the US for the first time (Bloomberg 2005). This situation, *seirei keinetsu* ('politically cold, economically hot' in Japanese), might epitomize the type that neoliberal institutionalists could easily embrace, in the sense that incessant market-led relationships may be a guide to some kind of international institutions (Keohane and Nye 2000). According to Kenneth W. Abbot and Duncan Snidal, states are inclined to prioritize softer legalization at the beginning because it has many advantages, including easier achievability and strategic uncertainty (Abbot and Snidal, in Goldstein et al. 2000).

While the Sino–Japanese relationship maintains this level, however, it is of use to contemplate the possible forms of greater legalization in East Asia. As Judith Goldstein and Lisa L. Martin argue, increased legalization has changed the information environment and the nature of government obligations, which in turn has affected the pattern of mobilization of domestic interest groups on trade (Goldstein and Martin, in Goldstein et al. 2001). Those reciprocal links between international institutions and domestic actors are indeed what neoliberal institutionalists attempt to emphasize. After China's entry into the World Trade Organization (WTO) in 2000 and its subsequent efforts to expand the free trade agreement (FTA) network with the Association of South East Asian Nations (ASEAN) countries, a soft legalization of the regional FTA regime comes into view and eventually a possible scenario towards building an East Asian economic community might become a reality, especially after the Chenmai Declaration was adopted in the ASEAN plus 3 (China, Japan and the Republic of Korea) Summit in 2004.

In a similar context, not a hard legalization but a move towards constructing a 'soft regime' of export controls on an East Asian regional basis looks to be under way at Japan's initiative. The primary steps toward this end were taken in the late 1990s after India and Pakistan detonated nuclear bombs in 1998. Furthermore, the move has accelerated after September 11 since targets of non-proliferation expanded from the concerned states to non-state actors, such as terrorist groups, along with the scandal of a year-long programme of illicit transfers of nuclear materials and technologies by Pakistani nuclear scientist A.Q. Khan to some 'pariah' states, such as Libya and North Korea. In view of these developments, an urgent need to make a regional export control regime in East Asia has been recognized in Japanese government circles. Even though China has not yet become a full member of the global multilateral export control regimes, except the NSG which it joined in May 2004, it has already enacted a national export control law, has stated officially its intention to abide by international norms of non-proliferation including, albeit reluctantly, the Proliferation Security Initiative (PSI) and the Container Security Initiative (CSI), and has also conducted its own export control administration more rigorously than before September 11 (Yamamoto 2004). Other ASEAN countries and South Korea have taken the same steps towards the regionalization of an export control regime in a soft way toward the international legalization of the security trade, especially after the passing of United Nations (UN) Security Council Resolution 1540 in 2004. It goes without saying that this process of constructing a 'soft regime' of export controls on a regional scale remains weak and at a basic level as compared to other regions, such as the European Union. It should be said, however, that the process might possibly lead to soft legalization of non-proliferation norms on a region-wide basis if and when the states concerned can coordinate and harmonize their respective systems of export control in line with fundamental norms and rules of existing global export control regimes.

Social constructivists, to the same extent, highlight identity formation in shared security norms. ASEAN would typify an East Asian case (Buzan, Waever and de Wilde 1998; Buzan and Waever 2003). While maintaining much informality, the members of ASEAN have rather socially constructed some norms, typically the so-called 'ASEAN Way' which has facilitated confidence-building and succeeded in reducing frictions among them (Acharya 1998). On the one hand, ASEAN members have in common been concerned from the beginning about China's military dominance in the region, as partly illustrated by the territorial disputes over the Spratly and Paracel Islands. However, Japanese economic ascendancy in the region could be seen in a similar vein by the members. In spite of this sense of insecurity on the part of the ASEAN countries, as the regional security complex (RSC) theorists assert, certainly after the 1990s the patterns of regional security interdependence in Asia underwent an external transformation because of the knitting together of north-east and south-east Asia into a single RSC, as exemplified in the growth of the ASEAN Regional Forum (ARF) as a cooperative security regime, and by the ascendance and deepening of functional cooperation in the framework of ASEAN plus 3 (Buzan and Waever 2003). Nevertheless, those factors of inter-regional securitization, between south-east and north-east Asian sub-regional security complexes, might have cast a shadow of turbulence in constructing a regional export control regime.

Furthermore, social constructivists call attention to 'the inter-subjectively constituted structure of identities and interests' (Wendt 1992). If regionalization is to proceed in East Asia, it will largely depend upon the degree to which states in the region share common identities and interests; therefore, it will likely be some sort of combination of socially-bound institutions like ASEAN, ASEAN plus 3, and interest-driven institutions like Sino–Japanese economic and industrial relations as a whole. Regardless of the weak sense of common identity at political and societal levels between Japan, China and South Korea, commonality of security interests in terms of export controls have been inter-subjectively nurtured during this decade among these nations. In the case of the de-nuclearization of the Korean Peninsula, the governments of these three countries have fundamentally taken a common approach for preventing North Korea from going nuclear, even though China retained something of a supportive stance towards North Korea. At the same time, as mentioned above, especially since September 11, these three countries have pursued policies of non-proliferation export controls respectively at national levels. ASEAN countries have developed their own export control systems as well, in line with norms and rules of multilateral export control regimes. They have done this, first, because they are now facing the invisible imminent threat of terrorist attacks, as illustrated in suicide-bombing in Indonesia in October 2005, and second, because of a recognition that they are now the secondary sources of proliferation of WMD-related goods and technologies and a basis for transit or trans-shipment of those materials to 'pariah' states and non-state actors including terrorist groups. Considering these developments, a sense of security interdependence and, therefore, common structure of identities and interests in terms of non-proliferation export controls has quite naturally grown in East Asia.

In close relation to the constructivist paradigm, the theoretical relevance of an 'epistemic community', as developed by Peter Haas in environmental protection as well as by Emanuel Adler in the arms control, is arguably adaptable to the regionalization dynamics of export controls. An 'epistemic community' is defined as 'a network of individuals or groups with an authoritative claim to policy-relevant knowledge within their domain of expertise. The community members share knowledge about the causation of social and physical phenomena in an area for which they have a reputation for competence, and they have a common set of normative beliefs about what will benefit human welfare in such a domain' (Haas 1992). In this context, Emanuel Adler argues that an American epistemic community played a key role in creating the international shared understanding and practice of nuclear arms control, especially shared understanding and interests of mutual nuclear deterrence between the US and the Soviet Union (Adler 2005).

In line with this analysis, it seems possible to analogize an epistemic community of export controls in which government experts, business practitioners and academics develop theoretical expectations and create a domestic system of export controls and also diffuse them internationally. In retrospect, since the establishment of COCOM in 1949, the domestically embedded mechanism of export controls in the US was created by a nation-wide group of experts and afterward disseminated to the allies. The structure of identities and interests among the national epistemic communities of export controls had led to more sophisticated mechanisms of periodic consultations with member countries and review of individual export applications to COCOM. At the same time, an American epistemic community of export controls attempted to extend their outreach activities to friendly countries like Japan, and supported the development of a cooperative mechanism with them (Bertsch, Cupitt and Yamamoto 1996). After the break-up of COCOM, the fundamental characteristics of the epistemic community of export controls have been largely ceded to multilateral non-proliferation export control regimes. In this context, as mentioned earlier, it should be noted that a regional framework of an export controls epistemic community seems to have arisen in East Asia.

Based on the understanding of these schools of thought and approaches to international relations, this chapter will consider a possible export control regime in East Asia. In order to examine the regionalization dynamics of constructing a 'soft regime' of export controls in the region, the politico-military and economic environment in East Asia will be briefly discussed.

Geo-strategic Interactions among Countries in East Asia

Since the Cold War ended in 1989, geo-strategic interactions between the US and Russia have dramatically changed in both political and economic terms, in the sense that the US and its allies not only strongly supported the marketization of the Russian economy, that is, the diversion of Russian war economy, but also succeeded in a series of arms control agreements, such as START I, START II, Comprehensive Test Ban Treaty (CTBT) and the Moscow Treaty of 2002. The dissolution of COCOM in 1994 resulted from these dramatic changes in the world strategic environment. As a matter of course, the two ideologies of 'democratization' and 'marketization' have been newly embedded in the international system since the early 1990s as the new global standard of political legitimacy in national and international governance (Yamamoto 2003).

In East Asia, however, there still remain authoritarian and semi-democratic regimes, albeit with some gradual success of 'marketization', in such countries as China, North Korea, Vietnam, Myanmar and others. In this sense, the newly embedded global paradigm of political legitimacy for governance has become a grave source of political tensions in East Asia, notably over how to acclimatize them to democratic standards of governance like pluralistic representation and human rights. Moreover, North Korea has never changed its Stalinist style of governance in both political and economic terms even after the death of Kim Il-Sung in 1994. Regardless of benevolent efforts made by the international community in the form of enormous gifts of food and energy since the mid-1990s, the mutual distrust between North Korea and its neighbours, and especially with Japan, has not been alleviated. Meanwhile, relations between China and Taiwan have been aggravated since the mid-1990s when Lee Ten Hoi was democratically elected as the President of Taiwan and announced his *de facto* independence stance with regard to China. In spite of huge increases in investments and mutual trade between China and Taiwan, political relations worsened, even more than during the era of Lee's presidency, when China adopted the Anti-State Independence Law in 2005 against the pro-independence stance taken by Taiwanese president Chen Shui-bian. In this context, Cold War aspects stubbornly remain in north-east Asia, so much so that the over-securitization of political–military relations might continue to be a part of the north-east Asian sub-security complex for the foreseeable future (Buzan and Waever 2003).

In a situation such as this, all in all, there are at least two troublesome issues with regard to export controls in East Asia. The first is how to deal with China as a trading partner in the region. It is true that its huge market and manufacturing potentials are far beyond levels that can be ignored. However, there have been several cases in which it has exported missile manufacturing technologies to Pakistan and Middle Eastern countries like Iran, as well as possible covert transfers of nuclear and missile-related technologies to North Korea, although China has repeatedly stated its intentions to abide by the norms, principles and rules of the existing WMD-related multilateral export control regimes since the country's enactment of the Law of Security Export Regulation, and its amendment in September 2002. In addition, a Chinese nuclear espionage incident in the Los Alamos National Laboratory stirred anti-Chinese sentiments in US governmental and congressional circles. More specifically, in May 1999, the US House of Representatives published the so-called Cox Report concerning Chinese overt and covert actions aimed at acquiring sensitive information related to militarily relevant technologies from the US (US Congress 1999). The report summarizes China's efforts and its alleged ability to acquire US-origin technologies to enhance its nuclear technological abilities and missile capabilities (US Congress 1999). Even though the US administration has attempted to put stricter regulations on exporting sensitive goods and technologies, export drives of private companies to the Chinese market are making this a difficult task. There were at least two major cases in which US high-tech companies have committed violations. One was a case in which two satellite companies, Loral Space and Communications and Hughes Electronics, violated US export control regulations. The other was the case of problematic sales of machinery equipment by McDonell Douglas, in which China diverted this machinery to the possible production of cruise missiles.[d] These two cases illustrate the difficulty of the politico-economic relationship with China regardless of the 'engagement policy' of the Clinton administration *vis-à-vis* China (Yamamoto 2000b, 2003).

The second is how to deal with the repeated 'brinkmanship policy' over nuclear and missile developments pursued by North Korea since the mid-1990s. Although a possible second Korean War was avoided by the Framework Agreement signed in October 1994, threats of the proliferation of WMD-related goods and technologies by North Korea to other concerned states and non-state actors have not disappeared. Rather, it seems very likely that this issue will continue to be an important diplomatic point of leverage for North Korea. Nuclear and missile proliferation issues have been used as effective bargaining chips by North Korea in order, not only to acquire more food and energy-related financial resources from the US, Japan, South Korea and the European countries, but also to make the US ease negative economic sanctions against North Korea. It is widely known that North Korea has continued to procure raw materials and components for both its ballistic missile programmes and production activities of weapons grade highly enriched uranium (HEU) from various foreign sources, especially through North Korean firms based in China as well as in Pakistan, as shown in the revelations regarding Pakistani scientist A.Q. Khan's unravelled proliferation network.

Furthermore, North Korea is capable of producing and delivering via munitions a wide variety of chemical and biological agents (see US CIA 2000). Although little attention has been paid to North Korea's purported chemical weapons and biological weapons activities (Harris 2004), there is a heightened sense of insecurity in the international community over missile and nuclear proliferation behaviour by North Korea. Some Japanese companies were reportedly engaged in exporting missile related goods like stainless steel, which are not strictly regulated under the present export control system.[5] North Korea is, even after the South–North Summit talks in June 2000, designated as one of the 'pariah' states and a target of stiffened export controls in the multilateral export control regimes. The US and other member countries in these regimes have been, nevertheless, ironically forced to treat it as a like member of the MTCR throughout bilateral missile talks, mainly because of its high capabilities and strong intentions to sell missiles to other concerned countries for the sake of earning hard currency. Most of the supply-side countries, especially the US, are now in a dilemma with regard to North Korea over whether it would be advisable to treat North Korea as if it were a quasi-member of the regime. From a geo-strategic viewpoint, this dilemma is clearly reflected as an appeasement dealing with North Korea. The tripartite partners, the US, South Korea and Japan, continuously and closely cooperated in terms of joint non-proliferation efforts in the Korean Energy Development Organization (KEDO) until 2002 when North Korea's covert development programme of HEU was revealed by the US, although North Korea several times furiously blamed the violation of the Framework Agreement and the delay of the light water reactor plant project on the US and its allies. The justification of North Korea to produce HEU, however, has no political legitimacy because it has no direct relations with the problems of electricity supply, as agreed in the Framework Agreement. Rather, it should be said, such a move by North Korea has been a gross violation of nuclear non-proliferation norms, so much so that the hardline policy of the Bush administration against North Korea in terms of WMD non-proliferation cannot be seriously repudiated as a hostile attitude.

Since some features of the Cold War remain in East Asia, US foreign policy inevitably has a major impact on the strategic interactions among state actors in the region. While pursuing a cautious policy on technology transfers to China for national security reasons, on the one hand, the Clinton administration in the 1990s adopted the policy of 'constructive engagement' *vis-à-vis* China on the other. During the period from 1995 to 1996, however, provocative missile tests launched by China over the Taiwan Strait resulted in making pro-Taiwan groups, including many Republicans in the US Congress even more antagonistic to the policy of engagement by the Clinton administration – they considered it as an appeasement to an authoritarian regime. In addition to these missile test launches, the mobile-type intercontinental ballistic missile (DF-31) test on 2 August 1999 accelerated the argument for the need to deploy a theatre missile defence system around north-east Asia, naturally including the Taiwan Strait. Even after President Clinton's official visit to China, the Clinton administration had become more deeply involved in the national and theatre missile defence programmes and had shifted its policy of 'constructive engagement' to the traditional policy of 'strategic ambiguity' toward China, especially in relation to the territorial defence of Taiwan.[6]

The Bush administration, on the other hand, has characterized China as a 'strategic competitor' since President George W. Bush took office in 2001. Although US foreign policy *vis-à-vis* China changed significantly after September 11, the basic stance of more stringent export controls on goods headed for China has been maintained. Indeed, even under the second term of the Bush administration, the US has pursued rather more cautious policies toward China, on the assumption that China has become the new threat to the US in terms of both economic and military security. As a matter of fact, the Sino–US relationship has been aggravated in the economic field especially since the trade deficit of the US to China ignited a sense of economic insecurity in the US Congress and in administration circles as well. From a geo-economic viewpoint, it should be said that the threat perception of the US in the economic field has dramatically shifted from targeting Japan in the late-1980s and the early-1990s to the current focus on China. The growing sense of insecurity arising from the decline of the defence industrial base of the US, following the export drive by China to the US market, is a case in point. In addition, it should be noted that China has increased military expenditures every year at an average rate of over 10 per cent since the late-1990s. The military build-up in strategic and conventional arms by China has been a source of growing wariness in the US as well as in Japan. It goes without saying, therefore, that the sense of insecurity in both economic and military fields has mounted year after year in the US.[7]

Furthermore, the Bush administration has pursued a missile defence (MD) programme far more fervently than the Clinton administration, and has clung to a unilateral approach in most foreign policy positions, exemplified by the refusal to ratify the CTBT, its reluctant attitudes toward reviewing the verification protocol of the Biological Weapons Convention (BWC), and the withdrawal from the Anti-Ballistic Missile (ABM) Treaty and so on. Meanwhile, Japan has continuously kept its basic position supporting the US in development and possible deployment of the MD system. Moreover, the Koizumi government finally decided to join the MD co-research and co-development programme and also to dispatch Japan's defence forces to Iraq in 2003 as a partner in the coalition of the willing. The US–Japan security relationship has been, therefore, further stepped up and strengthened after the Bush administration pushed ahead with the anti-terror wars and the MD programme, and also changed gears from a multilateral approach during the Clinton administration years to a unilateral one in international affairs, although a change from a staunch unilateralism to a multilateralism *à la carte* in the second term might have been observed. As the joint statement between President Bush and Prime Minister Koizumi in November 2005 shows well, the US–Japan alliance will undoubtedly continue to be a central part and linchpin of the regional security complex in East Asia.

The other US allies in the region, South Korea and Taiwan, have also continued, to a considerable degree, to follow along with the changed attitude of the Bush administration as long as their security interests are guaranteed by the military presence of the US in the region, even though the Kim Dae-jung and Roh Moo-hyun governments pursued a rather more independent stance *vis-à-vis* North Korea. It is a case in point that Presidents Bush and Roh reconfirmed the strong security tie between the US and South Korea in the joint statement of the 2005 summit talks. Indeed, recent trends in South Korea, such as anti-American movements among young people, remarks likening the South Korean position to a balancer between China and the US–Japan alliance by President Roh in the summer of 2005, and growing inter-Korean rapprochement amidst the North Korean nuclear crisis, have raised critical concerns regarding the future of the bilateral alliance with Washington. Regardless of these negative developments, however, the basic strategy of both countries to maintain the alliance relationship will likely continue to be pursued. It should be noted that anti-American social movements are not necessarily similar to anti-Americanism in the context of national security culture in South Korea, firstly because Korean people share the identity and value of democratic governance with the US, and secondly because they know well the deterrent effect of a US military presence in South Korea and its synergistic effects in leading to a positive settlement with North Korea. Consequently, even though American perception of the alliance shifts from time to time, the alliance between the US and South Korea 'is still healthy enough not to warrant an early epitaph' (Moon 2005).

The Bush administration's standpoint is even clearer on North Korea. The well-known statement by President Bush in his State of the Union Address in 2002 labelling North Korea as part of the 'axis of evil' is a lucid example. Especially after the secret operation of producing HEU by North Korea surfaced in 2002, the hawkish attitudes of the Bush administration have left the region with a sense of heavy insecurity. As a reaction to the growing crisis over the HEU problem, visits by China's and Russia's top leaders were made. Chinese President Hu Jin Tao paid a state visit to Pyongyang in October 2005 in order to persuade North Korea to give up its nuclear development programme. In view of the establishment of the Shanghai Cooperation Organization (SCO) in May 2001, the recent statement regarding US engagement in East Asian security affairs produced at the summit talks of the SCO held in 2005, and the conclusion of the Treaty for the Friendship and Cooperation between Russia and China, the geo-strategic combinations of major countries in East Asia may be gradually going toward a region-wide bipolarization of powers; that is to say a quadrilateral alliance between the US, Japan, South Korea and Taiwan versus the Sino–Russian–North Korea tripartite entente. It is uncertain at the present stage whether this scenario will go further or not. In this case, the basic norms, principles, rules and decision-making procedures of multilateral non-proliferation export control regimes would be faced with unseen challenges.

Towards a Regional Export Control Regime in East Asia

The revealed network of illicit flow of sophisticated nuclear weapons-relevant goods and technologies to Libya, North Korea and Iran by A.Q. Khan raised serious concerns regarding the current situation of structural and functional vulnerabilities of multilateral non-proliferation export control regimes on the one hand, and gave a suggestion of the importance of building a regional framework of security trade controls including the PSI and the CSI in East Asia on the other. The network was composed of highly complicated procurement strategies for acquiring sensitive materials from foreign suppliers along with a clandestine funding mechanism. There are at least two lessons, it seems, to be learned from this case. First, in the era of economic globalization the new focus of more effective export controls should be set on the second-tier proliferation ring as well as the first-tier proliferation ring (Braun and Chyba 2004; Kampani 2002). Second, as the Khan network demonstrated, the current rapid economic development of East Asian countries has, more and more, facilitated the transfer of state-of-the-art dual-use technologies and goods among these countries, such that the establishment of a regional framework for harmonization of the export control policies of related countries for synchronization of control practices, including enforcement and intelligence sharing becomes necessary.

In the grey-market network of A.Q. Khan, both first-tier and second-tier suppliers of East Asian countries, such as Malaysia, Singapore and Japan were deeply involved, whether intentionally or unintentionally. Just after the end of the Cold War, second-tier suppliers' capabilities were arguably at the lower end of the nuclear export spectrum, and the export actions these suppliers did undertake were for the most part cautious (Dunn 1990). A.Q. Khan's network, however, showed that since the late 1970s, combined and complex rings of first-tier and secondary suppliers had been formulated across a number of countries. Indeed, most of the secondary sources of nuclear proliferation were detached from multilateral non-proliferation export control mechanisms, rather developing proliferation rings with the first-tier suppliers, to whom the export or re-export of regulated items in their home countries was stringently restricted. This new challenge of second-tier proliferation shed light on the necessity for change in non-proliferation strategy from essentially supply-side-based approaches to a mixed approach of supply-side plus demand-side restrictions.

In order to meet this new challenge, the fortification of existing multilateral export control regimes and the improvement of the current structural and functional flaws of these regimes must, among other things, be taken into consideration. Some ideas and proposals from government circles as well as some research agencies have been suggested since the revelation of A.Q. Khan's network. A policy proposal, for example, to reform the current redundancy, unnecessary costs and disunity of effort of existing multilateral export control institutions by creating a unified regime is a noteworthy one, with a view to streamlining and strengthening the control systems (Gahlaut et al. 2004). Moreover, it seems more desirable to institutionalize a region-based sub-regime, especially in East Asia, in parallel with a strengthened and unified global export control regime, also exemplified in further institutionalization of export controls in the European Union.

After the economic turmoil in the late 1990s, East Asian countries developed a regional network of FTAs, at both bilateral and multilateral levels, for expanding economic and industrial safety networks in order to guard them from such a quaking shock as was seen during the breakdown of capital markets and the rapid reduction of export markets in the 1997–8 economic crisis. As a result, voluminous flows of dual-use items between and among these countries have been rapidly accelerated. This acceleration has aggravated danger of inconspicuous and invisible outflow of these items to states and non-state actors of concern. The regional dynamics of soft legalization of the FTA system in East Asia could lead ironically to a paradox of increasing the insecurity complex of the region as a whole. This should be categorized as a worst case scenario under which the regional security interdependence system might be seriously undermined. Therefore, hypothetically speaking, the more inconspicuous and more invisible the outflows of dual-use goods and technologies, including so-called 'deemed exports', become, the more the global regimes of export control should be sophisticatedly reformed in a unified way and simultaneously tackled by establishing new sub-regimes on a regional basis.

For the multilateral non-proliferation export control regimes to have legitimacy in preserving international security and stability, there is a need to have a commonality of security interests, at least among the member countries. In reality, however, there often remain spontaneous disagreements especially at a time when commercial interests are at stake among the member countries in the export control regimes (Yamamoto 2003). In the same vein, if and when a regional sub-regime of export controls in East Asia, albeit a non-legally-binding 'soft regime', is built and starts to function, controversies over how and whether export controls should be imposed could be expected to arise frequently.

Even in the Cold War era, there were several serious controversies among the members of COCOM as well as among the members of CHINCOM (China Committee) over to what extent and whether the export of certain dual-use items should be regulated against targeted countries, as demonstrated in the case of 'pipeline sanctions' against some western European members of COCOM by the Reagan administration. It is quite natural that the economic interests of the member countries might not always coincide with each other. Nevertheless, the rationale to maintain and to strengthen the multilateral export control regimes continues to have relevance primarily because proliferation of WMD-related goods and technologies to states of concern like North Korea would cause more insecurity in the region as a whole. Furthermore, the re-transfer of such goods and technologies among third 'pariah' states could also be their source for earning hard currency, as exemplified in the A.Q. Khan case of illicit sales to North Korea. Therefore, one of the problems is which of the states in East Asia should be included as original members of a possible regional regime of export controls, even if loosely and softly instituted at the outset. As key members, Japan, China, South Korea and the US should conceivably be included in an export control mechanism in the region.

Certainly, member countries of the existing export control regimes have restricted the export of high-tech goods and services to China, firstly because China has caused, even if unintentionally, a negative impact on the regional security situation through the export of missile and nuclear related items to several states of concern like Pakistan and North Korea, and secondly because China has been the subject of economic sanctions on the ground of human rights abuses after the massacre of protesters at Tiananmen Square in 1989. However, it is meaningless not to include China in a regime because China has considerably developed its own defence industrial and technological base as an emerging economic giant, so that it will increasingly become one of the main sources of export (and re-export) of sensitive dual-use items to actors of concern. It is necessary to include China in any regime of export controls, even if certain international activities by China throw a shadow on its global rise in power and notwithstanding China's role as the principal patron of North Korea (US Government 2005).

Thus, it was desirable for China to become a full member of the NSG in 2004 following its accession to the Zangger Committee in 1997. Firstly, because this is a first step towards fortifying the existing export control regime, and secondly, because as a full member, China must practice stringent internal controls of exports of nuclear-related goods and technologies, otherwise it would be blamed as a defector of the agreed rules and be sanctioned by other members. In other words, China is entangled with the 'shadow of the future' in the institutional framework of the NSG. In addition, China intends to step up its commitment to the MTCR after submitting an application for membership in September 2004. It has also maintained channels for exchange of views on a regular basis through the AG and the Wassenaar Arrangement, and maintains its intention to implement its own national export controls in accordance with the multilateral standards for export regulations of these institutions. The problem is rather how to treat Taiwan. Currently, Taiwan is not a full member of any multilateral export control regime. It seems unlikely that it will get a membership in the existing export control regimes as long as China refuses to allow Taiwan to be an independent actor in international institutions. However, Taiwan has developed high-tech industries since the mid-1980s, comprising one of the 'four dragons' which have achieved miraculous economic growth. At the same time, it introduced its own national export control system after the end of the Cold War and adopted a highly cooperative approach, acting as a *de facto* full member, with the export control guidelines of the multilateral regimes, including the sister initiatives of the PSI and the CSI. These phenomena demonstrate the necessity of accepting Taiwan into a regional regime of trade controls. Nevertheless, the only potential political stumbling block is China's seemingly intractable posture on the Taiwan issue. At this point, it might be desirable for Taiwan to maintain an observer status, such as it does in the Asia Pacific Economic Cooperation (APEC) and other international organizations.

The US allies in the region have, more or less, followed with the shift in US export control strategy. In other words, Japan, South Korea and Taiwan have been, whether intentionally or intentionally, involved in the US's grand strategy of 'geo-science and technology' in the sense that the US has consistently pursued geo-strategic interests in which its comparative edge in science and technology plays a decisive role *vis-à-vis* any potential rival, resulting in regional stability.[8] In this context, these countries, especially Japan and Taiwan, have supported the current strong attitude of the Bush administration against moves by European countries towards the lifting of arms embargos against China for two reasons. Firstly, lifting the export ban on sophisticated weaponry might eventually result in a shift of the power balance in the region in favour of China, especially between China and Taiwan. Secondly, it would enhance further the potential of the defence industrial and technological base of China and, as a result, undermine US advantage in the field of science and technology. As long as these strategic thoughts of 'geo-science and technology' compete with each other, they may constitute factors which could significantly hamper the building of whatever 'soft regime' of export controls might otherwise be possible in East Asia.

Meanwhile, south-east Asian countries have constructed certain common points of identity among themselves within the institutions of ASEAN, as discussed earlier. There have been several attempts to expand it in the region, driven by economic interests, such as the East Asian Economic Caucus (EAEC), the Pacific Economic Cooperation Conference (PECC) and the ASEAN Free Trade AREA (AFTA). The economic transactions between south-east and north-east Asia increase year after year in a wave of trade liberalization. At the same time, a number of Japanese manufacturing and trade corporations, including medium- and small-sized companies, are widely rooted in the region and deploy their business networks around Asia in general. Furthermore, China embarked on building a stronger economic relationship with ASEAN soon after it joined the WTO in 2000 (Kuik 2005). As mentioned above, in spite of a cooling in relations in the political arena, there is nevertheless a continuing 'hot relationship' in economic transactions between China and Japan. Therefore, regionalization dynamics in East Asia in terms of further economic interdependence are ongoing, owing to an expansion of bilateral and multilateral networks through the FTAs. As a result, the technological levels of ASEAN countries have upgraded more and more and economic activity including trade in high-tech goods has increased dramatically, so that the establishment and strengthening of export control systems in those countries has become an urgent priority in order to guard against the emergence of major sources of leakage to states of concern and non-state actors as well.

However, most ASEAN countries have not yet satisfactorily established and practised stringent internal systems of export controls, including monitoring, enforcement, customs and port control, as well as internal compliance programmes within both state-controlled and private companies, although they have enacted domestic laws and regulatory decrees. There is an increasing need, therefore, for these countries to strengthen their systems of transit and trans-shipment controls. Hong Kong and Macau, the sovereign titles which reverted to China in the late 1990s, exemplify these problems. Although they are engaged in export controls at their own discretion, several cases of illicit traffic of sensitive goods and money laundering via these two jurisdictions have been reported. For example, there has been anecdotal evidence of the transit of sensitive Japanese items which were allegedly stopped by the Hong Kong authorities just before trans-shipment to North Korea.[9] Regarding illicit transactions via Macau, North Korea established a stronghold there for the sake of acquiring dual-use goods, money laundering, counterfeit dollars and even drug trafficking. The more awareness of the importance of transit and trans-shipment controls after September 11 grows, the more expectations will be placed upon the roles played by these jurisdictions and Singapore in the regional export control regime, including in PSI and CSI operations. In this sense, it is an epoch-making development that the Cooperation Agreements between the Ministry of Economics, Trade and Industry of Japan (METI), the Singaporean Customs Authority, and the Department of Industry and Trade of Hong Kong were concluded in 2004 for the exchange of information as well as for the facilitation of cooperation for preventing export diversion.

Regarding the PSI operations, although East Asian countries except Japan are not original participants in the initiative, they have, by and large, adopted cooperative postures. On the one hand, Japan and Singapore (and Australia) in particular, have actively participated in the operations because they share a common interest in preventing dangerous materials from passing through their waters, particularly since the countries rely so heavily on their numerous harbours for commerce. China, on the other hand, is not yet fully ready to take part in the PSI. They seem reluctant to cooperate fully with the PSI due to the hawkish attitude of the Bush administration toward North Korea. However, China has on occasion cooperated in PSI operations with the US on a case by case basis. In the summer of 2003, for example, acting on an intelligence report provided by the US, China stopped a train on its way to North Korea and confiscated its cargo – a nuclear-related material known as Liquefied Tributyl Phosphate (TBP). China agrees, therefore, in cooperating with the US on some individual cases with the understanding that the nuclear weaponization of North Korea has a significant negative impact on the security of north-east Asia and on China's own vital interest *vis-à-vis* the US. Such a cooperative approach by China is also illustrated by the fact that it formally joined the CSI by signing the CSI Declaration of Principles with the US on 29 July 2003, and agreed to pre-screen high risk cargo containers in Shanghai and Shenzhen ports (Yamamoto 2004).

After all, East Asian countries commonly feel it necessary to meet these new challenges posed by secondary proliferators linked with the invisible first-tier proliferation ring. In other words, most East Asian countries have not only shared a sense of identity in preventing them from accessing sources of secondary proliferation, but have also developed their internal trade control systems in accordance with the norms and common standards of export controls established within the existing multilateral regimes. Even though there still remains a large difference in domestic systems of export controls among these countries, regionalization of export controls in East Asia is growing from a no-regime reality to a 'soft regime' in which harmonization and coordination of politics among related actors including business communities works gradually on a regional basis.

It is a significant step, in this sense, that a regular mechanism of periodic dialogues among East Asian governments has been established by the initiative of the Japanese government, that is, the new institutional framework of the Asian Senior-level Talks on Non-Proliferation (ASTOP) which has been institutionalized since 2003. This step can be said to be a track-1 approach taken by governmental actors in the area of export controls in East Asia. A new approach of 'cooperative trade security', as it were, was adopted by the related governments through the Japanese initiative. The first round of ASTOP was held in Tokyo on 13 November 2003, with participation from all members of ASEAN, the US, South Korea and Australia (Japan Ministry of Foreign Affairs 2003). It is noteworthy that China joined in this mechanism of dialogues from the second round of ASTOP in February 2005, through which it sent a message of its intent to keep in step with other East Asian countries. According to the Japanese Ministry of Foreign Affairs, the agenda for this meeting was as follows:

- To make an overview of the recent trend in the proliferation of WMDs and their means of delivery in East Asia, such as the North Korean nuclear issue, proliferation of missiles by North Korea and the underground network of nuclear proliferation of Dr A.Q. Khan and others, as the issues of major concern in the region, while reflecting on the recent non-proliferation efforts made by Asian countries.
- To endeavour to enhance the understanding of participating countries towards new non-proliferation measures which have been introduced to further strengthen the existing non-proliferation regime, such as the International Atomic Energy Agency (IAEA) Additional Protocol, the Hague Code of Conduct against Ballistic Missile Proliferation (HCOC) and the PSI.
- To deepen understanding among participating countries regarding the difficulties and obstacles Asian countries may face in implementing treaties and norms related to disarmament and non-proliferation within their countries, and to discuss the possibilities for cooperation in overcoming the obstacles (Japan Ministry of Foreign Affairs 2005).

When the East Asian governments agree on taking a common step toward a regional mechanism of cooperation and coordination in line with this agenda, this attempt to establish ASTOP may be remembered as the catalyst for 'soft legalization' of a regional regime for export controls. In fact, the Japanese government has taken initiatives in this direction. For instance, it proposed, jointly with the US, a draft for introduction and implementation of an effective export control system at the APEC ministerial meeting. This proposal was adopted in the joint statement of the ministerial meeting on 18 November 2004 as the 'APEC Key Elements for Effective Export Control' in which the framework of restrictions by national laws, licence procedures and enforcement systems desired for effective export controls in respective the countries was incorporated on the basis of a best practices model. As this case shows, it should be taken into consideration that the US has to be involved, more or less, in the process of 'soft legalization' as the initiating leader of global export control regimes and a major player in security affairs in the APEC region. As aforementioned, a slowly evolving regional export control system in East Asia might be positioned as a sub-regime of the existing multilateral control systems. All in all, from these discussions, a diagram can be sketched on structural linkage of a possible regional regime of export controls in East Asia with global regimes (see Figure 9.1).

In fact, a series of export control seminars were initiated and sponsored by the Japanese government from July 2004 in ASEAN countries after the 'Japan–ASEAN Joint Program for Common Conduct' was adopted in the special summit talks between Japan and ASEAN held in December 2003.[10] An exchange of views was held with the Taiwanese representative in Tokyo on 26 April 2004, over more effective export controls in Northeast Asia. A further meeting was held on 25–27 January 2005 in Singapore with the US and Australian governments at a Commodity Identification Training (CIT) seminar, which was held with a view towards improving identification techniques for finding restricted items in the customs office of Singapore. The Japanese government also hosted a seminar for progress of abilities of licence and audit for export controls of the Singaporean government from 31 May to 1 June 2005.

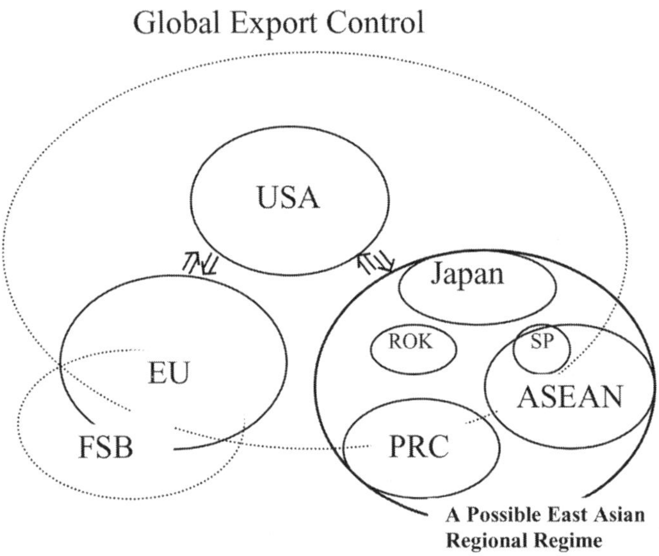

Figure 9.1 A Possible East Asian Regional Regime

Furthermore, such non-governmental actors as business communities and academics in the related countries have developed, even on a small scale, regional frameworks of cooperation on both bilateral and multilateral basis. Especially, as business communities expanded their transnational business activities around the region, they strongly want to share the information needed to preserve their own business interests.[11] They know well, when and if they violate the rules of the game in terms of domestic and international trade controls, they will be severely sanctioned by their respective governments. They are increasingly sensitive to being targeted by proliferators, and have been forced to pay for more financial and human resources to strengthen their self-policing systems, including internal compliance programmes (CP). Actually, they can not help but be involved, more or less, in cooperation with each other beyond national boundaries in order to preserve their own interests from a perspective of corporate governance.

Here too, the Japanese business community has played an active role in organizing and expanding outreach activities for making a network of business cooperation in export controls around the region. The Center for Information on Security Trade Control (CISTEC) has been its centrepiece. It has organized and sponsored the

Asian Export Control Seminar on an annual basis since the 1990s, in order to train specialists from Asian countries and exchange views with each other on export control exercises of respective countries. Experts on security affairs including arms controls have also talked about to what extent and how policy alternatives to current weak systems of non-proliferation export controls could be implemented, for example, in the talks in the Conference on Security and Cooperation in Asia and the Pacific (CSCAP) organized by civilians. It is certain that these non-governmental frameworks of cooperation have not yet become full-fledged. It seems, however, these developments in non-governmental sectors show a desire to go further toward formulating a region-wide epistemic community of export controls. In other words, these trends may be summarized as a track-2 approach in the area of export controls.

At any rate, the current features of the growing Asian system are oriented not around military security affairs *per se* or major power relations, but around the increasingly dense web of economic, technological and societal ties being forged among East Asian nations. The core actor in this region is not necessarily nation states, but rather a plethora of non-state actors and processes in which multiple threads have been woven in a complex system of interdependence (Shambaugh 2004). Therefore, an evolving regional 'soft regime' of export controls is, for the time being, desired to be developed in a sophisticated manner of intertwining state and non-state actors without impeding this growing complex interdependence system.

Continuity and Change of Japanese Export Control Systems

Eighteen years have passed since the illegal export of highly sophisticated numerically-controlled milling machines to the former Soviet Union by Toshiba Machine Tool Company, a subsidiary of Toshiba Corporation. The incident caused serious damage to US–Japan security ties because it endangered the advantage the US possessed over the Soviet Union in second strike capabilities by submarine-launched ballistic missiles (SLBM) in terms of anti-submarine warfare (ASW) operations. The Reagan administration sanctioned the Toshiba Corporation, prohibiting government procurements of all goods made and imported by the corporation to the US.

Since then, the Japanese government has drastically strengthened its domestic export control mechanism, notably under the Nakasone government in 1987 by the revision of the Foreign Exchange and Foreign Trade Law enacted in 1948. This revision was so great that the Japanese business community has often expressed strong complaints to the government about stringent licensing procedures, including administrative red tape in the export control bureaucracy of METI. The Federation of Economic Organizations (KEIDANREN), the most influential group representing the Japanese business community, requests, every year, that the government deregulates export controls of dual-use technologies as well as enhance further the transparency of the export control administration. For example, on 15 October 2002, the KEIDANREN submitted its annual official request to the government for further deregulations of unnecessary controls in light of the international standard, and for more transparency and simplification of procedures of export administration. It should be noted, among other things, that it asked the government to abolish the present requirement to submit the compliance programme of any export-related company to METI. At the same time, it requested the abolition of administrative red tape, such as the confirmation system of 'no-licence items', and also to deregulate 'other military uses' in case of general licences and to simplify the complicated system of regulations in export controls (see KEIDANREN 2002).

Therefore, although the Japanese business community has maintained its complaints over the government's stringent export control practices, it should be taken into account that despite the Toshiba Machine Tool Company's illegal export case, Japan has been the most cooperative state among the industrialized countries since Japan joined COCOM in 1952. At the same time, in spite of maintaining strong complaints over stringency, the Japanese business community has largely complied with government regulations with regard to export controls in order to share in the security interests of the US. As a result, the community has lost many business opportunities in foreign markets other than the US (Yamamoto 2003).

Moreover, the business community has recognized the importance of corporate social responsibility (CSR) activities including internal compliance of export controls, from the lessons of the Toshiba case. Internal export control practices are now very important components of CSR for good corporate governance in most Japanese transnational companies. Toshiba Corporation, for instance, has been organizing annual seminars on internal export controls for employees who are engaged in daily export control work since 23 August, the day when the Omnibus Trade Act of 1988 took effect and sanctions against it had begun, as a lesson from its illegal export and subsequent damage to business activities in the US market.

In addition, Japanese transnational corporations have less efficient and effective checking mechanisms for their supply-chain system than do US companies. Export control systems in advanced countries cannot function well unless internal compliance programmes work well in individual companies. Japanese companies have such complicated supply-chain mechanisms across national borders that they have been forced, more than before, to organize more effective ones.

After the end of the Cold War, member countries in the multilateral export control regimes have respectively practised domestic regulations of export of WMD-related and high-tech conventional weapons-related goods and technologies on national control lists. Just after September 11, METI established a sub-committee for introducing a 'catch-all' system of regulations throughout the national export control system. The US introduced this system in 1991 and the European Union followed in 1995. The major purpose of this system is to widen the range of controls to items whose components and technologies would have the possibilities to be used or diverted for the production of WMD. All of the goods and technologies which had not been controlled on the list which would be possible to be used for WMD have become the subject items for 'catch-all' control since April 2002. For example, stainless steel, automatic potentiometric titrators, ion-exchange membranes, presses, bearings have been listed as 'catch-all' items. Before its introduction, Japanese export controls were practised according to the Export Trade Control Order Attachment List 1 (from Item 1 to Item 15) and were also complementarily administered through Item 16 of the Attachment List 1 in which 87 WMD-related goods and technologies were included. Before the introduction of the 'catch-all' system, the export control community in Japan had called this complementary export control the 'catch-87' system. In the 'catch-87' system, two mechanisms of 'knowledge' regulation and 'informed requirement' regulation had functioned.[12] Therefore, every exporter was obliged to perform its own daily self-policing works, including end-user and end-use checks for satisfying these requirements. After the introduction of the 'catch-all' system, METI published two lists in order to contribute to more efficient and effective export controls in Japan under the new system:

1. The Foreign Users List, in which dubious and concerned users are named on a country basis. When an exporter needs to export goods and technology to listed users, it is required to obtain validated licences for export. Currently, 165 foreign concerned users are listed (see Table 9.1).

2. The Examples List of Cautious Goods, by which exporters are informed of goods available for use in WMD production and development. Forty items are listed as of April 2005.[13]

Table 9.1 The Numbers of Foreign Users List

Country	Pre-review	Post-review	Plus–minus
North Korea	33	39	+ 6
Israel	5	5	0
Iran	35	39	+ 4
India	39	35	– 4
Syria	4	6	+ 2
Taiwan	1	1	0
China	14	14	0
Pakistan	25	24	– 1
Libya	2	0	– 2
Afghanistan	2	2	0
Total	160	165	+ 5

This administrative guideline for export controls in Japan, as a matter of course, is so complicated that most high-tech manufacturing and trade companies have worried about increased daily work to obtain export licences. As suggested earlier, the KEIDANREN had understandably requested the government to streamline and simplify the rules and export administration. In addition, Japanese companies have usually adopted the rule of cyclical changes in the postings of their personnel for two or three-year terms. By the same token, government officials engaged in and responsible for security trade controls have regularly changed their posts following the same cyclical term as company personnel. This is, in a sense, traditionally rooted in social custom in the Japanese labour system. Therefore, those companies are forced to regularly educate and train new personnel in charge of the company's internal export control matters. This means that expertise in export controls could be weakened in high-tech manufacturing and trade companies, even if temporarily. If and when the domestic export control system in Japan is strengthened, this would be one of the biggest structural problems that is inseparably connected with the Japanese business culture.

After the introduction of the 'catch-all' system, therefore, Japan has undoubtedly entered into the forefront of the most stringent national security export controls together with the US and the EU. At the same time, it should be said that despite bearing a larger burden than before, the Japanese business community is under the same obligations to abide by common standards and norms of non-proliferation in terms of 'catch-all' systems as American and European competitors. METI and CISTEC have actively sponsored seminars for education to officials in developing countries of East Asia in charge of export controls on a yearly basis as mentioned before.[14] Most of the relevant companies have, directly or indirectly, supported these efforts and have provided their own knowledge and expertise on export controls. In this sense, Japan is taking an initiative for the regionalization and harmonization of non-proliferation export control systems in terms of 'catch-all' in East Asia (Yamamoto 2003).

Another problem is that there are a lot of small companies engaged in manufacturing high-tech goods (including component parts), and in developing computer software. These companies include venture capital businesses in which there are few experts on export controls, leading to insufficient resources not only to implement their own compliance programmes, but also to comply with domestic rules and procedures for the control of technology transfer to foreign clients. This is mainly due to their lack of knowledge on and technique for export controls, and also to the weakness of information sharing systems. It is, therefore, urgently necessary for the government to take measures for reform of such structural weakness of the export control system in general.

At present, we only have the information gathering and sharing system of CISTEC, established in 1987, just after the Toshiba Machine Tool Company's illegal export incident, to which METI and the business community gave strong support. Although CISTEC plays an important role in providing public information through publications and seminars, outreach activities inside and outside Japan, and training of export control officials in Asian developing countries, it is merely a small think-tank and a financially weak organization.

There has nevertheless emerged a new phenomenon for encouraging the export control community to share its common knowledge for a well-scrutinized structure of a nation-wide export control system in Japan. It is noteworthy that the Japan Association of International Security and Trade (JAIST) was established in May 2005, to which a number of persons engaged in export controls in the government, industry and academic circles have joined for the purpose of sharing knowledge and expertise on export control affairs from scholarly as well as practical aspects. JAIST may expand, sooner or later, its geographical reach from the metropolitan Tokyo area to other industrial areas like Osaka and Fukuoka. At the same time, it is expected to be an intellectual base for formulating a regional epistemic community of export controls in East Asia in the foreseeable future.

It has been argued correctly that North Korea's longstanding efforts to develop a nuclear weapons capability is a serious problem for all of North Korea's neighbours. Although the fifth round of six party talks over the denuclearization of North Korea succeeded after a game of diplomatic shadow boxing in reaching a provisional accord in freezing its nuclear activities and doing away with its nuclear development programme, the US, Japan and South Korea have not dropped their common cautious attitude toward North Korea. Indeed, North Korea reacted verbally against the decision to terminate the decade-long light water reactor project thorough KEDO by the US, Japan and the EU on 22 November 2005. So, there still remains uncertainty as to whether North Korea will finally and firmly promise to abandon all of its nuclear activities including for civilian purposes.[15] Moreover, despite the Pyongyang Declaration after the historical visit of Prime Minister Koizumi to North Korea in 2002, there has been a growing sense of distrust against North Korea among the Japanese public, which has been especially irritated by North Korea's continuing provocative attitude toward Japan on issues, such as the longstanding abduction issues, widely spread rumours of illicit drug trafficking from North Korea into Japan, and some past incidents of the unauthorized entry of unknown North Korean vessels into Japanese territorial waters. As long as these negative interactions with North Korea continue, Japan will be forced to strengthen its own export control strategy toward North Korea in cooperation with other member countries in the multilateral export control regimes.

It seems likely that Japan will be at the forefront of efforts to continue a kind of 'containment' policy against North Korea. The Koizumi administration has embarked on stringent port controls since June 2003 in Niigata, Maizuru, Otaru and other large ports where North Korean cargo ships routinely call. In addition to stringent port control and on-site inspection by the Japanese authorities of North Korean cargo ships, the Japanese government has intensified its efforts as one of the original core members of PSI with a view to prevention of illicit transfer of WMD-related goods to North Korea. The government's sponsorship of the multilateral training operation of PSI, which was held in Tokyo Bay on 24–25 October 2004, is a typical case in point. Furthermore, the Japanese Diet passed a bill for the Prohibition of Specified Ships to Enter into Japanese Ports, allegedly targeting North Korean ships, in May 2004, which is likely to have a negative effect on trade with North Korea.

Conclusion

On 11 September 2001 in the US, 26 October 2002 in Moscow, 12 March 2004 in Madrid, 7 July 2005 in London and 1 October 2005 in Bali, the world witnessed a series of tragic scenes of terrorist attacks around the world. We are faced with innumerable terrorist groups as well as some 'pariah' countries supporting terrorism. These tragedies have given us a new challenge of how we should protect ourselves from attacks by terrorist groups or 'pariah' states with WMD, cyber weapons, and small and light weapons.

Whether we like it or not, we are obviously facing new challenges from non-governmental entities, such as terrorist groups and illegal exporters, and we are compelled to build a new paradigm for export controls in light of such invisible threats. In this context, we need to embark on reforming and restructuring the existing multilateral non-proliferation export control regimes as aforementioned. Current arguments for countering the threat of terrorism have focused on a wide range of WMD-related technologies as well as on gathering good intelligence (see US Government 2000). In addition to these arguments, we need to focus more on building an institutional framework of 'cooperative trade security' on a regional basis from a wide spectrum of 'comprehensive common security' frameworks in East Asia. Japan experienced the detestable and unenviable attack by nerve gas in a Tokyo subway in 1995 by the religious cult group, Aum Shinrikyo. Although transnational linkage between this cult and foreign terrorist groups was not evident, this incident gave us some lessons about how to meet the new challenges posed by the invisible enemy. Firstly, the roots of extremism in every industrialized state are found in their own societies. These states are, therefore, obliged to resolve societal sources of insecurity in their own countries and on a regional basis as well. Secondly, it is necessary for us to prepare for any possible terrorist attack in terms of durable systemization of crisis management. It should be understood, in this context, that a possible regional export control regime in East Asia would eventually contribute to further development of domestic export control systems.

In retrospect, Japan has accumulated profound experience in export controls since the early 1950s when the US supported its membership in COCOM. Japan faced a big dilemma at the time when the US proposed to build a Far East-COCOM headquartered in Tokyo, because the United Kingdom and France were strongly opposed to this proposal, mainly out of fear of institutional duplication with COCOM. As a result of a compromise CHINCOM was established as a sub-organ of COCOM. After its entry into COCOM and CHINCOM, Japan pursued an intermediary stance between the US and western European members when harsh controversies over some critical issues on concrete cases of export approval in COCOM (or CHICOM) arose. In a sense, it might be said that Japan played a bridge-building or mediating role for compromise between them, even though both of them accused Japan of profiting from the situation (Yamamoto 2001). Again, it is expected that Japan will play such a mediating role when possible controversies or acute perception gaps between East Asian countries, especially between China and the US arise, in the process of constructing a regional export control regime. Constructing a geo-governance system of trade controls is a promising goal for most East Asian countries for national and international security reasons, primarily because they are involved in a multi-layered intertwining of first and second-tier proliferation rings. It goes without saying that Japan's responsibility for taking a leadership role in making and maintaining the system is of significant importance as the most experienced nation in terms of export controls in the region.

References

Acharya, A. (1998), 'Collective Identity and Conflict Management in Southeast Asia', in E. Adler and M. Barnett (eds), Security Communities, Cambridge University Press, Cambridge.

Adler, E. (2005), *Communitarian International Relations: The Epistemic Foundations of International Relations*, Routledge, London.

Anthony, I. (2001), 'Multilateral Weapon and Technology Export Controls', in Stockholm International Peace Research Institute (ed), *SPIRI Yearbook 2001: Armaments, Disarmament and International Security*, Oxford University Press, Oxford and New York.

Asahi Shimbun (2004), 22 February 2004.

Baldwin, D.A. (1985), *Economic Statecraft*, Princeton University Press, Princeton, NJ.

Bertsch, G.K., Cupitt, R.T. and Yamamoto, T. (eds) (1996), *U.S. and Japanese Nonproliferation Export Control: Theory, Description and Analysis*, University Press of America, Lanham, MD.

Bloomberg (2005), 'China, Hong Kong Surpass US as Japan's Largest Trade Partner', updated 26 January 2005, <www.bloomberg.com/apps/news?pid=10000101&sid=aCPOGKiyfhnc&refer=japan>.

Braun, C. and Chyba, C.F. (2004), 'Proliferation Rings: New Challenges to the Nuclear Nonproliferation Regime', *International Security*, Vol. 29, No. 2.

Buzan, B. and Waever, O. (2003), *Regions and Powers: The Structure of International Security,* Cambridge University Press, Cambridge.

Buzan, B., Waever, O. and de Wilde, J. (1998), *Security: A New Framework for Analysis,* Lynne Rienner, Boulder, CO.

Cupitt, R.T. (2000), *Reluctant Champions: Presidential Policy and Strategic Export Controls: Truman, Eisenhower, Bush and Clinton*, Routledge, New York.

Dunn, L. (1990), 'The Emerging Nuclear Suppliers: Some Guidelines for Policy', in William Potter (ed.), *International Nuclear Trade and Nonproliferation: The Challenge of Emerging Suppliers*, Lexington Books, Lexington, MA.

Gahlaut, S., Beck, M., Jones, S. and Joyner, D. (2004), *Roadmap to Reform: Creating a New Multilateral Export Control Regime*, Centre for International Trade and Security, University of Georgia, Athens, GA.

Goldstein, J.L., Kahler, M., Keohane, R.O. and Slaughter, A-M. (eds) (2000), *Legalization and World Politics*, MIT Press, Cambridge, MA.

Haas, P.M. (1992), 'Introduction: Epistemic Communities and International Policy Coordination', *International Organization*, Vol. 46, No. 1.

Harris, E.D. (2004), 'Threat Reduction and North Korea's CBW Programs', *The Nonproliferation Review*, Vol. 11, No. 3.

Hwang, B.Y. (2003), 'Curtailing North Korea's Illicit Activities', Policy Research and Analysis, Heritage Foundation, 25 August 2003, <www.heritage.org/Research/AsianandthePacific/bg1679.cfm>.

Japan Ministry of Foreign Affairs (2003), 'Chairman's Summary', Asian Senior-level Talks on Non-Proliferation (ASTOP), Tokyo, 13 November 2003, <www.mofa.go.jp/policy/un/disarmament/arms/astop/summary0311.html>.

—— (2005), 'The Second Asian Senior-Level Talks on Non-Proliferation (ASTOP)', 3 February 2005, <www.mofa.go.jp/policy/un/disarmament/arms/astop/talk0502.html>.

Kampani, G. (2002), 'Second Tier Proliferation: The Case of Pakistan and North Korea', *The Nonproliferation Review*, Vol. 9, No. 3.

KEIDANREN (2002), *The Annual Request to the Government in Relation to Export Activities*, 15 October 2002.

Keohane, R. and Nye, J. (2000), *Power and Interdependence*, 3rd edn, Longman, London.

Kuik, C-G. (2005), 'Multilateralism in China's ASEAN Policy: Its Evolution, Characteristics, and Aspiration', *Contemporary Southeast Asia*, Vol. 27, No. 1.

Martin, L.L. (1992), *Coercive Cooperation: Explaining Multilateral Economic Sanctions*, Princeton University Press, Princeton, NJ.

Mastanduno, M. (1992), *Economic Containment: CoCom and the Politics of East-West Trade*, Cornell University Press, Ithaca, NY.

Moon, C-I. (2005), 'S. Korea–US Alliance Faces Challenges', *Korea Times*, 30 October 2005.

New York Times, 20 October 1999.

Shambaugh, D. (2004), 'China Engages Asia', *International Security*, Vol. 29, No. 1.

US CIA (2000), 'Unclassified Report to Congress on the Acquisition of Technology Relating to Weapons of Mass Destruction and Advanced Conventional Munitions, 1 July through 31 December 2000', US Central Intelligence Agency Report, December 2000, <www.cia.gov/cia/reports/721_reports/july_dec2000.htm>.

US Congress (1999), 'Report of the United States House of Representatives Select Committee on US National Security and Military/Commercial Concerns with the People's Republic of China', 105th Congress, 2nd Session, Report 105-851, <www.house.gov/coxreport/>.

US Government (2005), '2005 Report to the US Congress of the US–China Economic and Security Review Commission', 109th Congress Session, November 2005, <www.uscc.gov/annual_report/2005/annual_report_full_05.pdf>.

US Government (2000), 'Countering the Changing Threat of International Terrorism: Report of the National Commission on Terrorism, Pursuant to Public Law 277', 105th Congress, 2 August 2000, <www.fas.org/irp/threat/commission.html>.

Wendt, A. (1992), 'Anarchy is What States Make of It: The Social Construction of Power Politics', *International Organization*, Vol. 46, No. 2.

Yamamoto, T. (2000a), 'Economic Sanctions and Security Dilemma', *Waseda Journal of Political Science and Economics* (Waseda SEIZI KEIZAIGAKU ZASHI), No. 341.

—— (2000b), 'Clinton Administration's Policy towards China and Domestic Politics in the US', *Monthly Journal of International Affairs* (KOKUSAI MONDAI), No. 479.

—— (2001), 'Strategic Interactions and Political Dynamics in Japan's Entry into COCOM in 1952', *Waseda Political Studies*, No. 32.

—— (2002), 'Power, Wealth and Technology Transfer In World Politics: Political Dynamics of Science and Technology Activities in East Asia', *Waseda Political Studies*, No. 33.

—— (2003), 'Political Gridlock on Regional Export Control Regimes in East Asia: Who Could Cut the Gordian Knot?', *Waseda Political Studies*, No. 34.

—— (2004), 'Japanese Engagement in the PSI', *The Monitor*, Vol. 10, No. 1.

Yomiuri Shimbun (2005), 24 November 2005.

Yomiuri Shimbun (2005), 25 November 2005.

Notes

1. See Wassenaar Arrangement (undated), 'What is the Wassenaar Arrangement' <www.wassenaar.org/docs/talkpts.html>.
2. See Wassenaar Arrangement (undated), 'History of the Wassenaar Arrangement' <www.wassenaar.org/docs/History.html>.
3. In fact, Japan and the Republic of Korea (ROK) are the only full members of the WA in East Asia.
4. In the latter case, the Federal Grand Jury indicted MacDonell Douglas, a unit of the Boeing Company and Douglas Aircraft Company with 13 counts, including conspiracy, false statements and misrepresentations in connection with a 1994 export licence to sell 13 pieces of machining equipment to China. It also contains 12 charges against the buyer of the equipment, the China National Aero Technology Import and Export Corporation, or Catic, and Catic Affiliated in Beijing and California.
5. Although there is no concrete evidence, a North Korean defector claimed in Washington on 16 May 2003 that North Korea imported 90 per cent of its missile components from Japan. See Hwang (2003).
6. I name this policy of 'strategic ambiguity' in the last stage of the Clinton administration as the policy of 'constructive ambiguity', mainly because although it had been rather more involved in Taiwan's security in terms of sophisticated conventional weapons sales, it had tackled with and finally succeeded in gaining China's admission to WTO in order to make the reformist China a full member of the international free trade regime (Yamamoto 2000a).
7. The rising sense of insecurity in economic and military fields in the US is well illustrated in the 2005 annual report by the US–China Economic and Security Review Commission to Congress (see US Government 2005).

8. I use the term 'geo-science and technology' as a connecting and intervening variable between geo-politics and geo-economics. Technology export control policy, as a matter of course, should be included in this category of 'geo-science and technology' (see Yamamoto 2002).
9. In early May 2003, Tokyo police searched a company named Meisin suspected of attempting to export to North Korea electronic devices that could be used in North Korea's HEU programme to develop nuclear arms. See Hwang (2003).
10. The seminars were held in Indonesia, the Philippines, Thailand, Vietnam, Cambodia, Laos and Brunei until March 2005.
11. The Japan Federation of the Economic Organization (KEIDANREN) insists on establishment of a cross-ministry system to achieve comprehensive security in defence, economic, technological and other fields. (see <www.keidanren.or.jp/english/policy/2005/006.html>). This stance coincides with the official position of the Japanese government who pursue a comprehensive framework of regional security including a region-wide export control system.
12. 'Knowledge' regulation means that any exporting company must regulate itself in the export of goods and technology if and when the company is aware that the end-user would use the goods or technology for development and manufacturing of WMD. 'Informed requirement' means that any exporter must not export goods and technologies when informed by the authorities that the exports could possibly be used for the development and manufacture of WMD.
13. The list was first published in 2003. At the outset, 36 items were listed. Recently, aramid fibre, unmanned vehicle designed for installation of atomizer, and two other items were added to the list.
14. The 12th seminar was held 19–21 October in Tokyo. Eighty people from 21 countries participated, including China, Macau, Hong Kong and the US.
15. North Korea strongly reproached this decision as non-compliance behaviour against the Framework Agreement of 1994.

PART IV
The Future of International Export Controls

Chapter 10

The Proliferation Security Initiative: An Anti-Institution?

Richard T. Cupitt
Scholar-in-Residence, School of International Service, American University[1]

Chris Jones
PhD Candidate, School of International Service, American University

Stop the *So San*

During early December 2002, multilateral forces tracked the freighter *So San*, of Cambodian registry, through the Indian Ocean. The United States suspected that the freighter carried weapons of mass destruction (WMD)-related items from North Korea to the Middle East. Nearly a decade earlier, proliferation concerns had led the US to pressure China to direct the freighter *Yinhe* to a Saudi Arabian port for inspection. When the inspection uncovered none of the suspect items (thiodiglycol and thionyl chloride), the Chinese insisted on an apology and compensation for the action (Winner 2005, 130–31). Would the US face another embarrassment with the *So San* (Ricks and Slevin 2002)?

Acting on a request from the US, Spanish military personnel rappelled from helicopters to board the *So San* off the coast of Yemen on 9 December 2002. Unlike the *Yinhe*, the captain of the *So San* had struck its flag, which made it a vessel without nationality and legal to board and inspect the vessel (Winner 2004). The Spanish soon discovered falsified shipping documents and found missile parts hidden beneath some of the official cargo of cement mix (Joseph 2004). With this evidence of likely illicit activity, the Spanish turned the *So San* over to the US Navy, who re-routed the ship towards the US naval facility in Diego Garcia. At Diego Garcia, American experts uncovered 15 North Korean Scud missiles and 85 drums of missile fuel, as well as spare missile parts (Romero 2003).

After some discussions, including contact between the Yemeni government and senior US officials, Yemeni President Ali Abdullah Saleh announced that the missiles belonged to Yemen and insisted on their return (Knowlton 2002). As President Saleh had agreed not to purchase weapons from North Korea in 2001, he also asserted that Yemen had finalized the purchase in 1999 and that Yemen intended to use the missiles solely for defensive purposes (Knowlton 2002).

The US relented. Although they had followed a compliance approach of catch, expose or shame, then release, which heightened awareness of the transaction, the limits on Spanish and US legal authority to continue to hold the ship and its cargo contributed to this decision (Joyner 2005). On 11 December, the *So San* resumed its voyage and three days later she docked at the port of el Hodeida, where the Yemeni military received the cargo (Deutsche Presse-Agentur 2002). For its part, Yemen promised not to sell the missiles to any third party (Knowlton 2002). Most observers pointed to the US interest in having Yemen support for the war on terrorism as the real basis for the release of the *So San*.

Yemeni papers declared the event a 'triumph for Yemeni–American bilateral relations' (BBC 2002). Many Europeans, in contrast, ridiculed the Bush administration for its 'hard-liner activism' (Jarreau 2002). In Spain, for example, the press attacked the government for its role in the boarding (*El Mundo* 2002). Further embarrassment came one year later, when allegations surfaced that the missiles had gone to Libya (Drago 2003).

In the US, some pundits asked why the White House had not finalized plans for disposing of the missiles before the seizure (Safire 2002). Nonetheless, the Bush administration gave events a positive spin. Ari Fleischer, Press Secretary for President Bush, claimed that 'in the long term it might help the anti-proliferation cause by demonstrating the case for additional, tougher international measures' (Knowlton 2002).

Less than a year later, another case produced a profoundly different result. In early October 2003, German, Italian, United Kingdom and US forces worked together to intercept the German-flagged *BBC China*, which they believed had loaded WMD-related items in Dubai destined for Libya (Squassoni 2005). The multilateral force diverted the ship to Taranto, Italy, where they found more than 1,000 gas centrifuges and components that Libya could have used to further its attempts to acquire a nuclear arsenal (Squassoni 2005). This successful interdiction seemed to contribute to the Libyan decision to abandon its WMD programmes, and the opening of its programmes to examination by the international community. What made this case so different from that of the *So San*?

Initiative, Institution or Anti-Institution?

Taking 'tougher multilateral measures' to stop proliferation seemed an unlikely course for the Bush administration. Many critics had accused it of having a disdain for multilateralism. For evidence of this bias, one could point to the US withdrawal from the Kyoto Protocol, its role in blocking approval of the verification protocol for the Biological and Toxic Weapons Convention (BWC), and the invasion of Iraq without an additional specific mandate from the United Nations (UN) Security Council. Concomitantly, the US successfully led a campaign to unseat Jose Bustani as the Director-General of the Organization for the Prevention of Chemical Weapons (OPCW) and pursued a less successful effort to replace Mohamed ElBaradei as

Director-General of the International Atomic Energy Agency (IAEA) when their approaches to non-proliferation diverged from that of the Bush Administration. Many critics questioned their commitment to multilateral, truly multilateral, action.

Yet, as the administration had hoped, the *So San* episode appears to have sparked several governments to consider alternative approaches to more conventional non-proliferation policies, such as the treaty verification regimes and export controls. In 2003, results of this new thinking blossomed with the establishment of the Proliferation Security Initiative (PSI), announced by President Bush in May 2003. Eleven countries, during 12–13 June 2003, launched the practical efforts by joining in a senior policy meeting in Madrid to discuss how their countries could improve their capacity to interdict suspect shipments.[2]

The PSI proved very popular. Within a year of its inception, the governments of more than 60 countries had expressed support for the PSI. Reviewing that first year, Secretary of State Colin Powell stated that the PSI went in 12 months 'from a hopeful vision to establishing an active network of partnerships that has already shown tangible results' (Polish Ministry of Foreign Affairs 2004a, 80). In April 2004, the PSI even won implicit global endorsement through UN Security Council Resolution 1540 (2004).[3] More important, success did not mean the attraction of merely rhetorical expressions of support. By June 2005, new US Secretary of State Condoleezza Rice could note that in the previous nine months alone, eleven PSI partners had cooperated in eleven interdictions (Nicola 2005).

From the beginning, the founders of the PSI strove to make it an institution for action, not debate. A government, for example, did not 'join' the PSI. Admittedly, the founding countries became known as the 'core group' of the PSI, but such a designation held few practical benefits (or costs) to distinguish it from participation in the PSI generally.[4] Core group countries accrued one major benefit – only they participated in the six PSI meetings of senior policy makers that first year (see Table 10.1).

Table 10.1 Plenary Meetings in the First Year of the PSI June 2003–June 2004

Date	Location	Actions and decisions – highlights
12–13 June 2003	Madrid, Spain	• Agreed to address certain proliferation threats (interdiction against state and non-state actors) • Agreed to assess and strengthen existing interdiction authorities • Agreed to seek wider support
9–10 July 2003	Brisbane, Australia	• Agreed to hold interdiction exercises • Agreed to engage key flag, transit and coastal states • Agreed to strengthen their existing national legal frameworks

Date	Location	Actions and decisions x- highlights
3–4 September 2003	Paris, France	• Issued the Interdiction Principles • Confirmed their commitment to a schedule of training exercises
9–10 October 2003	London, United Kingdom	• Agreed that the PSI would welcome any state or international body that supports the PSI Principles • Agreed on a long list of training exercises
4–5 March 2004	Lisbon, Portugal	• Identified national points of contact • Reached an agreement on an approach to sharing law enforcement and intelligence information

Source: Polish Ministry of Foreign Affairs (2004b)

This opportunity to participate sounds significant, but these meetings had a sharply limited role. At the very first policy plenary in Madrid, the original eleven participants agreed that some countries (and some non-state actors) posed a greater WMD proliferation threat than others. They did not agree, however, to name such countries in public. More important, by the Paris policy plenary in September 2003, the core group countries issued their Interdiction Principles, stating that PSI states would:

1) Undertake effective measures, either alone or in concert with other states, for interdicting the transfer or transport of WMD, their delivery systems, and related materials to and from states and non-state actors of proliferation concern. 'States or non-state actors of proliferation concern' generally refers to those countries or entities that the PSI participants involved establish should be subject to interdiction activities because they are engaged in proliferation through: (1) efforts to develop or acquire chemical, biological, or nuclear weapons and associated delivery systems; or (2) transfers (either selling, receiving, or facilitating) of WMD, their delivery systems, or related materials.
2) Adopt streamlined procedures for rapid exchange of relevant information concerning suspected proliferation activity, protecting the confidential character of classified information provided by other states as part of this initiative, dedicate appropriate resources and efforts to interdiction operations and capabilities, and maximize coordination among participants in interdiction efforts.
3) Review and work to strengthen their relevant national legal authorities where necessary to accomplish these objectives, and work to strengthen when necessary relevant international laws and frameworks in appropriate ways to support these commitments.
4) Take specific actions in support of interdiction efforts regarding cargoes of WMD, their delivery systems, or related materials, to the extent their national legal authorities permit and consistent with their obligations under international law and frameworks, to include:

a) Not to transport or assist in the transport of any such cargoes to or from states or non-state actors of proliferation concern, and not to allow any persons subject to their jurisdiction to do so.
b) At their own initiative, or at the request and good cause shown by another state, to take action to board and search any vessel flying their flag in their internal waters or territorial seas, or areas beyond the territorial seas of any other state, that is reasonably suspected of transporting such cargoes to or from states or non-state actors of proliferation concerns, and to seize such cargoes that are identified.
c) To seriously consider providing consent under the appropriate circumstances to the boarding and searching of its own flag vessels by other states, and to the seizure of such WMD-related cargoes in such vessels that may be identified by such states.
d) To take appropriate actions to (1) stop and/or search in their internal waters, territorial seas, or contiguous zones (when declared) vessels that are reasonably suspected of carrying such cargoes to or from states or non-state actors of proliferation concern and to seize such cargoes that are identified; and (2) enforce conditions on vessels entering or leaving their ports, internal waters, or territorial seas that are reasonably suspected of carrying such cargoes, such as requiring that such vessels be subject to boarding, search, and seizure of such cargoes prior to entry.
e) At their own initiative or upon the request and good cause shown by another state, to (a) require aircraft that are reasonably suspected of carrying such cargoes to or from states or non-state actors of proliferation concern and that are transiting their airspace to land for inspection and seize any carrying such cargoes transit rights through their airspace in advance of such flights …
f) If their ports, airfields, or other facilities are used as transshipment points for shipment of such cargoes to or from states or non-state actors of proliferation concern, to inspect vessels, aircraft, or other modes of transport reasonably suspected of carrying such cargoes, and to seize such cargoes that are identified (Polish Ministry of Foreign Affairs 2004b, 11–12).

Critically, the PSI core group made these four principles *non-negotiable*. This helped to ensure that PSI meetings and operations would not succumb to polemical debates, but to focus on when, where, and how to act. When a country decided to support and participate in the PSI, they had to accept these principles without bargaining, compromise, or concession.

In addition, the core group chose not to agree, at least in a formal way, on any specific target countries, entities, persons, or items of concern. They also chose to work within the confines of existing national and international frameworks. As with making the Interdiction Principles non-negotiable, this strategy helped to keep PSI discussions from delving too deeply into the policy differences among core group countries or other PSI supporters regarding end-users and end-uses, nor diving into the extremely technical and uncertain world of controls on transfers of dual-use goods and technologies or maritime law.

In theory, PSI partners would make decisions on a shipment by shipment basis. Any PSI partner could call on other PSI members regarding a particular shipment to see if it generated sufficient interest among other states to begin a joint interdiction operation. While the like-minded nations of the core group subsequently took up other issues, such as overall strategies for the sharing of intelligence and law enforcement information and coordination of their outreach efforts, these early decisions allowed core group countries to place far greater emphasis on coordinating their operational activities. In other words, these decisions allowed them to concentrate on means for specific activities rather than the overall ends of the initiative.

In contrast to policy meetings, participation in operations theoretically remained open to any country that subscribed to the PSI Interdiction Principles and wished to contribute some of their assets to the particular effort. Practically, interdiction depends on timely coordination of intelligence, law enforcement and other national assets. While policymakers may need to condone or veto a particular operation, a sustained debate on the merits of cooperation, much less on how to coordinate their efforts, would prove self-defeating. To this end, PSI adherents formed an Operation Experts Working Group to address the more practical issues of cooperation and coordination. By April 2004, it had met six times (Wright 2004, 39). In many instances, this need to coordinate internationally appeared to spawn reform efforts within countries. Canada, for example, created an interagency working group from twenty ministries and agencies, which created a host of new individual and bureaucratic links, as part of its efforts to participate in PSI (Wright 2004, 40).

Table 10.2 Operational Training Exercises in the First Year of the PSI May 2003–June 2004

Date	Leading nation	Location	Type
12–13 September 2003	Australia	Coral Sea	Maritime
8 October 2003	United Kingdom	London	Air (desktop)
14–17 October 2003	Spain	Mediterranean	Maritime
25–27 November 2003	France	Mediterranean	Maritime
3–4 December 2003	Italy	Mediterranean	Maritime
11–17 January 2004	US	Arabian Sea	Maritime
19 February 2004	Italy	Mediterranean	Air
31 March–7 April 2004	Germany	Frankfurt	Land
19–21 April 2004	Poland	Poland	Land
19–22 April 2004	Italy	Mediterranean	Maritime

Source: Polish Ministry of Foreign Affairs (2004b)

For some, expressing support for the PSI Principles became an end in itself. By getting supporters to make public declarations of their commitment to the PSI, the core group created more opportunities for action, which could produce a greater global deterrent effect. Not surprisingly, some core group countries engaged in an assertive global outreach campaign to get more governments to support the Principles. Officials from the US Departments of State and Defence, for example, visited many countries to promote support for the PSI. Other outreach efforts had a regional focus, such as the meeting hosted by Poland for countries in central and eastern Europe in January 2004, the Japanese non-proliferation missions to the ASEAN countries in February 2004, and the meeting organized by Portugal for several African nations in March 2004 (Arai 2004, 63; da Silva 2004). Countries also attempted to enlist support from states that permit vessels, for a minor fee, to fly their flags. These 'flags of convenience' allow vessels owned by countries, entities or persons of criminal or terrorist concern to ply the seas hidden under an often deep and ill-regulated façade (Richardson 2005).[5]

Finally, PSI partners also took steps at outreach to the general public. Officials briefed and provided statements for the media, which helped generate extensive, and generally positive, coverage of the initiative. The operational exercises usually included a media component, including a press strategy and press releases. Several governments put information on the internet, while the Canadians volunteered to take the lead in maintaining a web site dedicated to the PSI at <www.proliferationsecurity.info> (Wright 2004, 40).

The public outreach effort had other objectives besides increasing the deterrent impact of the initiative. Initial suspicion about the purpose of the PSI ran high. Many critics thought that the core countries sought to use the PSI to challenge ancient laws of the high seas or the more modern rules established through the United Nations Convention on the Law of the Sea (UNCLOS). While some core countries may indeed wish to change such laws in the long term, the PSI Interdiction Principles and the outreach efforts made clear that interdictions would obey existing rules, which dissipated some of this concern. More important, no evidence exists that PSI contributors have contravened existing international law or cavalierly treated current international non-proliferation norms, which would undermine the credibility of the outreach message.

Similarly, officials needed to reassure industry. With more companies working on real-time production schedules, diverting a large ship to port to inspect a single container buried deep among several thousand imposes an immense economic cost for time lost alone, much less the liability associated with accidents or damage such actions may bring. Nonetheless, as recently as February 2005, participants at a Chatham House conference speculated 'that there must have been hundreds of interdictions' under PSI (Chatham House 2005, 3). If true, one might expect significant complaints from industry, which did not occur.[6] While no evidence exists that 'hundreds' of interdictions have taken place under PSI, PSI countries did work with the private sector to assuage concerns by noting that interdictions would not occur often and, when they did, authorities would target very high risk shipments.

Countries also included some companies in operational exercises, such as Lufthansa Cargo AG, recognizing the critical role legitimate industry plays in disrupting illicit trade networks (Kleinschmidt 2004). Finally, in August 2004, Denmark hosted a formal PSI outreach effort for industry to address the role of the major shipping lines within the context of PSI.

Outreach to the private sector has another important benefit besides showing that the PSI countries would not engage in aberrant practices: it can improve the links between the major legitimate cargo carriers (and, in a trickle down effect, their feeder companies) and key law enforcement, military and intelligence personnel. Good companies know more about their customers, competitors, products and the latest trade practices than governments ever will, making them an important connection for effective interdiction efforts.

Supporting the PSI

In addition to a public statement endorsing the PSI, the outreach programme called on prospective PSI participants to take other steps, including:

- reviewing and providing information on their current legal authorities to undertake interdictions on air, land, and at sea (a step the founding states also took);
- developing a set of specific national assets that might contribute to the interdiction of suspect shipments;
- identifying points of contact and creating appropriate internal processes for cooperating on interdictions;
- willingness to participate in training exercises;
- willingness to join in interdictions; and
- willingness to consider signing boarding, overflight, or other international agreements that could contribute to more effective interdiction efforts (Squassoni 2005, 2–3).

Most of the initial operational exercises during the first year focused on interdictions by military forces at sea (see Table 10.2). As the *So San* case made clear, governments had limited experience in multilateral military interdiction operations in the high seas. With more than 90 per cent of all trade, and more than 80 per cent of global trade in manufactured goods, going by sea, and the suspicion that al Qaeda alone controlled more than a dozen cargo freighters, the initial emphasis on maritime interdiction focused on a major gap in interdiction capabilities (Koch 2004; Mintz 2002). As important, the core group countries have considerable assets applicable to interdiction at sea, when compared with air or land interdiction efforts, which makes illicit sea-borne cargo of WMD or WMD-related items particularly vulnerable to strategies of prevention and denial.

Tactically, the exercises allowed participants to build cooperative mechanisms, create informal points of contact, and generate 'lessons learned'. Knowing who to contact and something about the character, knowledge, skills and abilities of that contact breeds the trust needed to generate quick and effective coordination. The Spanish-led Sanso 03 exercise in the western Mediterranean, for example, helped officials better understand how to integrate legal advice into the operation (Paez 2004). Over time, PSI participants also expanded their efforts to include air and land interdiction exercises, with similar tactical goals for learning how to coordinate action (see Table 10.2). For example, the 'Airbrake' operational exercise, which took place over Sicily in February 2004, taught participants about the need to have policy-level points of contact to meet the time constraints for effective air interdiction (Annunziata and Sardo 2004, 69).

Participants also increasingly recognized the need to integrate law enforcement and other executive agencies, such as customs or licensing authorities, into the process, particularly after the March 2004 policy plenary in Lisbon, Portugal. There officials began to identify law enforcement authorities that countries might bring to bear in interdictions (Polish Ministry of Foreign Affairs 2004b). On a practical level, military forces usually do not have the appropriate expertise or authority to delineate legal from illicit shipments, which made including those agencies that do have the expertise a prerequisite for effective interdiction. This principle holds even more truly for land route interdictions, where customs and border forces have traditional authorities not given to the military. In many, perhaps most, countries this kind of interaction demanded the evolution of new patterns of cooperation *within* governments as well as among governments (Wright 2004).

The Interdiction Principles also calls on states to strengthen their national and international legal authorities to perform interdictions. The development of new bilateral ship-boarding agreements provides the most obvious example of this endeavour. Typically, PSI partners patterned these agreements, such as the one signed between the US and Panama, on existing drug interdiction agreements. By reaching agreement with states that register a substantial number of flags of convenience, such as Liberia and Panama, PSI countries have expanded the opportunities for interdiction considerably. Finally, while the United Nations Security Council did not identify the PSI by name in Resolution 1540 (2004), it clearly legitimized PSI measures in paragraph ten of the Resolution.

Analysis

When compared to more formal international approaches to non-proliferation, such as the creation of the Nuclear Non-Proliferation Treaty (NPT), the establishment of the PSI moved at astonishing speed. Moreover, participating in the PSI involves real costs, from reorganizing domestic bureaucracies to employing military resources in physically risky operations. In contrast, while 156 of the 170 signatory states have ratified the Chemical Weapons Convention (CWC), five years after the CWC entered into force, more than 45 countries had yet to establish a national authority and an unknown, but presumably far greater number, had not taken steps to produce (much less implement) the necessary national legislative framework (Organization for the Prohibition of Chemical Weapons Secretariat 2001). What characteristics distinguished the PSI from other more formal forms of international cooperation such that it attracted support from very diverse quarters and prompted swift multilateral action? Will this support and momentum have a lasting impact on international relations?

Certainly, the PSI resembles a transitory self-help defence system as defined by the realist school of international relations (Morgenthau 1978). Although aimed at disrupting proliferation networks of both state and non-state actors, the PSI Interdiction Principles call only on states to do so and describe how states should take action, leaving the role of supportive non-state actors in ambiguity. Similarly, its initial operational exercises emphasized military action, following the example set with the case of the *So San*, as befits a realist approach. Moreover, the core group countries specifically avoided the creation of a permanent institutional structure or regular meetings of policymakers, which characterize most international governmental organizations, keeping the initiative state-centric.

At the same time, key members of the PSI core group have sought to use the PSI as a means to initiate or support efforts to reform existing international norms and international law. PSI members, for example, discussed and generally supported proposed amendments to the Convention for the Suppression of Unlawful Acts against the Safety of Maritime Navigation (SUA) that would make the transportation of WMD, their means of delivery and related materials criminal acts. Taken together, one can view the PSI as part of an effort to bring about long-term, permanent change in the framework of international relations. The focus of the PSI on interdicting the physical movement of goods in waters beyond the control of the original supplier country clearly filled a niche that more traditional prohibitions or restrictions on the production, accounting, physical protection or export of items had left open. As some have argued:

> [i]f, as seems obvious, sovereign states are involved in clandestinely developing and acquiring weapons of mass destruction and delivery systems (or using surrogates to deliver these weapons of terror), then the law must adapt and a new legal paradigm adopted to allow sovereign states to effectively respond without themselves being labeled international rogues (Roberts 1999, 483).

Many scholars of international relations note that long-term cooperation occurs even among countries with divergent interests, if sufficient mutual benefits exist, a condition not easily amenable to self-help explanations. In situations of unequal interests, achieving cooperation often requires one or more participants to generate side payments to induce support (Cupitt and Grillot 1997; Stein 1984). As officials crossed the globe promoting the PSI, they certainly had plenty of opportunities to offer inducements. No evidence exists, however, that the US or the other core group countries offered any form of carrot (or stick) to governments for supporting the PSI, beyond the intrinsic security benefits the initiative might produce. While this does not preclude the possibility that more diffuse forms of reciprocity had an important impact on state behaviour, that countries supported the PSI because of a common belief in the dangers of proliferation, and that improving interdiction capabilities could serve as another important tool in the anti-proliferation effort, makes for a simpler answer.

The PSI also fits uneasily into emerging models of global governance (Kahler and Lake 2004). Rosenau (2002), for example, identifies six major types of global governance, including the traditional state system, but none of these appear to include informal, top-down, state-led structure. The PSI does not – purposefully – even follow the more traditional yet informal forms of the supplier organizations, such as the Nuclear Suppliers Group or the Missile Technology Control Regime. The PSI does not, for example, use the decision-making principle of consensus and eschews high-level meetings of policymakers. Instead, the PSI relies on mini-coalitions of the willing functioning within a larger set of like-minded countries, and emphasizes operational action rather than information sharing and policy coordination.

From Initiative to Anti-Institution: The Long-Term Future of the PSI

As the Council of the European Union asserted in its endorsement of the PSI, the initiative complements the European Union (EU)'s '[s]trategy against the proliferation of WMD' and 'can provide an effective basis, consistent with national legal authorities and relevant international law and frameworks … to impede and stop trafficking in' WMD and their means of delivery (Council of the European Union 2004). To achieve this promise, however, PSI countries need to sustain their commitment to the PSI approach to interdiction, to continue to have successful interdiction operations, and to create new international norms and law that lead to increased effectiveness in disrupting illicit proliferation networks through interdiction. Squassoni (2005, 3) succinctly states the issue facing the Bush Administration and other political actors:

> PSI has no international secretariat, no offices in federal agencies established to support it, no database or reports of successes or failures, and no established funding. Many consider the lack of formal mechanisms an advantage …. Others, however, question the seriousness of the Administration's effort as well as its sustainability, as long as no formal mechanisms are created.[7] The current configuration holds nothing particularly to bind PSI adherents to this cooperative endeavor.

Will the PSI play out as a fad, one solely dependent on US interest? If so, then new priorities will arise that will attract the attention, time and resources of the government, and the PSI, as with the adage about old soldiers, will fade away. Will the PSI remain among the policy priorities for the next US administration of either political party? Can the US and its PSI partners sustain the operational coalitions that characterize PSI activities?

Serious policy failures could undermine current support for the PSI. Just a couple of spectacular interdiction failures could erode support quickly, within the US and among PSI supporters as a whole. An interdiction that finds nothing illicit, thereby halting purely legitimate traffic at considerable expense to the shipping company and the owners of the contents of thousands of containers, would certainly undercut the initiative. Cargo lines, compared with more itinerant tramp operators, make their profit on providing regular and dependable service on specific routes, which any maritime interdiction disrupts. If the PSI generates a number of 'false positives', serious questions and complaints about the costs and benefits of the initiative will arise. Worse, an interdiction that found something but, as with the *So San*, could not legitimately prevent the shipment from continuing on to its destination, coupled with a few false positive interdictions, could inflict a mortal wound on the initiative. Given the many highly public failures of intelligence related to WMD in recent years, governments can not discount these potential miscues. This suggests that the PSI partners should develop robust decision criteria regarding the choice to begin an interdiction. Issues such as the imminence and severity of the threat, the credibility of the intelligence, and the specifics of the disposition and end result sought need to appear on the agenda in any PSI decision-making process.

Equally as important, the more PSI succeeds, the more likely that non-state actors will use methods not subject themselves to PSI-like interdictions as have happened with traditional export controls. They will likely try to use PSI-proof routes, to bury the transactions even deeper under legitimate traffic, emphasize more indigenous development of items of concern, to rely more on 'home-grown' terrorists, increase use of the internet, and so forth, which will distract focus from the considerable energy required to sustain the PSI.

Nonetheless, one should not discount several positive elements now in place for long-term cooperation. The PSI has had several successes, and done so without interfering significantly with the flow of legitimate global commerce. Without the formal institutional restrictions that make change difficult in more structured international institutions, the PSI may adapt swiftly to changes in strategies among proliferators. In practice at least, PSI countries have adapted their operational exercises with alacrity through a 'lessons learned' process. As noted earlier, for example, they quickly expanded integration of and training for law enforcement as the limitations of a primarily military strategy became clearer.

In the end, the most serious challenge may come from policy fatigue. Political administrations often seek something to distinguish themselves from previous administrations, and continuing to highlight an initiative of a prior administration usually does not meet that need. In this case, support for training exercises alone requires a considerable investment in resources. If the PSI proves successful in the short term, however, determined proliferators will find other channels to meet their needs. Under such circumstances, transactions susceptible to PSI operations may no longer characterize an important channel for proliferation. In other words, if its niche disappears, then support for the expense of the training and networks needed to sustain PSI may falter.

In the long term, the PSI will have to prove its value as an effective and efficient tool alongside other non-proliferation programmes, such as export controls or materials protection, control and accounting. The cost of almost any specific maritime interdiction will exceed the cost of stopping the illicit transaction before the shipment takes place. In some instances, nonetheless, PSI countries will have no effective tool other than interdiction. More important, as with any non-proliferation or even counter-proliferation policy tool, interdiction will only buy time for PSI partners to address the larger of the demand for WMD. If PSI partners fail to make use of the time interdiction and other non-proliferation policy measures create, then they will waste any successes these tools may produce.

References

Annunziata, G. and Sardo R. (2004), 'Air Brake First LIVEX Air: Interdiction Exercise', *Proceedings of the Conference*, First Anniversary PSI Meeting, Krakow, Poland, 31 May–1 June 2004, Polish Ministry of Foreign Affairs, Krakow.

Arai, T. (2004), 'Japan's Efforts for Promoting Non–proliferation in Asia', *Proceedings of the Conference*, First Anniversary PSI Meeting, Krakow, Poland, 31 May–1 June 2004, Polish Ministry of Foreign Affairs, Krakow.

BBC (2002), 'Yemeni Daily Says Korean Vessel Incident "Triumph" for Relations with USA', *BBC Monitoring International Reports*, 17 December 2002.

Byers, M. (2004), 'Policing the High Seas: The Proliferation Security Initiative', *American Journal of International Law*, Vol. 98, No. 9.

Chatham House (2005), 'The Proliferation Security Initiative: Is It Legal? Are We More Secure?', <www.chathamhouse.org.uk/pdf/research/il/ILP250205.pdf>.

Council of the European Union (2004), 'Non-Proliferation Support of the Proliferation Security Initiative (PSI)', 10052/04 (Presse 189), <http://ue.eu.int/Newsroom>.

Cupitt, R.T. and Grillot. S. (1997), 'COCOM is Dead, Long Live COCOM: Persistence and Change in Multilateral Security Institutions', *British Journal of Political Science*, Vol. 27.

Da Silva, F.M.H. (2004), 'Proliferation Security Initiative: Outreach Dimension', *Proceedings of the Conference*, First Anniversary PSI Meeting, Krakow, Poland, 31 May–1 June 2004, Polish Ministry of Foreign Affairs, Krakow.

Deutsche Presse-Agentur (2002), 'Briefly Seized Scud Missiles Arrive in Yemen', 14 December 2002.

Drago, T. (2003), 'Spain: US Should Explain Libya Missile Shipment, Madrid Says', Inter Press Service/Global Information Network, 9 December 2003.

El Mundo (2002), 'Spain Criticizes USA for Handing Over Missiles Seized to Yemen', 12 December 2002.

Foley, M. (2004), 'The Proliferation Security Initiative: A New Multilateralism', *National Security Law Report*, Vol. 26, No. 2, Standing Committee on Law and National Security, American Bar Association.

Jarreau, P. (2002), 'Washington Authorizes Delivery of North Korean Scud Missiles to Yemen', *Le Monde*, 13 December 2002.

Joseph, J. (2004), 'The Proliferation Security Initiative: Can Interdiction Stop

Proliferation?', *Arms Control Today*, Vol. 34, No. 5, <http://www.armscontrol.org/act/2004_06/Joseph.asp>.

Joyner, D. (2005), 'The Proliferation Security Initiative: Non-proliferation, Counterproliferation and International Law', *Yale Journal of International Law*, Vol. 30, No. 2, pp. 507–48.

Kahler, M. and Lake, D.A. (2004), 'Governance in a Global Economy: Political Authority in Transition', *PS: Political Science & Politics*, Vol. 37, No. 3.

Koch, C. (2004), 'Remarks', Unpublished manuscript for the Proliferation Security Initiative Global Container Line Security Workshop, Copenhagen, 3 August 2004.

Kleinschmidt, G. (2004), 'Hawkeye Interdiction Exercise', *Proceedings of the Conference*, First Anniversary PSI Meeting, Krakow, Poland, 31 May–1 June 2004, Polish Ministry of Foreign Affairs, Krakow.

Knowlton, B. (2002). 'US Frees Freighter Carrying Missiles; Ship Allowed to Take North Korea Scuds on to Yemeni Port', *International Herald Tribune*, 12 December 2002.

Lehrman, T.D. (2004), 'Rethinking Interdiction: The Future of the Proliferation Security Initiative', *The Nonproliferation Review*, Vol. 11, No. 2.

Mintz, J. (2002), '15 Freighters Believed to Be Linked To Al Qaeda; US Fears Terrorists at Sea; Tracking Ships Is Difficult', *Washington Post*, 31 December 2002.

Morgenthau, H.J. (1978), *Politics among Nations*, Alfred A. Knopf, New York.

Nicola, S. (2005), 'Lawmaker Criticizes US Anti-WMD Initiative', Global Security Newswire, <www.nti.org/d_newswire/issues/2005/6/14/FB2B6527-DB80-427B-BABB-7C969193FF9D.html>.

Organization for the Prohibition of Chemical Weapons Secretariat (2001), 'National Implementation Measures: Legal Questionnaire: Further Analysis of Responses to the Survey of National Measures to Implement the Chemical Weapons Convention', <www.opcw.org>.

Paez, F.J. (2004), 'Spanish Experience on Maritime Interdiction Operations', *Proceedings of the Conference*, First Anniversary PSI Meeting, Krakow, Poland, 31 May–1 June 2004, Polish Ministry of Foreign Affairs, Krakow.

Persbo, A. and Davis I. (2004), 'Sailing into Uncharted Waters? The Proliferation Security Initiative and the Law of the Sea', *Research Report*, Washington, DC, British-American Security Information Council, <http://www.basicint.org/pubs/Research/04PSI.htm>.

Polish Ministry of Foreign Affairs (2004a), *Proceedings of the Conference*, First Anniversary PSI Meeting, Krakow, Poland, 31 May–1 June 2004, Polish Ministry of Foreign Affairs, Krakow.

—— (2004b), 'Calendarium: Crakow to Crakow', *Proceedings of the Conference*, First Anniversary PSI Meeting, Krakow, Poland, 31 May–1 June 2004, Polish Ministry of Foreign Affairs, Krakow.

Richardson, M. (2005), 'A Time Bomb for Global Trade: Maritime-related Terrorism in an Age of Weapons of Mass Destruction', *Viewpoints*, Singapore: Institute of South East Asian Studies <www.iseas.edu.sg/viewpoint/mricsumfeb04.pdf>.

Ricks, T.E. and Slevin, P. (2002), 'Spain and US Seize N. Korean Missiles; Scuds Were on Ship Bound for Yemen', *Washington Post*, 11 December 2002.

Roberts, G.B. (1999), 'The Counterproliferation Self-Help Paradigm: A Legal Regime for Enforcing the Norm Prohibiting the Proliferation of Weapons of Mass Destruction', *Denver Journal of International Law and Policy*, Vol. 27, No. 3.

Romero, J. (2003), 'Spanish Forces Intercept Scuds', *US Naval Institute Proceedings*, Vol. 129.

Rosenau, J.N. (2002), 'Governance in a New Global Order', in D. Held and A. McGrew (eds), *Governing Globalization: Power, Authority and Global Governance*, Blackwell, Malden, MA.

Safire, W. (2002), 'Bush's Stumble: The So-San Affair', *New York Times*, 19 December 2002.

Shanker, T. (2002) 'Threats and Responses: Arms Smuggling; Scud Missiles Found on Ship of North Korea', *New York Times*, 11 December 2002.

Squassoni, S. (2005), 'The Proliferation Security Initiative', *CRS Report to Congress*, 7 June 2005, < www.usembassy.it/pdf/other/RS21881.pdf>.

Stein, A.A. (1984), 'The Hegemon's Dilemma: Great Britain, the US, and the International Economic Order', *International Organization*, Vol. 38, No. 2.

Szyliowicz, J.S. (2004), 'International Transportation Security', *Review of Policy Research*, Vol. 21, No. 3.

US Department of State, Bureau of Non-Proliferation (2004), 'Fact Sheet: Proliferation Security Initiative', <www.state.gov/t/np/rls/fs/32725.htm>.

Winner, A.C. (2004), 'The PSI as a Strategy', *The Monitor*, Vol. 10, No. 1.

—— (2005), 'The Proliferation Security Initiative: The New Face of Interdiction,' *The Washington Quarterly*, Vol. 28, No. 2.

Wright, J. (2004), 'Co-ordination and cooperation in Support of the PSI: The Canadian Experience', *Proceedings of the Conference*, First Anniversary PSI Meeting, Krakow, Poland, 31 May – 1 June 2004, Polish Ministry of Foreign Affairs, Krakow.

Notes

1. Currently Expert and Technical Assistance Coordinator for the United Nations Resolution 1540 Committee (Special Committee of the Security Council). Formerly Special Assistant to Under-Secretary of State Kenneth Juster, US Department of Commerce Bureau of Industry and Security.
2. Australia, France, Germany, Italy, Japan, the Netherlands, Poland, Portugal, Spain, the United Kingdom and the US made up the original eleven.
3. See United Nations Security Council Resolution 1540 (2004), operational paragraph 10.
4. Several countries sought to become part of the 'core group' and eventually it did expand to include Canada, Denmark, Norway, Romania, Russia and Singapore.
5. Flags of convenience include Antigua and Barbuda, Aruba (Netherlands), Bahamas, Barbados, Belize, Bermuda (UK), Burma, Cambodia, Canary Islands (Spain), Cayman Islands (UK), Cook Islands (New Zealand), Cyprus, German International Ship Register

(GIS), Gibraltar (UK), Honduras, Lebanon, Liberia, Luxembourg, Malta, Marshall Islands (USA), Mauritius, Netherlands Antilles, Panama, St Vincent, Sri Lanka, Tuvalu, and Vanuatu (Mintz 2002).

6. The regulatory and enforcement authority of the governments involved, their economic power, and the private sector recognition of the threat that WMD proliferation poses to the global economy would mute some criticism. Nonetheless, compared with a condition where hundreds of interdictions took place, it seems unlikely that complaints would not emerge.
7. See transcript from Senate Government Affairs Committee, Subcommittee on Budget and International Security hearing on WMD and counter-proliferation, 23 June 2004.

Chapter 11

Restructuring the Multilateral Export Control Regime System[1]

Daniel H. Joyner
Lecturer, University of Warwick
Senior Research Fellow, Centre for International Trade and Security, University of Georgia

With the recent coalition action in Iraq, attention among international lawyers interested in the system for normative ordering of international security relationships has largely been focused on the arguments for and against the establishment of pre-emptive strike principles in both national security policy and international law to deal with the proliferation of weapons of mass destruction (WMD). The maintenance and legitimacy of such a principle, it is argued by some, are necessary to protect against the threats arising from such proliferation, including the acquisition and use of such technologies by states and non-state actors perceived to pose a threat to international peace and security.

While such arguments, and the exigencies presented by perceivably hostile states already in possession of destabilizing quantities of WMD-related material upon which they are based, are of interest and worthy of thorough study, they are not the focus of this chapter. This treatment will rather examine what is herein argued to be an even more important element in the overall programme of national and multilateral non-proliferation efforts than the doctrine of pre-emption – timely and effective prevention.

Benjamin Franklin noted in his *Poor Richard's Almanac* that 'an ounce of prevention is worth a pound of cure'. Although it is safe to assume that he never dreamed of the relevance of this classical maxim to modern security realities, its sage message is perfectly applicable. After all, it has become abundantly clear through revelations in the last decade that the lax export control standards of both national and multilateral regulatory frameworks contributed significantly to the development of the clandestine Iraqi WMD programme, a primary cause of two multinational wars in 12 years aimed at containing the perceived threat produced thereby (Holmes and Bertsch 2003). Due in part to these revelations and to the attacks of 11 September 2001, a number of important members of the international community have now pledged their resources to a perennial 'war on terrorism' with the explicit purpose of eliminating the threat of potential sources of WMD proliferation. And while current security imperatives may well justify this emphasis on active and invasive counter-proliferation initiatives, it would be well for the international community to remember that had more comprehensive and effective preventive measures, in the form of more developed export control regulatory frameworks, been in place at both national and multilateral levels, such a high level of continuing expenditures of resources and lives for the cause of security might not now be necessary.

These preventive frameworks will be the subject of the balance of this study. The multilateral export control regimes, which will be defined and discussed in detail later on, in particular have the potential to contribute significantly to the maintenance of a more harmonized and efficient overall non-proliferation regime at both the national and international levels, and thereby to the preventive programme of the international community in the area of WMD-related materials and technology and their proliferation to hostile or terrorist entities. The regimes have, however, been criticized in recent years as ineffective in performing their core roles of promulgating norms and facilitating coordination and cooperation among member states in the area of export control law and policy. This treatment will examine these claims of inefficiency and will seek both to provide commentary on their substance, and, more important, will propose means of institutional restructuring within the current multilateral export control regime system to remedy existing regime shortcomings.

As a policy matter, detailed study of the multilateral export control regimes and proposals for their strengthening could hardly be of more pressing and timely importance as they bear on the maintenance and improvement of one vital arrow in the quiver of the international community's non-proliferation efforts. From a theoretical perspective as well, however, these regimes are interesting examples of continuously functioning international soft law arrangements, which, while based upon non-binding foundational documents, yet have elements of institutional structure such as regularized meetings, sophisticated information sharing networks and procedures for continuing norm generation. In the context of these policy arguments, therefore, this treatment will also examine some modern thinking in both international legal theory and international relations theory, and utilize these understandings both to explain the character of the regimes more fully and in making proposals for the future direction of the regimes.

The Regime System

Consideration will first turn, however, to an explication of the regimes and their role and essential attributes, as well as some characteristics of the modern security environment in which they exist. The multilateral export control regime system is currently comprised of four separate and almost wholly independent functional supplier state regimes: the Nuclear Supplier's Group (NSG) in the nuclear weapons and materials context, the Wassenaar Arrangement (WA) in the conventional weapons context, the Australia Group (AG) concerned with chemical and biological weapons proliferation, and the Missile Technology Control Regime (MTCR) in the missile and related delivery system technologies area. Several of these export control and non-proliferation regimes supplement the provisions of binding, multilateral treaties primarily focused on the development and possession of weapons technologies, including the 1968 Nuclear Non-Proliferation Treaty (NPT), the 1972 Biological Weapons Convention (BWC) and the 1993 Chemical Weapons Convention (CWC).[2]

While differences exist among the particulars of the respective regimes, their essential attributes share a great deal of similarity. All are informal political arrangements, with no elements of legal formality in the commitments of member states either in the originating regime documents or with regard to subsequent guidelines and decisions made by or within the regimes. The regimes may perhaps best be described using the framework for characterization of security communities, as a subset of international institutions, laid out by Emanuel Adler and Michael Barnett.[3] This framework identifies security communities as arrangements between states wherein members share identities, values and meanings concerning issues related to their survival, and have an expectation of peaceful cooperation among themselves. These communities are typified by interaction among members exhibiting an appreciation of both short-term and long-term communal interests in cooperating on issues of security concern. Security communities may be either loosely or tightly joined together as gauged by the degree of interaction and structural formality of the arrangement (Adler and Barnett 1998).

Adler and Barnett classify security communities in their movement from loose to tight interaction and commonality of perspective using a categorical nomenclature of nascent, ascendant and mature communities. The multilateral export control regimes have varied in their placement within this categorization scheme both among themselves and also collectively over the course of their evolutionary track, at times arguably regressing within this hierarchy of developmental status. However, in general they may be described as bordering between nascent and ascendant communities, typified by their character as thoroughly informal, voluntary and vague associations of states who maintain discretion in implementing regime policies, but which at the same time have become influential in the promulgation of norms and in possessing some elements of institutionalization, including in some cases the appointment of permanent secretariats with staff and a standing physical presence.

Their primary purpose being to coordinate and harmonize national policies regarding non-proliferation export controls, the core membership of the regimes has traditionally been those states already in possession of significant amounts of such technologies, and therefore a proliferation threat (that is, supplier states). In addition to facilitating coordination and cooperation, the regimes have also become important promulgators of multilateral norms used in efforts by the regimes and by international civil society of compliance pressuring, directed both at regime members and non-members.

The central features of each regime include a control list, composed of items both of a single use (that is, of only military practical usefulness) and of a dual-use character (that is, with both legitimate civilian as well as WMD or high-end conventional weapons-related potential application) which are to be monitored with utmost diligence by member states within their national regulatory systems, and which should be a part of each member state's export licensing programme. These lists are regularly updated as their covered technologies develop. The regimes operate without exception on the principle of member consensus. Such consensus is needed either to change originating documents and amend control lists or promulgate additional guidelines or hortatory normative statements establishing minimal standards for member state behaviour in the context of export controls. These guidelines are uniformly vague and lacking in precision and are, of course, subject to national discretion in their implementation in state law and policies.

In most of the regimes, there are procedures for information sharing among member states particularly relating to licence denials. When a denial of an export licence for an item on a control list is made at the national level, member states under this rule are to notify the regime. This is a crucial element in ensuring member states that the restrictive policies of the regime will not be abrogated to the financial gain of one or a few members, to the corresponding loss of the remainder of member states whose positions have thereby been undercut and to the mooting of regime principles.[4]

Three out of four of the regimes can trace their origins to the Cold War period, and were initially formed by relatively small groups of 'like-minded' states the chief goal of many of which was to counter the influence of the Soviet Union and protect the security interests of the West through harmonized control of WMD-related materials and technology transfer (see Bertsch, Cupitt and Elliot-Gower 1994). However, particularly since the fall of the Soviet Union, the regimes have been faced with an identity crisis, and their character as supply-side regimes comprised of like-minded states has been challenged through the addition of new members, many of whom were former targets of regime controls, including Russia itself, and many of which are either questionable in their categorization as supplier states, have widely divergent perceptions of threat identification and security interests, or which are substantively lacking in resources to devote to export control efforts (see Gahlaut and Zaborsky 2003).

The regimes have in recent years been faced with other challenges flowing from global politico-economic macro phenomena.[5] These include the expansion in number of states possessing sufficient quantities of dual-use technologies to qualify as significant supplier states. This expansion, coupled with general trends of increased trade and the interlinking processes of globalization of business transactions and interests particularly in defence industries, has contributed to the threat of proliferation and the resulting complexity of regulating trade in WMD-related technologies at the multilateral level (see Reinsch 1999; Keller and Nolan 1997). Complicating matters further is the fact that some of these new supplier states have elected to remain outside of the existing regimes.[6]

In addition, public control of trade in dual-use items has been rendered more difficult through the phenomenon of privatization of dual-use goods production. In the Cold War years, development of dual-use goods and weapons-related technology was largely conducted by government-funded research, and thus was relatively easy to keep track of and regulate. More recently, however, production of dual-use technologies has shifted, in large degree, to elements of the private sector, as national governments have found that higher quality and lower prices are available 'off the shelf' in private markets. This shift has had the result of significantly decentralizing the production of sensitive items and requiring increased coordination between the private and public spheres and the institutionalization of corporate compliance measures in the private sector, a programme which has met with mixed results internationally.[7]

Also with the end of the Cold War, proliferation of WMD-related materials and technology has until recently taken a back seat in the minds of many policymakers, as the newly arrived unipolar moment and resultant 'new world order' has seemed to justify turning attentions elsewhere. As a result, there has been a lack of high-level political attention given to the multilateral export control regimes in the past 13 years. Part of this problem no doubt stems from the complexity of the issue area generally and the disparate nature of the regimes, with four separate (and not always functionally named) groups with independent mandates and lists of covered materials. The true possessors of expertise and keepers of institutional wisdom and concern relative to the regimes are to be found at mid-level official posts. This fact, while not harmful to the daily functioning of the regimes, has resulted in some stagnation in regime policies, as the natural difficulty of consensus building among nations to make desired changes is supplemented by the fact that those most 'in the know' regarding needed alterations do not have the authority to bring them about.[8]

Finally, Iraqi post-1991 WMD revelations along with fears concerning WMD development programmes, notably in North Korea and Iran, combined with the terror attacks of 11 September 2001, have thrust into the public spotlight the nexus of WMD proliferation and global terrorism as the most serious challenge facing the international community in the twenty-first century, and have highlighted the degree to which sophisticated states and non-state actors have acquired or are threatening to acquire WMD. In the wake of this modified calculus of geopolitical threat, the multilateral export control regimes have in recent years, and particularly in the wake of September 11, been the target of criticism by some, both within national governments and without, who claim that the regimes have been insufficiently adapted to the challenges posed by these and other forces of both external and internal character (see Cirincione 2000). Some commentators have claimed that the regimes have been ineffective in accomplishing the goal of stopping the proliferation of their subject materials and technology, and have insufficiently addressed the nexus of threat of terrorism and WMD proliferation in their policies. Some have even questioned the regimes' relevance and value to the international community's non-proliferation efforts going forward (see Latham and Bow 1998).

This chapter will proceed to consider the concerns raised by these commentators relative to the effectiveness and legitimate role of the multilateral export control regimes in the international community's twenty-first-century non-proliferation programme, and will posit that the regime system is in fact currently at a defining moment due to the clash of increased expectations for regime performance with inherent structural limitations of the regimes themselves. It will consider both policy and process level issues relating to this moment, and will propose significant efforts of restructuring of the regimes to remedy these inherent structural problems and to meet modern challenges to their effectiveness in filling their core non-proliferation roles.

Regime Effectiveness

From the start, it must be noted that analysis of regime effectiveness, as customarily cast in terms of member compliance with commitments undertaken in the context of the multilateral export control regimes, is an exercise in uncertainty and definitional difficulty. As will be explained in greater detail below, the guidelines of the regimes are extremely vague in outlining the parameters of member state commitments. For example, when considering the transfer of Category II items, including complete rocket systems (ballistic missiles systems, space launch vehicles and sounding rockets) and unmanned air vehicles (including cruise missile systems, target drones and reconnaissance drones), the MTCR Guidelines state only that 'Particular restraint will also be exercised in the consideration of transfers … if the Government judges, on the basis of all available, persuasive information, evaluated according to factors including those in paragraph 3, that they are intended to be used for the delivery of weapons of mass destruction, and there will be a strong presumption to deny such transfers'. Thus, the determination of threat and status of the end-user, along with the criteria for adjudging intent, as well as the level of 'restraint' appropriate in each case, is left wholly to national discretion based only upon a number of listed factors without authoritative interpretation or objective standards and with no transparent process for verification.

In any case of alleged non-compliance with regime commitments, therefore, there is precious little in the way of objectively ascertainable standards by which to determine such compliance, with the result that reliable or objectively legitimate studies or reports on levels of member compliance with regime norms have been impossible to produce. This fact has made efforts of reform of the regimes all the more difficult, as there has been very little data to point to establishing a compliance problem. This combined with the further reality that some influential nations have a vested interest in maintaining lax or ambiguous multilateral export control standards have made proposals for restructuring relatively easy for those officials to dismiss as unnecessary.

The compliance problem in the regimes can therefore be best described not only as one wherein existing rules are not being complied with, or implemented sufficiently in national legal systems, but also one in which what rules there are, are incapable of authoritative interpretation and determination, due to the institutional characteristics of the regimes (discussed further below), on which to base a determination of non-compliance. That being said, there is a general understanding among observers of the regimes that a number of key regime members have acted in the past and are continuing to act in significant disharmony with interpretations of their commitments commonly held by a majority of regime members. Common targets of such criticism have included Russia and, in some cases, France and the United States, with regard to their commitments in the context of regimes of which they have been members.

Of course casting the concept of regime effectiveness in terms of member compliance with existing commitments is in fact only half of the picture. The other half is the substance of the norms themselves. A hundred per cent member state compliance with norms insufficiently constructed to address proliferation problems would still not produce a regime system effective in achieving its goals in this regard. In reality, therefore, the ineffectiveness of the multilateral export control regimes is necessarily viewed as a two-fold problem, consisting both of levels of compliance with existing norms, and with the insufficient character of the norms themselves. However, both aspects of this larger issue of regime effectiveness can be viewed as being framed within the context of the gap between heightened expectations for regime effectiveness, to be found in statements of policymakers and others, and institutional facets of the current structure of the regimes themselves.

Structural Problems

Critics have identified a number of problems with the institutional structure of the regimes as currently constituted which are claimed to be at the root of problems of regime ineffectiveness. It is proposed herein that it would in fact be more accurate to describe these structural elements as limitations rather than problems in the most fundamental sense. For, as the insider government officials who constitute the functioning members of the regimes are quick to point out, the regimes were never designed to fulfil the expectations which have been placed upon them of late. Indeed, as previously noted the origin of the multilateral export control regimes is to be found in small groups of supplier states (of generally uniform identity throughout the regimes) relatively speaking of a 'like mind' concerning perceptions of threat (that is, states to be the target of regime controls) and their security interests in general.

The primary function of the regimes during their formative stages was to aid in the harmonization of national export control policies and to provide fora for cooperation, information sharing, and the promulgation of norms to govern trade in sensitive items and technologies. The regimes were not originally mandated to take on separate lives as organizations, charged with taking independent measures in the struggle against proliferation, and were certainly not chartered as institutions focused upon the very nebulous and at that time immature phenomenon of international terrorism. In fact, most officials maintain that the regimes have performed relatively well given their modest mandates and have been effective in accomplishing their goals of facilitating cooperation among member states relative to their national non-proliferation efforts.[9]

However, there is a simple tautological truth in the statement that voluntary, normatively vague organizational and rule-making structures are efficient in accomplishing their aims only when those aims are of a character which can be satisfied by levels of uniformity in member-state compliance consistent with voluntary, vague and, thereby, unenforceable rules. This almost insultingly simple maxim-like statement has however profound implications for the multilateral export control regime system. As will be more fully discussed below, if the current regime system is to be instrumental in effecting increased levels of harmonization among national export control policies and compliance with a multilaterally conceived set of normative bases for the deterrence of WMD proliferation, as is desired by many in the security community, it will by necessity need to be endowed with an institutional structure capable of the clarity, independent interpretive discretion and precision necessary to bring about such results (see Beck and Gahlaut 2003).

Informality

Among the limitations in existing elements of regime structure which have been identified, the most problematic and influential is the informal nature of the regimes as institutions (see Beck 2000). As previously noted, each of the regimes was established by its members with no legally binding character attaching either to originating documents (which as a rule were adopted only by joint declaration and without signatures) or to subsequent guidelines or decisions of the regimes, including those relating to the harmonization of members' national licensing systems with regime control lists. For this reason, many have quite accurately likened the current structure of the multilateral export control regime system to a collection of 'supplier states clubs', bereft of normative or legal foundation or compulsory procedures to produce compliance with regime rules.[10] In addition to this weakness in the 'letter' of regime documentary foundations, is the further fact that the regimes as previously noted have been endowed with uniformly vague substantive rules, an aspect of their structures which has traditionally bedevilled efforts of promoting compliance even with the 'spirit' of the regimes.[11]

A further particularly poignant example of this vagueness in substantive regime rules is the lack of consensus in any of the regimes regarding end-users of concern. The technological annexes to the regimes are, as a general rule, highly detailed in their specification of items subject to regime regulation. Thus, when contemplating an export, a regime member may be reasonably assured of the sensitivity level of items in question. However, due to the lack of consensus on bad end users, there is very little either in the guidelines or annexes of the regimes to guide a member state as to proper and improper destinations for the items. This absence of a collective determination of threat and end users of concern has had a significant undermining effect upon efforts to promote compliance with a multilaterally conceived set of normative prescriptions, and has left states to their own devices in making determinations of threat with no procedure for resolution of these issues having been achieved in the documentary foundations of the regimes.

International law has classically recognized two sources of binding norm generation in relations among states. The first is treaties, which are written agreements between two or more parties, the obligations of which apply solely to those executing the treaty. Treaties are binding upon their signatories and subject to adjudication in international judicial fora. The second is customary international law, which develops through the acts of states accompanied with sufficient *opinio juris*, or expressed sense of legal obligation, of state officials.[12] Custom may form parallel to or wholly independent from treaties and may bind not only those who participate in its creation, but potentially also other states who do not successfully obtain persistent objector status while the customary norm is in creation (see Chayes and Chayes 1994; Szasz 1994). While not without theoretical and practical weaknesses as a true system of law, these two sources have traditionally been held to produce binding obligations, or 'hard' international law.

Such structures as the multilateral export control regimes by contrast are representative of a modern movement in international law and organization to give some credence to the normative utility of instruments and understandings between state parties that are not strictly speaking legally binding, but which are entered into with an expectation that they will influence the behaviour of their declarants (see Harris 1998).[13] Speaking of the proponents of this 'soft law' movement, one commentator has written:

> they stress that these instruments fulfill at least some, if not a great number, of the criteria required for rules to be considered rules of international law and cannot therefore be simply put aside as non-law. In other words, they acknowledge that there exists a considerable 'grey area' of 'soft-law' between the white space of law and the black territory of non-law. Simultaneously, they make the salient point that the 'grey area' may greatly affect the white one and explain, sometimes in considerable detail, in what ways 'soft law' can have legal effects (Van Hoof 1983).[14]

There are of course sound reasons why the framers of the various multilateral export control regimes chose to institutionalize the international regulation of the area of non-proliferation export controls using softer, as opposed to harder, forms of institutional structure and procedures. As noted in one of the leading treatments of the relative advantages of soft versus hard law structure in international organizations, hard law is best utilized to regulate areas of international interaction in which the value placed on making credible commitments is high, reduction of long-term transactions costs from continual re-negotiation is important, political strategies may be supplemented by adjudicative or otherwise legalistic international regimes, and where delegation of authority to international fora is an attractive means for remedying inherent problems of incomplete contracting (Abbot and Snidal 2000).

It concludes that soft law, by contrast, is most attractive in issue areas in which a premium is placed on low initial contracting costs, where the use of hard law would present unacceptable sovereignty costs (which are highest when proposed international legalization touches upon important issues of national security), and where the novelty and complexity of the issue area create a high degree of uncertainty and possibility for positional change which make hard law enshrinement of norms unattractive. It also recognizes soft law as being an efficient means of compromise between antagonistic positions between states, particularly in the early stages of normative consideration of a subject area (ibid.).

The area of non-proliferation export controls, particularly in the sub-categories of WMD-related and dual-use items, is an issue area intimately tied to perceptions of national security interest and fundamental national sovereignty concern. It additionally has from its inception constituted an attempt to regulate a variety of dynamic and often overlapping technologies and their transfer to end users the threat status of which is a source of considerable contention among regime members. Thus, it is an area convincingly argued to be best regulated, at least in the preliminary stages of regime formation, by softer, more cooperative organizational understandings as opposed to harder, more compulsory ones (see Stein 1993; Grieco 1993; Martin 1993).

Again, however, for the heightened expectations of observers of the regimes to be met, that is, for the regimes to be both more effective in the promulgation of adequate norms addressing problems of WMD proliferation and in facilitating member implementation of those norms in their national systems, it is this chapter's contention that attention will need to be paid to proposals for increasing the formality of the structure of the regimes. However, as a fuller discussion of this point below will establish, this formalization need not be effected by an increase in the binding nature of commitments relative to the regimes. Rather, employing modern trends in both international legal theory and international relations theory it will be argued that increases in specificity of those commitments, combined with the institution of an adjudicatory forum within the structure of the regimes to which will be delegated interpretive authority, can together constitute the necessary elements of formalization for increasing member compliance and regime effectiveness.

Consensus Rules

In addition to informality, another limitation in the structural make-up of the regimes which has been pointed to by critics is the practice in all the regimes of acting only upon the basis of consensus (Beck and Gahlaut 2003). The consensus rule applies across the board to changes in originating documents, changes to guidelines, membership decisions, as well as alterations to control lists. This consensus principle, while understandable considering the sovereignty and security relevance of the issue area of WMD non-proliferation export controls, has formed a significant hindrance to the effectiveness of the regimes in promulgating progressive norms and in facilitating harmonization of members' national export control systems. It has, according to experts, made the regimes slow to respond to technological changes, including intelligence on new military applications of existing technologies, new means of acquisition of illicit materials and technology by states of concern, and other emerging threats to international security.

Consensus rules have become a particularly difficult problem due to the more recent phenomenon of expansion of regime membership, and the inclusion of states with highly varied perceptions of threat and concern regarding trade in sensitive technologies. Due to the maintenance of consensus voting rules, regime action can be, and in fact has often been, held up by one dissenting member. This fact is even more troubling to members forming a majority view on such points as it is understood that any change in regime voting rules, or in the membership status of problematic members, is held hostage by the very same principle.

Consensus voting rules within the regimes are in fact the principal reason for the conclusion that, in order for meaningful restructuring of the regimes to take place, an entirely new institutional structure for the regimes will need to be created. Simply put, with the consensus voting rules in place no significant restructuring to meet modern challenges and heightened expectations, and to remedy structural limitations of informality and the very existence of such rules, will take place because at every turn in this process there will inevitably be aggrieved and dissenting regime members. Changes in structure to allow for greater formality and lesser unilateral control over regime decision-making will, by their very nature and purpose, affect a loss in autonomy of members to act according to their national discretion. In the security realm as in others, but poignantly so in this context, such concessions of national sovereignty are not made lightly by states and perspectives on details of the new regime order are likely to vary substantially among members. Thus it will fall to those states desirous of pushing forward the non-proliferation efforts of the international community to new levels of effectiveness to institute a bold new programme of reform and creation of a new regime *sui generis*, which while sharing many characteristics and attributes of the existing regimes will be a new and independent merged entity.[15]

This referenced division of perspectives will, of course, yet be the case even in the context of the creation of an entirely new institutional structure. The advantages of such a new programme of establishment, however, include the fact that the states who will again be at the nucleus of this revised effort are likely to be relatively like minded and therefore able to compromise and produce results due both to their like-minded and cooperative relationship as well as the fact that in this effort compromise is crucial, as no higher powers (such as veto powers) will have yet been granted to negotiating participants. To this new institution formed ideally by a small number of the most influential supplier states will undoubtedly be drawn the other supplier states, including emerging supplier states, whose membership will not only be a sign of maturity and inclusion in the international community, but whose prosperity can – as it has in the case of membership in the existing regimes – be linked in very real ways to accession to the new comprehensive regime structure.

In the interests of contributing to debate within both legal and policy circles relative to the potential design of such a merged and restructured multilateral export control regime system, this chapter will proceed to consider concrete proposals of institutional restructuring to aid in meeting the referenced modern challenges of politico-economic reality and increased expectations of the security community, and to remedy the identified structural limitations of the existing regimes.

New Regime Foundations

The advantages of a new restructured and merged regime system in the multilateral export control context include at the most basic level those efficiencies which naturally flow from centralization. Not least among these advantages is simple avoidance of redundancy and duplication of effort. Notwithstanding their different subject areas of control and the separate identities and developed cultural characteristics, as well as attached policy and technical expert communities of the four existing regimes, they yet boast nearly identical membership rolls. And while bureaucratic turf wars may ensue within national governments if member states are limited to one delegation to the regime system instead of four, it remains the case that issues and strategies to deal with the complex controls and end user issues present in all four current regimes are very similar if not identical and may therefore most logically and efficiently be addressed in one unified structural framework.

Second, the co-location in a single institutional context of all regimes focused on multilateral WMD non-proliferation export controls would facilitate inter-regime dialogue on issues of cross-cutting concern, including trans-shipment, transfers of intangible technologies, information sharing and end users of concern. Third, centralization of regime activities into one overarching forum would save scarce resources and cut down on what have become excessive practices of 'diplomatic tourism', in which the international working groups of official experts have been known to spend vast percentages of their calendars in travelling to the far flung meetings of each respective regime only to interact with the very same cast of diplomatic characters, simply wearing different regime delegation name tags.

Finally, a centralized multilateral export control regime system would counteract the previously identified problems of issue area complexity and confusingly dispersed and independent regime frameworks which have hindered the attraction of higher-level political attention to regime issues. These even more calendar-challenged and attention-sparse higher-ups would be significantly more likely to attend one comprehensive plenary meeting covering all subjects of export control concern, held in one locale, than they would to attend four annual plenaries, one for each sub-regime. Their participation and realization of the importance of and need for multilateral coordination of export control efforts would have an incalculable effect upon the future direction and success of such efforts, particularly in their ability to negotiate substantive changes to the regimes as needed to allow them to better adapt to the constantly changing international security environment (see Beck and Gahlaut 2003). In addition to these simple advantages of co-location, however, could be added more substantive structural modifications to the existing regime system.

Formalization

First, on the topic of informality. There is a substantial literature linking formalization in the institutional structure of international regimes, and particularly in the substance of obligations undertaken by regime members, to increased member-state compliance with regime rules. There are in fact at least two treatments that argue for such binding formalization in the specific context of the multilateral export control regime system (see Gualtieri 2000; Kellman 1994). According to this literature, formalization of commitments and institutionalization of commitments in regime structures is facilitative of state compliance because of its functions in clearly delineating legitimate and illegitimate state behaviour, reducing transaction costs, establishing clear standards for state behaviour, establishing linkages between issues and between regimes, improving confidence in information sharing, reducing motivations to cheat, enhancing the value of reputation, and making decentralized enforcement possible by creating processes of institutional monitoring (see ibid.; Chayes and Chayes 1995; Keohane 1984; Slaughter Burley 1993; Jervis 1983).

There is also, however, a considerable and growing literature disputing the claim that an increase in the binding nature of commitments at the documentary foundation of international regimes inescapably leads to increased levels of member compliance. Rather, say proponents of this opposing view, formalization in the structure of international institutions can be separated into at least three broad sub-categories – obligation, precision and delegation – the sum of the relative presence of each being the functional determinant of the degree of formalization, or legalization, present in the regime. As described by Keohane et al.:

> 'Legalization' refers to a particular set of characteristics that institutions may (or may not) possess. These characteristics are defined along three dimensions: obligation, precision, and delegation. *Obligation* means that states or other actors are bound by a rule or commitment or by a set of rules or commitments. Specifically, it means that they are *legally* bound by a rule or commitment in the sense that their behaviour thereunder is subject to scrutiny under the general rules, procedures, and discourse of international law, and often of domestic law as well. *Precision* means that rules unambiguously define the conduct they require, authorize, or proscribe. *Delegation* means that third parties have been granted authority to implement, interpret, and apply the rules; to resolve disputes; and (possibly) to make further rules (Keohane et al. 2000).

In some cases, it is argued, greater legalization of commitments, as through the conclusion of binding treaties, is not advantageous, particularly as those obligations cover areas of state interaction in which sovereignty costs and uncertainty are high (ibid.; Abbot and Snidal 2000; Trachtman 1999; Downs et al. 1996; Goldstein and Martin 2000). The clear relevance of WMD export controls to concerns of national security and the intimacy of security to perceptions of national sovereignty, along with the previously mentioned technologically dynamic aspects of export control regimes, serve to qualify perfectly the multilateral export control regime system as a candidate for informal obligation in the documentary structure of the regime.

However, it is also important to note that formalization in the structural attributes of international regimes, and its attendant positive impact upon compliance by member states, can be effected in the absence of legalized obligations by increases in either the precision of regime rules or by processes of delegation of some rule-making or interpretive authority to regime structures or by a combination of these elements. Examples of regimes in which formalization has been achieved through a combination of precision and delegation include the United Nations (UN) Committee on Sustainable Development (Agenda 21) with its accompanying non-binding normative instruments, including the Forest Principles adopted at the 1992 Rio Conference on Environment and Development (high precision and moderate delegation), the CSCE/OSCE's 1975 Helsinki Final Act (high precision and low delegation), and the UN Human Rights Commission (low precision, high delegation).[16]

Compliance

A note on compliance. In formulating theories of state compliance with international law prescriptions, it is easy and perhaps too common to project our assumptions flowing from individual and collective experience living under the vertical enforcement mechanisms of national legal systems onto the international legal system writ large. As most such exercises are, however, this fallacy of composition is based upon a fundamentally misinformed conception of the contours and substantive attributes of the international legal system, and therefore leads to false expectations for the behaviour of its processes and creations. Compliance with the dictates of international law, or the rules of international organizations, is in fact effected through a much more complex, much looser horizontal system of both domestic and international pressure by citizens and by other states and non-governmental actors (Chayes and Chayes 1993; Guzman 2002; Koh 1997). Its primary guarantor of enforcement relies upon a cost–benefit (or cost–value) analysis by the state-subjects of such rules, an analysis which is fuelled and informed by the enmeshing results of globalization, issue linkages, norm internalization and the increasing legalization of many aspects of international relations (see Elster 1989; Braithwaite 1989; Honneth 1995; Martin 1992; Checkel 2001).

There are substantial grounds on which to posit, therefore, that at least in some areas of international interaction, levels of state compliance with international norms within regimes are not significantly increased through the legalization of underlying commitments. Rather, in areas in which softness of obligations is either a theoretical utility or political necessity, attempts to increase the formalization of obligations of member states may in fact lead to an over-playing of the hand of the organization and of the international legal system in general, likely resulting either in a substantial increase in vagueness or generality in substantive rules and commitments or, if the former does not occur, in a compliance deficit which the organization does not have the institutional capacity to narrow. As Joel Trachtman has explained:

> hard law is not necessarily good law, and strengthened implementation, including possible direct effect, is not necessarily desirable. This seems obvious once we recognize that, putting aside for a moment transaction costs and strategic costs, states generally have the level of compliance that they want. The correct role for scholars and for lawyers involved with these issues is to help political decision-makers to identify circumstances in which, due to such problems, states have not achieved the desired level of compliance (Trachtman 1999).

Implicit in this assertion is that it is the weight of a norm as a recognized international community standard, with the corresponding moral, reputational, and precedential factors militating for its observance, that in fact effects compliance and not the precise status of the norm in the relative hierarchy of legality imposed by the international legal system.[17] Thus, in some cases it is highly preferable to have specific, soft commitments than to have more vague, binding commitments as the specificity of the norm is more likely to form a principled locus around which efforts of domestic and international compliance pressure may be focused (see Checkel 2001).[18]

This observation, that states are often no more likely to comply with a norm in its legalized incarnation than in its embodiment in softer, non-binding instruments, is inspiring of optimism in the modern era in which increasing use is being made of soft law based regulatory or cooperative regimes in a variety of international issue areas in order to overcome the difficulties of securing hard commitments particularly in areas of state sovereignty sensitivity.

The immediate implications for the multilateral export control regimes include the strong likelihood that an increase in specificity of regime rules and some form of albeit primitive delegation for the purpose of interpretive uniformity can lead to increased state compliance with a more cohesive set of regime rules even in the absence of more binding documentary structures, which are unlikely to be concluded by member states in this area in the near future. This proposal for reforming the multilateral export control regime system into a merged institutional structure still based on non-binding initial documents yet comprised of significantly more formalized substantive provisions and procedures is based upon an understanding and appreciation of the particular nature of multilateral regulation in this sovereignty-sensitive area. It is in the final analysis a far more politically palatable option for policymakers to consider, and hopefully even embrace, than is the position of some observers of the regimes, who in haste to recommend changes to deal with the apparent weaknesses of the regimes adopt overly-elementary and non-politically viable structural models for such modification.

Non-Consensual Voting Procedures

Second, on the topic of consensus voting rules, a restructured multilateral export control regime system could incorporate a diversified approach to institutional decision-making, leaving in place consensus voting procedures for those issues of first importance (that is, deal breaking issues such as new member admissions) and for elements of regime identity (that is, amendments to originating documents), but substituting super-majority or weighted voting procedures for an array of decisions in such areas as modification of control lists, identification of member violations, sanctioning and expulsion of members, passage of guidelines, and identification of end users of concern.

This substitution of non-consensual voting procedures is a vital part of any proposed restructuring effort and is becoming increasingly necessary particularly due to the new membership issues discussed previously and the admission to the regimes since the end of the Cold War of states with widely varying threat perceptions and value placed on export controls. It would enormously aid in the efficiency of the regime and the ability of members to make needed changes and take action deemed by a vast majority of members to be prudent without fear of being forever hung by procedure through the dissenting votes of one or a few members.

While it is relatively easy to propose the institution of non-consensual voting procedures for the new regime structure, this in fact is no modest proposition inasmuch as it is likely to face strident opposition by many current regime members. This again raises the question of status quo versus something different, and the clashing of higher expectations with current structural regime limitations. Despite this opposition, based in arguments of sovereign autonomy and the sensitivity and security relevance of regime decisions, it is likely to be the case that if the originating nucleus of states-proponents of the restructured regime commit themselves and their influence to the establishment of a merged and restructured entity including the elements of formality and voting procedures discussed in this section, there will be a domino effect of second-tier supplier states and others who will accept membership in the new regime to preserve their place in the international security community and to safeguard their prosperity in a globalizing economy, in which to be labelled a pariah by the most influential members of the international community, particularly in the area of WMD proliferation, is to unlock a Pandora's box of danger and difficulties.

New Regime Design

Having reviewed some general structural amendments which could be incorporated into a new multilateral export control regime system, this chapter will proceed to offer a more detailed proposal of an institutional model for the new merged and restructured regime. This in fact is an area in which this treatment hopes to make a significant contribution to existing debates concerning the future of the multilateral regimes, as to the author's knowledge no such detailed institutional proposals have ever been offered. This section will bring principles of institutional design and organizational structure to bear on the question of what institutional model would best suit the renewed multilateral export control regime system.

In many ways, forming an international institution is an exercise similar to that in which a private corporate lawyer engages when considering the structure of a new corporation. There are of course a number of legitimate models to choose from in the corporate design context, each coming with a particular set of advantages and areas of strength which must be fit to the corresponding facts of the case to determine which model will produce the best and most desirable fit. When forming an international institution, consideration must first be had of the particular needs and characteristics of the issue area in question and the desires and needs of potential member states. Then and only then can a proper institutional framework be divined by creative thinking and by reference to the vast array of designs already in place to facilitate international interaction in various issue areas.

Taking into consideration the needs and desires of the multilateral export control regime system and its concerned community, this chapter will advance the thesis that an institutional arrangement most analogous to that currently in employ in the World Trade Organization (WTO) will best suit those needs and lead to greatest efficiency and potential success for the restructuring effort. Before beginning this exercise, however, it should be clear that this chapter's contention is simply that elements of the structural and procedural attributes of the WTO system, and not necessarily the role or function of that system, could find useful application in the multilateral export control regime context. In so disclaiming, it is hoped that automatic cognitive reference to issues of current discussion and perhaps concern peculiar to the latter characteristics of the WTO system will be avoided.

That being said, however, the history of international regulation of general trade since the mid-twentieth century, as considered by analogy from an institutional development perspective, is in fact also quite instructive to the current discussion concerning the multilateral export control regime system.[19] Commercial trade between nations has historically been among the most sensitive of areas to regulate because of the potential far-reaching effect of such regulation upon perceived domestic prerogatives and the importance of successful international trade to national economies. After the Second World War, the largest economic powers concluded on a relatively loose association to preliminarily cover the area of international trade, established by the General Agreement on Tariffs and Trade (GATT). While technically a binding international agreement, the GATT was in actuality quite soft in a number of ways.

The GATT was subject to a number of institutional 'birth defects' having never been intended or structured to compose a true organization in the international legal sense and being adopted only provisionally after the failure of the International Trade Organization in 1950. Partially due to its unintended rise to prominence, the provisions of the GATT relative to rule-making and adjudication were fashioned quite broadly and vaguely, attributes of its structure which would come back to haunt it time and again as lack of clarity and precision in its provisions led to *ad hoc* and inconsistent application of its precepts, and very often simple neglect of its use. Its adjudication procedures as well were often hamstrung in their effectiveness due to the practice of requiring consensual adoption of panel rulings in order to bestow finality upon them – including the consent of the state against whom the adjudicatory panel had ruled.

These and other institutional imperfections, including the fact that the GATT was entered into as an executive agreement by the United States and never subjected to Senate ratification, also led to great doubt and disagreement as to the relevance of GATT rules and adjudicatory procedures to national law and policy. In the United States in particular, there was great debate in legal circles as to the binding character of GATT obligations in national law. This ambiguity relative to implementation of GATT policy further strained its institutional credibility and thereby undercut its effectiveness in regulating the area of international trade (Jackson et al. 1995). The GATT however served to introduce some normativization to the issue area, and in doing so illustrated in a fairly non-threatening way to its signatories the advantages of mutual cooperation in the area based on norms.

With the institution of the World Trade Organization in 1995, many of the inefficiencies proceeding from structural imperfection in the GATT were remedied. The provisions of the World Trade Organization Agreement were decidedly more clear and comprehensive, particularly in terms of the administrative structure of the organization, than were the GATT provisions on these subjects. The Dispute Settlement Understanding (DSU), attached as an annex to the agreement, set out a much clearer and more formal adjudication process for disputes arising among members. The DSU, for example, reversed the procedure for adoption of dispute panel rulings making such reports presumptively binding absent its unanimous disapproval by all member states. Also included in the WTO Agreement was the Trade Policy Review Mechanism (TPRM), an institutionalized procedure for promoting transparency and for assessing the overall effectiveness of the regime through a regular review of member states' trade policies.

The general institutional structure of the World Trade Organization is also quite instructive. The WTO Agreement itself is a mere ten pages long.[20] Its purpose is simply to establish a framework of organizational elements and organs to provide an administrative system for the institution. It therefore details the various bodies through which the organization functions at the general level. These include a Ministerial Conference, composed of all members, which meets approximately once every two years and which has authority to take decisions under all of the sub-agreements and to make substantive changes to all organizational documents. Also included in the organizational structure is a General Council, also composed of representatives of all members, which meets on a more regular and frequent basis, and which conducts the functions of the Ministerial Conference when it is not in session. The General Council additionally convenes as appropriate to discharge the responsibilities of the Dispute Settlement Body, and the Trade Policy Review body – that is, the same mid-level national officials which make up the General Council, simply wearing different functional hats.

Attached to this framework administrative structure are a number of sub-agreements which cover substantive areas of trade, including the revised General Agreement on Tariffs and Trade, the General Agreement on Trade in Services (GATS), and the Agreement on Trade-Related Aspects of Intellectual Property Rights (TRIPS). These three agreements, termed multilateral agreements, are currently binding upon all WTO members. In addition, however, there are two plurilateral agreements, the Agreement on Trade in Civil Aircraft and the Agreement on Government Procurement, which are only binding upon their signatories and not incumbent upon all WTO members.

These sub-agreements and their substantive provisions, while referenced by and subject to the general administrative organs in the WTO Agreement, are at the same time independent normative regimes and, in the case of the plurilateral agreements, are comprised of differing memberships. The WTO Agreement makes clear that states may maintain membership in the WTO while being signatories to and participating in either, both or none of the plurilateral agreements. Thus, states may be members of the framework administrative agreement and fully active at the general level of regime activity while not being a member of all WTO sub-agreements.

This structural model of a framework administrative agreement with attached substantive sub-agreements is representative of a modern trend in international organizational design, with other notable examples of its use being found in the Vienna Convention for the Protection of the Ozone Layer and associated Montreal Protocol on ozone-depleting gases, and the United Nations Framework Convention on Climate Change and associated Kyoto Protocol on greenhouse gases. It incorporates two aspects of institutional decentralization which are of note in consideration of the potential use of this model for a restructured multilateral export control regime system.

First, this structure provides for horizontal decentralization, in the sense that the existing multilateral regimes could be incorporated into the comprehensive framework in much the same form in which they presently exist – that is, as in many ways separate and independent subject-material focused normative regimes. Horizontal decentralization is potentially useful in this context for a number of reasons. It allows, as previously stated, for diversity of membership among the sub-regimes. This is an important area of institutional flexibility and strength of the WTO-type framework agreement design. While membership in the existing regimes is largely similar, there are some notable differences in regime membership rolls which could otherwise be extremely problematic to make allowance for in the merged regime context. For example, Russia, traditionally one of the states of greatest concern *vis-a-vis* the proliferation threat, is not a member of the Australia Group. In this particular case, it is not the state that refuses accession to the regime, but the regime which, for a variety of reasons, has consistently refused to accept Russia as a member. Thus, in the horizontally decentralized framework structure under consideration, Russia could be a member of the framework administrative agreement, including whatever compliance determination mechanisms which may be in place at that level, and be a member of only three of the sub-regimes. This aspect of the framework structure is advantageous in its inclusivity and provision of a formalized institutional structure through which to monitor compliance with regime rules, while yet allowing for plurilateral regimes from a membership standpoint at the sub-regime level.

Horizontal decentralization further allows for the existing regime-centric communities of specialists at both policy and technical levels to maintain feelings of identity and institutional ownership, values that have been expressed to be important by international officials in the export control issue area. This aspect of the framework structure contributes significantly to the political viability of the entire enterprise of restructuring the multilateral export control regimes, and is thus of great practical as well as theoretical value. Lastly, it allows for easier addition and subtraction of sub-regimes with a minimum of restructuring required to the system in the event of such changes.

The framework agreement structure also, however, incorporates vertical decentralization of authority and an almost federal-type system of multi-levelling in its design. Again, the primary purpose of the framework agreement itself is to provide for organs of general administration for the regime. At that level are carried out macro policy discussions and decisions on cross-cutting issues, inter-regime information sharing, and regime compliance review as well as activities encouraging issue area cohesion and a unified institutional presence with a permanent secretariat. The sub-regime level, however, could retain a great deal of its existing competencies with a renewed, formalized, documentary foundation. At this sub-regime level could be kept the ordinary functioning of and expertise regarding the control lists, including the authority and responsibility to regularly update lists. Intra-regime information sharing (with the possibility of information firewalls between sub-regimes in deference to membership differences), material-specific target lists, and regime guidelines could be continuing facets of the sub-regimes. This again would, from a practical standpoint, cause as little trauma to existing communities and to the functioning of the regimes themselves as possible in the process of restructuring. As noted, it is expected that the existing regimes would be re-negotiated and their foundational documents significantly revised in light particularly of the principles of formality and consensus voting already laid out as proposed characteristics of the restructured regime system before taking their place as sub-regimes within the framework structure.

Before continuing, it is important to note that the merged and restructured framework agreement structure under consideration is not proposed to be the last step in progression of the multilateral export control regime system. As discussed earlier, as regime members become more supportive of yet harder, more binding forms of institutionalization of commitments in this issue area (that is, treaties), such support and resulting hard agreements together with their compliance enhancing qualities can and should supplant the informal structures proposed here. However, it will also be noted that the framework structure which is herein discussed is eminently qualified to act as a facilitator of this process on a number of levels. First, in terms of facilitation of the requisite level of member support for such formalizing developments, the proposed regime structure should as previously discussed contribute significantly to issue area cohesion and closer cooperation both between states and between regimes in this area, hopefully fostering continued positive interaction and a level of trust conducive to contemplation of yet more enforceable commitments. This indeed is one of the strengths of soft law structures – as preliminary facilitators of exchange and overcoming of information barriers leading to the creation of political will to conclude harder law structures.

Second, simply in terms of institutional design, as in the case of the WTO the framework agreement model is easily adapted *in toto* into such forms of increased formality as a treaty-based organization. Thus if in the future the time should arrive in which the members of the restructured regime system desire to increase the formalization of the norms and relationships incorporated therein, there would need be no serious structural or functional upheavals. The job would rather fall to their lawyers to draft the necessary documents for signature, with the work of the regimes continuing unabated.

Export Policy Review Mechanism (EPRM) and Compliance Determination Understanding (CDU)

A couple of institutional facets of the proposed restructured regime system bear more detailed review and explication. Within the structure of the WTO framework agreement, two of the most novel structural elements in terms of international organizational design are the Trade Policy Review Mechanism and the Dispute Settlement Understanding, both of which have been alluded to previously. The inclusion of analogous processes, in addition to organs approximating the others established by the WTO Agreement, in the restructured multilateral export control regime system is proposed herein to be of great advisability.

Within the current organization of the regimes, there are no established, institutionalized processes for determining the compliance of member states with regime rules and policies. In fact, as many policy experts in the area are quick to point out, it is an assumption even to speak of member 'compliance' in the context of the multilateral export control regimes. Many have asserted that member acts and omissions in this area may at worst only be termed as not 'in keeping with the spirit' of the regimes. This is more than a simple semantic debate. It has reference first to the informal character of obligations undertaken by virtue of membership in the regimes as previously discussed, but is also importantly an indictment of the specificity of regime guidelines and the absence of any process of authoritative interpretation of regime rules. Thus, even though 32 of the 34 members of the Nuclear Supplier's Group agreed that Russia's shipments of fuel to the Terapur nuclear reactor in India in January 2001 were inconsistent with Russia's NSG commitments, no authoritative mechanism existed by which to render an interpretation of regime guidelines and officially sanction Russia (see US GAO 2002, 23).

As previously stated, the restructured multilateral export control regime system of which this chapter conceives, due to an existing lack of political will to establish harder more binding legal instruments, is proposed to be one founded on a soft law (that is, non-legally binding) documentary foundation. Thus while states under this structure will similarly not be legally liable for non-compliance with regime rules, the utility of instituting a process for authoritative, or official interpretation of regime rules and for passing judgments regarding the harmony of member state action with such established norms is proposed to be of significant worth. As discussed earlier, in the absence of vertical enforcement mechanisms the primary guarantor of enforcement of any rule of international law currently relies upon a horizontal system of internal and external compliance pressuring, a process in which the enmeshing results of globalization, issue linkages, norm internalization and the increasing legalization of many aspects of international relations affect the decisions of policymakers. Thus, while the character of norms as being derived from hard law versus soft law instruments is likely not a decisive factor in determining the level of state compliance which can be expected in reference thereto, the level of objective legitimacy, both procedural and substantive, which the international community perceives as being attached to a norm likely is an independent variable influencing compliance, as it is a moving factor for the types and degree of both internal and external compliance pressure which may be exerted upon officials of the member states in question (see Franck 1990).

In the context of the restructured multilateral export control regime system, this sense of legitimacy of regime norms could be significantly enhanced by the institutionalization of both an Export Policy Review Mechanism (EPRM) and a Compliance Determination Understanding (CDU) (based upon the WTO's TPRM and DSU mechanisms, though with some procedural alteration particularly with regard to the CDU), from which could be derived official pronouncements of interpretation and judgments regarding member state behaviour through a mutually agreed upon procedure and according to clear standards. In support of these determinations, it is proposed, there will be an increase in compliance pressuring, as clear standards are produced and official sanctioning rendered to which both other governments and international civil society may point in their castigatory rhetoric and around which they can organize more persuasive pressuring efforts. Thus even without an increase in formal legality or enforceability of obligations within the regime system, an increase of specificity and the delegation of interpretive authority to regime structures can constitute a form of formality likely to positively impact member compliance levels.

The main purpose of the EPRM in the multilateral export control regime context would be to provide a unified system with harmonized standards of review for producing reports on the export control practices of member states. This largely informational function is a novel suggestion in that there is no currently institutionalized procedure for such reviews. The work of an Export Policy Review Body, analogous to its role in the WTO context, would promote transparency in members' export control policies and regulatory frameworks and would contribute to general understandings regarding export controls, and would be of particular usefulness to nations with developing export control systems. This uniform system for review of member state export control policies would itself likely bring about improved member compliance with regime rules, as it would bring such non-compliances into the light of international civil societal scrutiny. It would further, however, contribute to the functioning of the Compliance Determination Understanding.

As previously mentioned, one of the most significant limitations of the current regimes is the lack of any institutional procedure through which to officially declare a members' actions in non-compliance with its commitments and with regime rules. In considering possible models for such a mechanism in the restructured multilateral export control regime context, first to be considered would naturally be an adversarial system such as that in place in many international organizations, including the WTO, through which individual members who feel their interests have been materially damaged due to another member's abrogation of regime commitments bring such claims to an adjudicatory forum for disposition and for the awarding of a judgement specifying remedial action on the part of a liable defendant state. This paradigm, however, seems fairly unworkable in the restructured multilateral export control regime context. Deficient export controls, with few exceptions, by their nature are not easily linked to particular damage suffered by specific member states. The damage flowing from lax or incongruent export controls is usually of a more generalized nature, in allowing for the export from a member state of sensitive items which may or may not be subsequently involved in a WMD development programme, the results of which then may or may not be proliferated either to hostile states or terrorist entities and used against the interests of another member state. Linking such a causal chain back to a defendant country would be an extremely difficult task and would, if jurisdiction were linked as is usually the case to such evidence of concrete damage, be an exercise in futility and very much in the 'too little too late' category.

If, however, the process of compliance determination were not to be jurisdictionally linked to particular damage but rather based upon the breach itself with an understanding that any such breach contributes *per se* to a latent threat to international security, it would of course not be possible to award damages to a particular party. It could rather be triggered procedurally not by the presentation of one specific aggrieved party, but upon the referral of any member state having information upon which to base a suspicion or allegation of non-compliance. In this sense the compliance determination process pursuant to the CDU would be more inquisitorial than adversarial in nature, finding a better analogy in the procedures of the UN Commission on Human Rights.

The compliance determination mechanism described above, in which the present or past non-compliance of a member state may be determined should be distinguished from the procedure for *ex ante* authorization of significant exports of sensitive goods which was an institutional feature of the Coordinating Committee for Multilateral Export Controls (COCOM), the Cold War predecessor of the Wassenaar Arrangement (see Cupitt and Grillot 1997; Dursht 1997). COCOM members wishing to export certain highly sensitive items were required beforehand to submit an application for review and approval by the entire COCOM membership. Unanimous member consent was required for the export to proceed. While both this *ex ante* procedure and the *ex post* compliance determination mechanism currently under consideration supplement the role of norm-promulgation processes, it is simply a current reality that the like-mindedness of membership within the regimes and the mutual identification of threat and end users of concern have become significantly diluted due to both macro-political changes and changes in regime membership since the disbanding of COCOM in 1994. Thus attempting to institutionalize an *ex ante* procedure for licence approvals requiring unanimity among regime members, while theoretically the most effective means of coordinating non-proliferation efforts, would without doubt be an unworkable prospect in the context of a restructured multilateral regime. The *ex post* system here proposed would however serve an important purpose in providing an avenue for official determinations of non-compliance and promulgation of norms, without pushing the procedural envelope and ineffectually challenging notions of sovereignty among increasingly un-like-minded member states.

Conclusion

This chapter has attempted to identify the tensions currently existing between the expectations of many in the international security community with regard to the role and effectiveness of the multilateral export control regime system, and inherent structural limitations within the current regimes. It has posited that this clash of expectations and structural limitations has produced a defining moment for international WMD non-proliferation efforts in the area of multilateral export controls.

In the hope of contributing to international debate on this issue, this chapter has advanced the proposition that a newly merged and restructured multilateral export control regime system incorporating some, but not all, elements of normative formality could in large measure overcome these structural limitations and contribute to the more effective functioning of the regime system in carrying out its vital role in international security, while at the same time remaining grounded in political reality and in an understanding of the particular characteristics of the multilateral export control issue area.

It has further posited that an organizational structure analogous to that designed in the agreements establishing the World Trade Organization would offer many structural advantages and utilities as an institutional framework for this restructured regime, including through the maintenance of a specially designed Export Policy Review Mechanism and Compliance Determination Understanding aimed at producing official interpretations of regime norms and determinations of member state compliance with agreed commitments.

In discussions with governmental officials during the writing of this chapter, it has become clear that there are currently two primary hindrances to the restructuring of the multilateral export control regimes along lines similar to those outlined herein. The first is the strong sense that many officials in regime circles feel and manifest regarding the maintenance of the status quo in this area; a sense that is no doubt wedded at least partially to their own personal investments of time in working within the existing regime frameworks and developing of regime-specific expertise, and to their having obtained influential positions in their national governments by virtue thereof.

The second is the lack of momentum currently present within national governments to bring about a newly restructured regime which, although concededly offering significant points of added value, has not yet received the mandate of catastrophe. Meaning, of course, that there has not yet occurred a WMD event of the location and magnitude necessary to martial political will at high enough levels of government to allow such a restructuring to be pushed through bureaucratic channels. While the first hindrance described above is understandable and expected in any new endeavour of regime engineering, the second is more troubling.

It is a fact that international organizations in the security context have a history of being one generation too late to in fact perform the functions for which they are designed. The League of Nations was instituted, for example, in order to establish a procedural system of checks and limitations purposed to prevent the sorts of miscommunications from occurring which were thought to have precipitated the First World War, but were not in fact the primary modern threat, and thus not well dealt with under the League of Nations Covenant system. The United Nations Charter as well was established with a firm grasp of the sorts of normative protections and frameworks which might have been useful had they been instituted in 1938, but which fairly soon after the Charter's establishment began to be criticized as being insufficient to cover more modern security realities.

It is unfortunate that the multilateral export control regime system seems destined to suffer the same fate, and that there is not enough farsightedness among government circles not just to act reflexively to calamities in their international institution building, but to proactively seek to prevent them *ex ante* by engaging in the sorts of relatively simple institutional reworkings considered herein. It is the more disturbing because the technologies which the multilateral export control regimes seek to regulate, and which they might more effectively control if properly institutionally endowed, are even less allowing of institutional amendment *ex post* than are the use of force regimes previously mentioned. In the field of WMD proliferation, it is not prudentially sound to try and get things right the second time around.

Thus, it is this chapter's contention that national policymakers should in this area particularly heed the advice of Benjamin Franklin, and commit themselves sooner rather than too late to a course of consideration and proactive implementation of measures to strengthen the multilateral export control system. It is hoped that the prescriptions for structural change as herein discussed may contribute to that consideration.

References

Abbot, K. and Snidal, D. (2000), 'Hard and Soft Law in International Governance', *International Organization*, Vol. 54.

Adamantopoulos, K. (ed.) (1997), *An Anatomy of the World Trade Organization*, London: Kluwer.

Adler, E. and Barnett, M. (eds) (1998), *Security Communities*, Cambridge University Press, Cambridge.

Beck, M. (2000), 'Reforming the Multilateral Export Control Regimes', *The Nonproliferation Review*, Vol. 91.

Beck, M. and Gahlaut, S. (2003), 'Creating a New Multilateral Export Control Regime', *Arms Control Today*, April 2003.

Bertsch, G.K., Cupitt, R.T. and Elliot-Gower, S. (1994), 'Multilateral Export Control Organizations', in G.K. Bertsch, R.T. Cupitt and S. Elliot-Gower (eds), *International Cooperation on Non-Proliferation Export Controls*, University of Michigan Press, Ann Arbor, MI.

Braithwaite, J.B. (1989), *Crime, Shame and Reintegration*, Cambridge University Press, Cambridge.

Bunn, G. (1999), 'The Status of Norms Against Nuclear Testing', *The Nonproliferation Review*, Winter 1999.

Center for International Trade and Security (2002), *Strengthening Multilateral Export Controls: A Non-Proliferation Priority*, Center for International Trade and Security report, September 2002.

Chayes, A. and Chayes, A. (1993), 'On Compliance', *International* Organization, Vol. 47.

—— (1994). 'Regime Architecture: Elements and Principles', in J. Nolan (ed.), *Global Engagement: Cooperation and Security in the 21st Century*, Brookings Institution Press, Washington, DC.

—— (1995), *The New Sovereignty: Compliance with International Regulatory Agreements*, Harvard University Press, Cambridge, MA.

Checkel, J. (2001), 'Why Comply?: Social Learning and European Identity Change', *International Organization*, Vol. 55.

Cirincione, J. (ed.) (2000), *Repairing the Regime: Preventing the Spread of Weapons of Mass Destruction*, Carnegie Endowment for International Peace, Washington, DC.

Cohn, T.H. (2002), *Governing Global Trade: International Institutions in Conflict and Convergence*, Ashgate, Aldershot.

Croome, J. (1999), *Reshaping the World Trading System: A History of the Uruguay Round*, Kluwer Law International, The Hague and Boston, MA.

Cupitt, R.T. and Grillot, S.R. (1997), 'COCOM is Dead, Long Live COCOM: Persistence and Change in Multilateral Security Institutions', *British Journal of Political Science*, Vol. 27.

Downs, G.W. et al. (1996), 'Is the Good News About Compliance Good News About Cooperation?', *International Organization*, Vol. 50.

Dursht, K. (1997), 'From Containment to Cooperation: Collective Action and the Wassenaar Arrangement', *Cardozo Law Review*, Vol. 19.

Elster, J. (1989), *The Cement of Society: A Study of Social Order*, Cambridge University Press, Cambridge.

Finnemore, M. (1996), 'Norms, Culture and World Politics: Insights from Sociology's Institutionalism', *International Organization*, Vol. 50.

Franck, T. (1990), *The Power of Legitimacy Among Nation*, Oxford University Press, New York.

Freedenberg, P. and Khripunov, I. (1992), 'Arms Control is Global Mission', *Defense News*, 27 January 1992.

Gahlaut Seema and Zaborsky Victor (2003), 'Do Regimes Have the Members They Need?', Centre for International Trade and Security Working Paper, February 2003, Centre for International Trade and Security, Athens, GA.

Galdi, Theodor W. (1993), *Proliferation Export Control Regimes: Options for Coordination or Consolidation*, Congressional Research Service, Washington, DC.

Goldstein, Judith and Martin, Lisa L. (2000), 'Legalization, Trade Liberalization and Domestic Politics: A Cautionary Note', *International Organization*, Vol. 54.

Grieco, J. (1993), 'Understanding the Problem of Institutional Cooperation', in D.A. Baldwin (ed.), *Neorealism and Neoliberalism: The Contemporary Debate*, Columbia University Press, New York.

Gualtieri, D.S. (2000). 'The System of Non-Proliferation Export Controls', in D. Shelton (ed.), *Commitment and Compliance: The Role of Non-Binding Norms in the International Legal System*, Oxford University Press, Oxford.

Guzman, A.T. (2002), 'A Compliance Based Theory of International Law', *California Law Review*, Vol. 90.

Harris, D.J. (1998), *Cases and Materials on International Law*, 5th edn, Sweet & Maxwell, London.

Hirsch, M. (1998), 'The Great Technology Giveaway', *Foreign Affairs*, September/October 1998.

Holmes, J. and Bertsch, G. (2003), 'Tighten Export Controls', *Defense News*, 5 May 2003.

Honneth, A. (1995), *The Struggle for Recognition: The Moral Grammar of Social Conflicts*, Polity Press, Cambridge.

Jackson, John H. (1998), *The World Trading System*, 2nd edn, MIT Press, Cambridge, MA.

Jackson, J.H., Davey, W.J. and Sykes Jr., A.O. (1995), *Legal Problems of International Economic Relations*, West, St Paul, MN.

Jervis, R. (1983), 'Security Regimes', in S. Krasner (ed.), *International Regimes*, Cornell University Press, Ithaca, NY.

Keller, W.W. and Nolan, J.E. (1997), 'The Arms Trade: Business as Usual?', *Foreign Policy*, Vol. 109.

—— (1997–98), 'Proliferation of Advanced Weaponry: Threat to Stability', *Foreign Policy*, Winter 1997–98.

Kellman, B. (1994), 'Bridling the International Trade of Catastrophic Weaponry', American University Law Review, Vol. 43.

Keohane, R. (1984), *After Hegemony: Cooperation and Discord in the World Political Economy*, Princeton University Press, Princeton, NJ.

—— Keohane, R.; Abbott, K.; Moravcsik, A.; Slaughter, A-M; and Snidal, D. (2000), 'The Concept of Legalization', special issue of *International Organization*, Vol. 54.

Koh, H.H. (1997), 'Why Do Nations Obey International Law?', *Yale Law Journal*, Vol. 106.

Krasner, S.D. (1983), 'Structural Causes and Regime Consequences: Regimes as Intervening Variables', in S.D. Krasner (ed.), *International Regimes*, Cornell University Press, Ithaca, NY.

Latham, A. and Bow, B. (1998), 'Multilateral Export Control Regimes: Bridging the North-South Divide', *Canadian Institute of International Affairs International Journal*, Vol. 53, No. 3.

Lipson, M. (1999), 'The Reincarnation of COCOM: Explaining Post Cold-War Export Controls', *The Nonproliferation Review*, Vol. 6, No. 2.

Martin, L.L. (1993), *Coercive Cooperation: Explaining Multilateral Economic Sanctions*, Princeton University Press. Princeton, NJ.

—— (1992), 'The Rational State Choice of Multilateralism', *International Organization*, Vol. 46.

Moodie, M. (1997), 'The Challenges of Chemical, Biological and Nuclear Weapons Enabling Technology', in P.G. Alves and K. Hoffman (eds), *The Transfer of Sensitive Technology and the Future of the Control Regimes*, UNIDIR.

Muller, M. (2000), 'Compliance Politics: A Critical Analysis of Multilateral Arms Control Treaty Enforcement', *The Nonproliferation Review*, Summer 2000.

National Academy of Sciences (1991), *Finding Common Ground: U.S. Export Controls in a Changed Global Environment*, National Academy Press, Washington, DC.

Reinsch, W.A. (1999), 'Export Controls in the Age of Globalization', *The Monitor: Non-Proliferation Demilitarization and Arms Control*, Summer 1999.

Sampson, G.P. (ed.) (2001), *The Role of the World Trade Organization in Global Governance*, United Nations University Press, Tokyo, New York and Paris.

Schachter, O. (1977), 'The Twilight Existence of Nonbinding International Agreements', *American Journal of International Law*, Vol. 71.

—— (1982), *International Law in Theory and Practice*, Martinus Nijhoff, Dordrecht.

Slaughter Burley, A-M. (1993), 'International Law and International Relations Theory: A Dual Agenda', *American Journal of International Law*, Vol. 87.

Spector, S. and Foran, V. (1992), *Preventing Weapons Proliferation: Should the Regimes be Combined?* Report of the Thirty-Third Strategy for Peace, U.S. Foreign Policy Conference, The Stanley Foundation, 22–24 October1992.

Stein, A. (1993), 'Coordination and Collaboration: Regimes in an Anarchic World', in D.A. Baldwin (ed.), *Neorealism and Neoliberalism: The Contemporary Debate*, Columbia University Press, New York.

Szasz, P. (1994), *General Law-Making Processes*, in O. Schacter and C. Joyner (eds), *United Nations Legal Order*, Cambridge University Press, Cambridge.

Sztucki, J. (1990), *Festkrift Hjerner*, Nostedts, Stockholm.

Trachtman, J. (1999), 'Bananas, Direct Effect and Compliance', *European Journal of International Law*, Vol. 10.

US Congress (1993). *Treaties and other International Agreements: The Role of the United States Senate*, Congressional Research Service Study, 103rd Congress, 1st Session, November 1993.

US General Accounting Office (2002), 'Strategy Needed to Strengthen Multilateral Export Control Regimes', GAO-03-43, General Accounting Office, Washington, DC.

US Government (1975), *US Department of State Bulletin*, Vol. 73, quoted in US Congress (1993), *Treaties and other International Agreements: The Role of the United States Senate*, Congressional Research Service Study, 103rd Congress, 1st Session, November 1993.

Van Hoof, G. (1983), *Rethinking the Sources of International Law*, Kluwer, Deventer.

Young, O. (1991), 'Political Leadership and Regime Formation: On the Development of Institutions in International Society', *International Organization*, Vol. 45.

Zeiler, T.W. (1999), *Free Trade, Free World: The Advent of GATT*, University of North Carolina Press, Chapel Hill, NC.

Notes

1. A version of this chapter was originally published in the Journal of Conflict and Security Law, Vol. 9, Issue 2, 181–211 in 2004. This version is republished with kind permission of Oxford University Press.
2. Treaty on the Non-Proliferation of Nuclear Weapons, opened for signature 1 July 1968; Convention on the Prohibition of the Development, Production and Stockpiling of Bacteriological (Biological) and Toxin Weapons and on Their Destruction, opened for signature 10 April 1972; Convention on the Prohibition of the Development, Production and Stockpiling and Use of Chemical Weapons and on Their Destruction, opened for signature 13 January 1993 and entered into force 29 April 1997.
3. For an excellent review of international relations theories on institutions in the context of multilateral export control regimes, see Lipson (1999). Regimes are defined by Stephen Krasner as the 'principles, norms, rules and decision-making structures' that influence the behaviour of states in various issue areas. See Krasner (1983).
4. The Wassenaar Arrangement is the only one of the regimes without these denial notification/no undercut policies.
5. See *Proceedings of the Fourth International Conference on Export Controls*, Warsaw, Poland, 30 September–4 October 2002.
6. Israel, India, Pakistan and China – all either declared or suspected nuclear weapons possessing states, and a number of which are suspected of involvement in secondary proliferation activities (that is, proliferation from sources outside of the regimes) – are, for example, not members of the Nuclear Suppliers Group.
7. On patterns of technology dissemination and the challenges presented thereby, see Moodie (1997). See also Keller and Nolan (1997–98) and Hirsch (1998).
8. See a full discussion of the current weaknesses of the multilateral export control regimes and proposals for restructuring in *Strengthening Multilateral Export Controls: A Non-Proliferation Priority* (Center for International Trade and Security report, September 2002) See also the United States General Accounting Office's 2002 report entitled *Strategy Needed to Strengthen Multilateral Export Control Regimes* (US GAO 2002).
9. See *Strengthening Multilateral Export Controls: A Non-proliferation Priority* (Center for International Trade and Security report, September 2002).

10. See the Congressional Research Service study *Treaties and other International Agreements: The Role of the United States Senate* (US Congress 1993): 'Non-binding agreements may take many forms, including ... declarations of intent, joint communiques and joint statements (including final acts of conferences) and informal agreements'.
11. See Beck (2000): 'A regime is effective to the extent that its members comply or abide by regime provisions. However, in the case of the export control regimes, the regime guidelines are often so vague that disputes can arise over what exports are contrary to regime provisions. For example, the Nuclear Suppliers Group guidelines set forth a "non-proliferation principle" whereby supplier states are called upon to only authorize exports of sensitive nuclear items when they are "satisfied that the transfers would not contribute to the proliferation of nuclear weapons" ... Moreover, the provision calls upon member states themselves to make risk assessments about the likelihood that an export will be diverted to unauthorized military uses'.
12. See the United Nations Charter, Statute of the International Court of Justice, Article 38 (listing the sources of international law). See also Bunn (1999) for an excellent review of the sources of international norms, including what Bunn refers to as 'politically binding' as opposed to 'legally binding' soft international norms. I have chosen in this piece to adopt the usage of 'soft law' common in international legal literature, though Bunn's usage and its implications are entirely accurate.
13. As Oscar Schacter, a preeminent international law scholar has noted, 'States entering into a non-legal commitment generally view it as a political (or moral) obligation and intend to carry it out in good faith. Other parties and other states concerned have reasons to expect such compliance and to rely on it ... [P]olitical texts which express commitments and positions of one kind or another are governed by the general principle of good faith' (Schacter 1982). See also Schacter (1977). While such soft law instruments are not submitted to the advice and consent and ratification procedures required for treaties under United States law, when questioned about them by the Senate Foreign Relations Committee, then Secretary of States Henry Kissinger once remarked that the United States is not 'morally or politically free to act as if they did not exist. On the contrary, they are important statements of diplomatic policy and engage the good faith of the United States as long as the circumstances that gave rise to them continue' (US Government 1975, 613).
14. The distinction between hard and soft law and the recognition of soft law instruments has met with disapproval by some in the international legal community, however. As expressed by Jerzy Sztucki: '*Primo*, the term is inadequate and misleading. There are no two levels or "species" of law – something is law or is not law. *Secundo*, the concept is counterproductive or even dangerous. On the one hand, it creates illusory expectations of (perhaps even insistence on) compliance with what no one is obliged to comply; and on the other hand, it exposes binding legal norms for risks of neglect, and international law as a whole for risks of erosion, by blurring the threshold between what is legally binding and what is not' (Sztucki 1990). However, as D.J. Harris has responded, 'While it may be paradoxical and confusing to call something "law" when it is *not* law, the concept is nonetheless useful to describe instruments that clearly have an impact on international relations and that may later harden into custom or become the basis of a treaty' (Harris 1998).
15. The idea of merging the multilateral export control regimes is not new. It was recommended a decade ago in a study by the National Academy of Sciences, *Finding*

Common Ground: U.S. Export Controls in a Changed Global Environment (National Academy of Sciences 1991, 131). See also Freedenberg and Khripunov (1992); Spector and Foran (1992); Galdi (1993). On the importance of state policies strengthening the multilateral regimes see Muller (2000) and Young (1991).

16. See Keohane et al. (2000) for this method of categorization of regimes.
17. This of course presupposes a degree of transparency in the workings of institutions such that there is adequate information disclosure regarding norms around which pressure can be brought to bear upon states in favour of is observance. See Finnemore (1996); Franck (1990).
18. This conclusion has some theoretical kinship to the arguments of the managerial school of regime theory, in which compliance with regime norms is asserted to be more likely achieved through persuasive and 'managerial' approaches rather than by the use of coercive sanctions built into the structure of regimes. See Chayes and Chayes (1995). It is also in keeping with the definition of international regimes put forward by Stephen D. Krasner as 'sets of implicit or explicit principles, norms, rules, and decision-making procedures around which actors' expectations converge in a given area of international relations' (Krasner 1983).
19. For this section see Jackson (1998); Sampson (2001); Cohn (2002); Zeiler (1999); Croome (1999); Adamantopoulos (1997).
20. As reprinted in the Documentary Supplement to Jackson et al. (1995). This is in stark contrast to the 22,500 pages of tariff bindings which complete the Uruguay Round Agreements establishing the WTO.

Index